Pedagogy of Language Learning in Higher Education

An Introduction

Recent Titles in
Advances in Foreign and Second Language Pedagogy
Gerd Bräuer, Series Editor

Volume One: Writing Across Languages
Gerd Bräuer, editor

Pedagogy of Language Learning in Higher Education

An Introduction

Edited by
Gerd Bräuer

Advances in Foreign and Second Language Pedagogy,
Volume 2
Gerd Bräuer, Series Editor

Ablex Publishing
Westport, Connecticut • London

Library of Congress Cataloging-in-Publication Data

Pedagogy of language learning in higher education : an introduction / edited by Gerd
Bräuer.
    p. cm.—(Advances in foreign and second language pedagogy ; v. 2)
    Includes bibliographical references and index.
    ISBN 1-56750-638-0 (alk. paper)—ISBN 1-56750-639-9 (pbk. : alk. paper)
    1. Language and languages—Study and teaching (Higher) I. Bräuer, Gerd. II.
Series.

P51.P37 2001
418'.0071'1—dc21   00-061791

British Library Cataloguing in Publication Data is available.

Library of Congress Catalog Card Number: 00-061791
ISBN: 1-56750-638-0
      1-56750-639-9 (pbk.)

First published in 2001

Ablex Publishing, 88 Post Road West, Westport, CT 06881
An imprint of Greenwood Publishing Group, Inc.
www.ablexbooks.com

Printed in the United States of America

The paper used in this book complies with the
Permanent Paper Standard issued by the National
Information Standards Organization (Z39.48-1984).

10 9 8 7 6 5 4 3 2 1

Contents

Series Foreword

Advances in Foreign and Second Language Pedagogy is a series focusing on the people involved in the process of language education: students, teachers, administrators, parents, and others related to the learner within a broader social context. Issues such as writing, reading, speaking, and listening are examined here for their potential for individual growth, learning partnership, and group dynamics. In the same context, it is of substantial interest for the authors of each volume to look at the pedagogical specifics of various fields of language learning, such as oral traditions, drama, music, or visual arts. The influence of alternative teaching methods and modern technology on learners and educators also raises substantial questions for this ongoing publication project.

The main approach for each volume of the series is one of practice-based research, wherein language practitioners become reflective researchers in order to deepen their own and the reader's theoretical understanding of their work and to develop practical consequences. For this purpose the relationship between practice and research is intimate, and the subtle interchanges between doing and reflecting are inseparable. Therefore, the contributors for this series focus on classroom practice: Empirical research is presented, case studies are introduced, individual teaching experience is discussed, and theoretical frameworks are developed. Nevertheless, all practical issues of language pedagogy are handled here in their theoretical contexts, with the aim of further deepening conceptual understanding of pedagogical phenomena and processes in language acquisition. A second, not less important goal of this series lies in bridging the gap in academic discourse between research and classroom practice and the integration of the wisdom of language educators from all areas of language education: primary and secondary schools, colleges and universities, and adult education.

As indicated, the prospective authors and readers of this series are expected to be future teachers, educators at all levels of instruction, and all those interested in pedagogical research. The wide range of creators and recipients of the series is geared toward a general collaboration among learners, rooted in the belief that people can profit from each other's knowledge and experience throughout the entire educational pyramid.

I want to expand the boundaries of this collaboration in the process of learning about the pedagogy of language teaching by bringing together in this series American teacher-researchers with their international colleagues in order to stimulate mutual learning and interdisciplinarity across languages and cultures. Ablex Publishing, as the host of this series, offers a great resource in spreading the word throughout the world.

Introduction

The second volume of the series is designed as an introduction to the *pedagogy of language learning in higher education*. Keeping the broad spectrum of this topic in perspective, this collection of articles concentrates on the four major issues constituting the main parts of the book: *learner motivation, classroom environments, relationships for learning, preparing the future of language education*.

Each theme provides deep insight into theory and practice of foreign language (FL) and second language (L2) instruction in college and university; it also reveals numerous links to high school language teaching and learning, as well as adult education. After all, the biography of the learner in higher education doesn't start with college, and it certainly doesn't end there. As future (language) teachers (and parents!) students will influence learner motivation, classroom environments, and relationships for learning as well as the work for generations to come in education with what they experience throughout their careers in school and college.

This book is very much about the potential for its future development that language instruction in higher education presently shows. Therefore, the publication is geared toward an audience drawn from across the educational pyramid. It should not least be read as an invitation to the writing of another introductory volume in this series: the pedagogy of language learning in elementary and secondary education.

The international scope of the series' first volume, *Writing Across Languages*, finds its continuation here with authors from Australia, Germany, and the United States, dealing with issues related to Portuguese, Spanish, Russian, Japanese, French, German, and English as both foreign and second languages. The extent of collaboration among the fifteen contributors discussing each other's work from very different (and sometimes contradictory) angles—such as the political agenda of higher institutions, language across the curriculum, service learning, adult education, artistic and aesthetic practice, intercultural awareness through electronic media, extracurricular consultation, and language learning outreach—made the coming into being of this volume truly unique.

Part I, Learner Motivation, explores some hidden aspects of language education: What is it that makes us want to get in touch with another language/culture? What is it that either keeps us learning that language or makes us turn away from what was initially hoped to be achieved?

Part I is introduced by Beverly Moser. Her chapter explores the challenge of maintaining viable language programs in a diversity of foreign languages and offers tangible strategies for strengthening language programs that are at risk. The author explores the irony of institutional rhetoric that favors "internationalization" of the curriculum while overlooking the centrality of foreign language instruction in achieving this goal. Moser suggests careful student advising at all levels, flexible programming for the advanced-level curriculum and study abroad, and a program of cocurricular activities to enhance the visibility of language programs and show administrators who have decision-making power why campus life is richer and more diverse because these languages are present.

Christine Jernigan examines university students' motivation for studying a less commonly taught language (LCTL) to see if a relationship exists between their perceived goal attainment and their continued motivation for language study. Since factors influencing the motivation of LCTL students may differ from those found with students of more commonly taught languages, this study employs expectancy theories as an alternative approach to conceptualizing student motivation. Participants in the study include students, teachers, and administrators in a Portuguese department, and both qualitative and quantitative data and analyses are used. Results indicate that continued motivational strength is affected by students' beliefs about language study and their perceived expectations for success and failure. Jernigan concludes her chapter with possible teacher interventions.

The study conducted by Frank Morris assesses whether participation in service learning by a Chicano/Latino community class influenced students'

motivation and attitudes toward learning Spanish and toward Spanish speakers and their culture. Qualitative and quantitative analyses indicate that there
was a positive change in the participants' motivation and attitudes. Based on
his findings, Morris suggests that service learning can be employed as a
pedagogical tool in enhancing motivation and promoting positive attitudes
toward second language learning and culture.

Timothy Collins discusses one of the most widely held beliefs among
teachers of ESL/EFL (not just in adult education), that in order to maximize
students' contact with a new language teachers need to prohibit the use of the
students' native tongue (L1). However, the examination of an actual adult ESL
classroom shows that the students' use of the L1 facilitates the language
learning process because of the many learning strategies available from their
educational native language background. Collins summarizes that teachers
need to find judicious ways to include students' L1 in ways that enhance the
learning process.

Part II, Classroom Environments, considers different spaces of language
learning, the real, the imaginative, and the virtual: What do we need them for?
How do we establish and maintain them? How do we travel from one
environment to the other? With what consequences?

Part II starts with a chapter by Kathleen March about creating an artistic
environment for foreign language instruction, for which she considers similarities and differences between children and adult learners. While recognizing that age is a factor in language learning, she claims that much can be
gained from stressing the similarities. She suggests that emphasizing the role
of performing language and encouraging creativity in its usage links both
children and adults. Comparisons are made to other performance activities,
such as music, athletics, and drama. March concludes her chapter with the
principle that the most effective learning occurs when foreign language
students perform their target language creatively, in a fluid manner, and at the
appropriate level.

Jean Marie Schultz specifies the exploration of the artistic environment
with a chapter on creative writing. She notes that creative writing generally
holds a marginal place in the foreign language curriculum. She sees it treated
there primarily as a diversionary activity subordinate to more academic
writing and often directed toward bolstering specifically targeted points of
grammar and vocabulary. On the contrary, creative writing can, Schultz
argues, play a significant role in the teaching of foreign language, fostering
acquisition by encouraging students' personal commitment to their writing
tasks. To maximize its benefits, the pedagogical approach to this mode must
be carefully defined. Based on the research conducted in an upper-division
creative writing program in French, Schultz explores the linguistic benefits
of creative writing and its particular pedagogy.

Margaret Gonglewski focuses on the electronic environment. Although
research on the use of the World Wide Web in L2 classrooms has increased

rapidly, little is known about the usefulness of this technological tool for L2 composition. In her chapter Gonglewski describes a pilot study on the use of hypertext (specifically, creating Web pages) to enrich L2 learning. Drawing from students' compositions as well as from interviews and survey results, she presents a qualitative examination of the concrete differences between the conventional and hypertext composing of one group of advanced German learners. Gonglewski concludes with suggestions for implementing hypermedia composition in L2 courses, providing teachers with strategies to help L2 writers make the most of the hypertext medium for their communicative needs.

Lina Lee continues the discussion of the electronic environment with a chapter on computer-based instruction (CBI). She first outlines CBI-related theory in foreign language instruction and then describes the design of her study, including the CBI and Internet tools, material developments, procedures for planning activities, and assessing learning outcomes. Finally, Lee reports on the results of the study and concludes with students' feedback, comments on the project, and suggestions for future improvement of CBI in the language classroom.

Adam Knee explores the role of film in the language class. He makes the case that despite the challenges they pose, feature films, in particular when presented through videotape or videodisc technology, can serve as a useful tool in the language classroom. He offers a brief outline of several justifications for using feature films as texts in the language instruction environment. On the basis of these justifications, he makes a general proposal about the specific ways features might be employed to help promote language learning. Knee concludes his chapter by providing practical suggestions for teachers trying to integrate film into their courses.

Part III, Relationships for Learning, looks into what happens or could happen among learners and between them and instructors: What are the consequences of certain relationships for acquiring another language, and how can we optimize their quality for successful language study?

Part III begins with a chapter by Robert Weissberg, who draws a rather intimate perspective on relationships for learning. He ponders the question of why, more than twenty-five years since the advent of communicative language teaching, many FL and L2 classrooms are still characterized by lockstep, teacher-fronted, whole-class instruction. Does this originate in the belief of some teachers that group work exposes language students to too many verbal errors? Can this be seen as a reaction to classroom experiences where groups didn't work well together? Or is it simply the result of language instructors feeling uncomfortable with the apparent chaos often accompanying social activities in class? The non–teacher-centered classroom is neither a quiet nor an orderly one, Weissberg exclaims, but teacher resistance to group work deprives students of the most natural and motivating environment in which to develop their language skills: the conversational give-and-take of people using language to accomplish something.

Stella Büker investigates to what degree foreign students in Germany can be supported successfully in their studies through extracurricular consultation. For this purpose, a writing consultation model is presented. After analyzing the common problems foreign students have with academic writing, Büker clarifies why this time-consuming form of intervention has been chosen. Through case examples she provides insight into specific features of the consultation work. From her own experience with the model, Büker argues in favor of extracurricular consultation in the field of academic writing for foreign students. She discusses advantages and current problems of the model put into practice.

Gerd Bräuer introduces the High School Language Learning Center as an effective way of collaborating between secondary and higher education. Drawing from recent American and European research on writing and reading and in educational studies, he sketches a model language center that, based on a strong notion of personally meaningful learning, fosters collaboration and independent study and aims for skills that encourage lifelong language learning. Focusing on possible undertakings of the High School Language Learning Center such as team teaching, peer tutoring, and student-teacher internship, Bräuer further explores those key aspects of student-centered pedagogy for their potential to bridge the traditional gap between secondary and postsecondary education.

Part IV, Preparing the Future of Language Education, investigates what needs to be done in order to successfully develop instruction and learning, not only in higher education but also in elementary and secondary schools, as well as in adult education, as the guarantor for generations of language learners to come.

Part IV is initiated by Tony Erben, who introduces the Australian system of instruction in languages other than English (LOTE) as being pushed in the last decade by state governments into the forefront of mainstream education. He explains the new demands toward LOTE education and describes how institutions for preservice teacher training try to prepare their students more adequately for those demands. Erben outlines two immersion degree programs for elementary and secondary school teachers of Japanese, where most of the content is being taught through the medium of the target language and with the pedagogical goal of imparting immersion teaching practices.

Lawrence F. Glatz pays tribute to the rapid changes in language learning involving technology of the last decade that he sees as having a great impact upon efforts to support up-to-date teacher training for language instruction. Due to tremendous advances in Multimedia-Based Content (MBC), Technology-Enhanced Language Learning (TELL), and Computer-Mediated Communication (CMC) technologies, especially those involving the World Wide Web (WWW), learners of foreign and second languages are pursuing self-paced, interactive study in the context of formal instruction. Glatz presents background information, outlines important developments, and discusses problematic issues in language learning technology as they have an impact on teacher training. He offers suggestions for specific innovations in peda-gogical courses and gives general recommendations for faculty who are guiding students embarking on the path to language teaching.

Mary Schleppegrell concludes this book with an outlook on the profes-sional field. She draws attention to the challenge language teacher educators face by having to prepare prospective teachers for a variety of possible settings. Graduates may teach at different proficiency levels, or they may need to focus on particular language skills. They may teach in environments in which the target language is available, or they may need to provide all language input in the classroom. The role of culture in language teaching will also vary with the setting. Schleppegrell describes how the teacher training program at her university addresses these challenges by exposing future teachers to second language acquisition research that has been conducted in varied settings, by helping them develop a flexible approach rather than just learning a set of techniques and methods, and by providing an internship experience enabling students to focus on pertinent issues and developing individually appropriate teaching skills.

Once again, this book would not have been possible without the help of many people. I want to especially thank my friends Kourtney Kuss and Elizabeth Soilis of the German Studies Department at Emory University and Soraya Bailey for their empathetic and generous help with every aspect of this publication. My deepest gratitude goes to all of the contributors to this book, with whom I have enjoyed working. Last but not least, I want to thank the production team from Ablex Publishing and William Cody, general editor, for their encouragement and guidance.

Part I

Learner Motivation

Maintaining Linguistic Diversity on College Campuses

Beverly Moser

In recent years, the language-instruction profession has seen alarming declines in enrollment in languages other than Spanish (Brod & Huber, 1992; Van Cleve & Willson, 1993; Siskin, Knowles, & Davis, 1996). At the same time, colleges are facing increasing pressure from state legislatures and boards of trustees to show how higher education is meeting the needs of students in an increasingly goal- and earnings-oriented model of education. College students are consumers, college courses are products, and universities are locales of education delivery. These shifts in conceptualizing higher education in the broadest sense, and the immediate enrollment trends of foreign languages more narrowly, pose a serious threat to linguistic diversity on campuses nationwide. As burgeoning classes in Spanish exert pressure on language departments to staff new positions, university administrators working under "accountability" models are focusing on the bottom line. It is clear that funding decisions will be made. Whether administrators have occasion to consider the intrinsic importance of offering a diversity of languages in this global age will depend largely on how well we do our job of communicating with them. As experts in our respective languages, it is our responsibility to stand firm against short-sighted economic arguments, to advocate for language choice for our students, and to position our courses and our diversity of languages firmly within the context of the college core. This is a mission for all of us who are foreign language educators, both for Spanish-teaching colleagues and for those of us teaching German, French, Russian, and other languages with a smaller student clientele. A diversity of languages reflects the diverse realities of the global marketplace where our students will make their way.

INTERNATIONALIZING COLLEGE CURRICULA: SOME MISCONCEPTIONS

Across the country, universities are taking steps to internationalize the college curriculum. Still, Wilga Rivers' leading question from the early 1990s has yet to find an answer: Internationalization of the university: Where are the foreign languages? (1993). The continuing integration of Europe has created an economic power that easily rivals our own. America's economic challenges are changing, and even in Europe there is a growing sentiment that proficiency in multiple foreign languages will be one of the keys to a successful future. Forward-thinking educators in the United States are pointing out that Arabic, Chinese, Hindi, and other less-commonly taught languages are increasingly relevant to changes in the global marketplace (García, 1998). Though no one can deny the geostrategic importance of Spanish to the American economy, America's trade interests are diverse and include nearly every area of the globe. The initiative Goals 2000 Educate America bill (1994) foresaw this and placed the issue of foreign language proficiency again in the spotlight (Rivers, 1994). While current trade relationships and NAFTA make Spanish a practical choice for existing American concerns, students of the future will be truly prepared for a global marketplace when they can leave home and seek international opportunities on equal ground with their European and Asian competitors. Opportunities to choose from a diversity of languages and college curricula that support the mastery of a foreign language to a high level of proficiency will be critical to attaining the goal of an internationalized curriculum.

Ironically, despite the move to internationalize higher education, those of us teaching languages other than Spanish have seen clear messages that the future of our programs is not secure (Byrnes, 1998b, pp. 10–11). Fiscal realities and enrollment fluctuations have merged smaller foreign languages into mega-departments; programs leading to the Russian major are imperiled; faculty lines in French and German are lost to attrition, split between two languages, or reappropriated for Spanish. However, on campuses where the support for foreign language study is especially strong, programs of foreign language across the curriculum have been developed to expose students to content courses in other disciplines offered all or in part in the foreign language (Knecht, 1999; Rivers, 1994). On these few fortunate campuses, these programs come closest to meeting the goals of a truly internationalized curriculum whereby students take courses in the target language much in the way an educated native speaker would.[1] However, on the majority of campuses, foreign language study is hardly a strong component of the university's mission to internationalize. This clearly needs to change.

One problem we face as a discipline stems from a broader misunderstanding entrenched both in higher education and in the general population: unrealistic expectations about the complexity and speed with which one can acquire a foreign language. This leads to the misconception, even in well-intentioned discussions of internationalizing the curriculum, that making room for two to four semesters of a foreign language should be sufficient to allow students to use the language in work settings or, conversely, that language courses themselves are at fault if students do not emerge "fluent" after two years. This gross underestimation of the complexity of the task is not shared by our European and Asian counterparts, who introduce foreign languages in grade school and know the importance of longer sequences of instruction. As masters of one or more foreign languages and as the university's liaison with other countries of the world, it is we who are best suited to position this issue in the continuing discussion of the university's mission to internationalize. As a group, we can build an awareness across campus that language study happens better when it happens early and happens best when it continues throughout students' four years of college. The message to students from all sides should be clear: Start a language as freshmen and continue until graduation.

An additional reality hampering efforts to have foreign languages play a more integral role in an international curriculum is the fully saturated nature of the college curriculum itself. If we encourage students to take more courses in a foreign language in order to become more fully proficient, how will an already-full program of study flex to make room for this? This is a real issue with curricular implications for various departments and financial implications for students. To overlook these concerns would be to invite opposition on all fronts.

This chapter examines these challenges facing languages programs today and suggests strategies for addressing them. It opens the volume's section on learner motivation by outlining broad-based steps for creating a community of learners in respective foreign languages, which would give students mutual support for making a long-term commitment to foreign language study. In opening, this chapter suggests that it is equally important to create among our colleagues a community of scholars across campus, so that the broader university context supports the extended study of foreign languages by students over time. Though derived from the broader vision that foreign languages are central to the curriculum of an internationalized campus, the focus here is on describing tangible, tried-and-true strategies to make this a reality.

The chapter complements others in the volume by dealing primarily with the importance of language diversity (see also Jernigan in this book) and with the viability of the upper-level program in various foreign languages (see Morris, Schultz, Gonglewski, and Schleppegrell in this volume). Though quality instruction at the lower level is always key, it will be discussed in other sections of this volume. The vitality of the upper-level program is the focus here because it is most critical to developing the high-level skills that make students professionally viable. The upper-level program is also the one most directly at risk when the pool of students shrinks. Though the chapter pertains most directly to the languages that have experienced enrollment declines in recent years (German, French, Russian), even heavily enrolled Spanish programs are addressed, as they share many issues with respect to attrition, student advising, ongoing language development, and other challenging aspects of advanced language study.

CREATING A COMMUNITY OF SCHOLARS

There has been much discussion here and elsewhere about demonstrating the contribution of foreign languages to the broader mission of the university (Swaffar, 1999; Roche, 1999). Rivers (1994) is careful to point out that the true benefits of "internationalization" come when students have reached high levels of foreign language proficiency, which is tied to their access to extended sequences of advanced-level instruction. From a programmatic standpoint, it is pointless for students to become excited about a foreign language only when they are ready to graduate. Careful advising before students select their first term of courses is a critical first link to enrolling freshmen early on. Since faculty and staff with varied backgrounds typically serve as general advisors to incoming freshmen, we must ensure that all members of the university community who come in contact with students understand the centrality of foreign languages to an internationalized curriculum.

HOW GENERAL ADVISORS ADVISE

Scene: College Advising Center at a major research university

Context: Student advising appointment, early August

Participants: Faculty advisor, a faculty member from discipline X; incoming freshman setting up schedule for fall

Student: What should I do about a foreign language? I had some French in high school.

Advisor: Oh, just get one of those cassettes from the bookstore, and see if you can place out.

This verbatim excerpt from a conversation in a well-staffed and generally well-trained advising center at a large state university in Tennessee documents the quality of faculty-student interactions in the worst-case scenario— when there is no input from foreign language specialists about the role of languages in the core curriculum. It also demonstrates one of the reasons that students postpone language study until very late: They are advised to do so by a faculty member they trust.

When students postpone taking a foreign language by even a year, they lose access to a whole year of advanced-level coursework in the language, and with it the chance to integrate upper-level language instruction into their general curriculum. Starting foreign language study early creates multiple options for students, regardless of the language they choose. By funneling students into language courses early, we give more of them the chance to become competent users of the target language.

Strategies

Liaison with Advising Centers. Foreign language faculty maintain ongoing representation in college advising centers, either by serving there in person or via regular, frequent meetings with the directors. With leadership from the advising director, the notion that foreign languages are something for students to "get out of the way" can be replaced with advice that encourages foreign language study. For example, the director will benefit from knowing about the varied careers that are open to students with language skills who combine foreign languages with another field of study.[2] When the director of advising knows that students need advanced-level classes to develop professionally viable skills, freshmen are routed into language classes early. The early continuation of language study in college also makes it less likely that work from high school is lost.

Direct Communication with Advisors. Faculty advisors from other disciplines need to know how foreign languages are part of an internationalized curriculum. Through direct contact with foreign language professors, they need to be aware of the benefits of starting foreign languages early and the opportunities available to students who do: study and work internships abroad. They need information on existing language placement exams and how or if college credit can be granted for language skills gained in high school. They need to be alerted to interesting, topic-based courses offered at the advanced level for students who are able to place out of the first two years of language, so that they can encourage students to take language placement exams seriously.

Freshman Orientation. An additional point of contact is with advisors and peer leaders of the freshman orientation programs that take place on campus during the summer. Orientation advisors need to know that the language placement exam is as important as math or English exams students take en masse. Peer orientation leaders need to convince their eighteen-year-old charges to actually attend and attempt the language exam. Ideally, placement exams need to be made a requirement for starting college, and a statement to this effect should be printed in the undergraduate bulletin.

Foreign Languages and Upper-level Graduation Requirements. General studies advisors need to know which advanced-level courses taught in a foreign language fulfill additional, upper-level requirements for graduation (in the humanities, social sciences, etc.). These connections to the upper-level curriculum may be obvious to those of us who teach the courses, but we cannot convey these benefits to students unless they enroll in our classes early on.

The reputation of foreign language study must be improved by such methods so that faculty and staff at all levels encourage language study rather than suggest it is a necessary evil. If we wish to reach students soon enough to leave them time to develop strong proficiency in a language, foreign language faculty must be more visible in the general advising process from the very beginning, and more vocal in discussions of the core curriculum throughout.

GALVANIZING SUPPORT FOR A DIVERSITY OF LANGUAGES

In addition to improving the level of communication with our colleagues who advise, campus-wide cocurricular programming reaches a different cross-section of the population. Colleagues in smaller language sections are particularly in need of demonstrating their presence on campus and showcasing the ways in which the university community is richer and more diverse because they are there. Faculty in less commonly taught languages can join forces to plan innovative programming; when the burden is shared, a variety of events can be offered each term. By strategies outlined here, a diversity of foreign languages is incorporated into campus life.

Strategies

Film. The foreign language department offers an international film festival each semester and targets its advertising toward specific professors who teach courses with international themes. Faculty members from other disciplines (communications, film studies) are invited as guest-presenters in the series; they bring their colleagues and students, and the community attends.

Poetry. Professors in French, Spanish, German, and Russian organize an international poetry reading each year, with pieces selected around a central topic and read in the original and in translation. Colleagues from the English department are recruited to present the translations or to add relevant contributions in English from world literature.

Music. Foreign language and music professors collaborate to schedule a series of recitals, each of which showcases the music of a specific country. The lyrics are provided in advance to the language faculty and are read in the original in class. The advanced preparation enhances students' comprehension of the works and allows them to appreciate the artists' interpretations. A language club sponsors an after-concert reception for the events, and the community, foreign language, and music students attend.

Art. A language professor contacts the art department to coordinate a traveling exhibit by an artist in a less commonly taught foreign language. The language department borrows the exhibit from the cultural division of the embassy of the target culture. Art is displayed prominently in the student center. An art professor is invited to present a brief lecture at the opening, and art and foreign language students attend.

History. A language professor contacts faculty teaching European Civilization to invite them to a documentary exhibit targeting a specific historical period, which has been borrowed from the target country's embassy. As a class project, advanced-level students translate captions, writing, and other language in the exhibit panels to make them accessible to English monolinguals. The target language is displayed as a living, breathing language that has something to communicate. In the translations, language students demonstrate their ability to make the texts accessible to those who don't know the code. Language students, students from history, and others across campus attend.

Publicity. Ensuring the success of all events is the willingness to do long-term planning and robust advertising. The student newspaper, faculty newsletter, and local and regional newspapers are contacted; flyers announcing the events are distributed. Deans, provosts, and university presidents are invited.

When possible, such events are incorporated into the regular teaching of foreign language courses. Advanced students write a reaction paper after attending an exhibit, intermediate students write a synopsis of a foreign film, and introductory students write a paragraph describing their favorite song at a recital. Just as language courses diversify what happens on campus, connections with outside disciplines invigorate what students do in the foreign language. The interconnections build excitement for language students and make it clear on campus that foreign languages have something to offer everyone.

FROM COCURRICULAR TO CURRICULAR

The campus-wide cocurricular programming just described reaches a broad student population. Jedan (1996, 1998) and DiDonato (1998) offer useful strategies for translating students' interests in the culture into college courses aimed at this broad base. For example, developing bona fide courses in film (Russian Culture Through Film, French Culture Through Film) attracts students who do not speak the language, but who may become interested in it by working with a popular medium. When film specialists from other departments are invited to co-teach or guest lecture, these courses also become opportunities for faculty collaborations.

COLLABORATING FOR SUPPORT OF A SPECIFIC LANGUAGE

Byrnes (1996, pp. 50–51) suggests Germanists improve their lot by enhancing their visibility to constituents at various levels: to colleagues, by collaborating with them, and to administrators, by participating in university governance within the administrative hierarchy. Roche (1999, pp. 16–17) highlights many other points of connection outside the academy: with high schools, professional schools, alumni contacts, and the community at large, all of whom have an interest in promoting a given foreign language.

One practical and straightforward option is to form unofficial alliances on campus between all members of the faculty, regardless of their discipline, who speak or share an interest in a common foreign language. If we formalize our colleagues' commitment to maintaining a target language on campus and keep them apprised of developments that may affect language study, professors in related disciplines support our work and multiply our institutional clout.

Strategy

Language Affinity Groups. Once per semester, faculty members from all disciplines who speak a common foreign language gather to discuss developments in their respective departments and how they might program for the year ahead.[3] As new faculty with language skills are discovered, they are immediately incorporated into the group. Research and teaching collaborations have a chance to take shape as faculty discover how many other professors on campus share their background in the target language. Faculty-student advising is enhanced because contact people in each discipline can be identified to language students with academic interests in a second area. An e-mail list keeps faculty apprised of language-related events on campus, and professors in all disciplines promote events involving the target language.

By creating a community of scholars who together support the goal of extended foreign language study, we have a better chance of finding and reaching our students. Seeking out research and teaching collaborations with other disciplines, joining forces with sympathetic promoters of each endangered language, participating visibly and vocally in university governance, adding foreign language vision to the practice of general advising, making sure diverse languages are active in campus life—in sum, being visible at all levels—are strategies available, perhaps even necessary, for maintaining a diversity of languages in the future.

CREATING A COMMUNITY OF LEARNERS

Surveys of incoming freshmen reveal that today's students see college as means of securing prestigious, well-paid employment (*Chronicle of Higher Education,* 1999). A survey of 275,811 freshmen in 469 two- and four-year institutions underscores this in the crassest of terms[4]: The most frequently cited rationale for deciding to go to college was "to be able to make more money." The most strongly rated personal objective considered "essential" or "very important" by freshmen was "being very well off financially." For those of us raised in decades where the humanities were not spurned as impractical, it may be difficult to reconcile ourselves to the need to argue in economic terms for the value of language study. But by understanding the goals of the current population of students, we can speak to what moves them. Fortunately, once we have enrolled our students, we can satisfy their concern for practicality as well as offer compelling personal motivation for continuing with a language until they are proficient.

MOVING BEYOND THE TRADITIONAL CLASSROOM

Many articles in this volume demonstrate our interest in enhancing students' motivation for language study (see Jernigan, Morris, and Collins in this book). It is unlikely we will reach today's students if we offer the kind of traditional language courses that we ourselves may have braved. Students say they want to learn to speak the language, though they are not always aware that this is a time-consuming process in which they will not experience immediate results. We know they have an interest in culture, but we must make room for it in our courses. What seems needed is a way to expand the walls of the classroom and give students opportunities to make the language a part of their lives. This begins by improving their ability to make tangible progress in the language and set realistic goals for long-term study. Immersion and mini-immersion experiences accomplish this goal.

IMMERSION AND MINI-IMMERSION EXPERIENCES

The age-old belief that immersion is the most effective way for students to make faster progress may have its place in the college curriculum (see also

Erben in this volume). Immersion weekends in relaxed, off-campus settings supplement classroom learning and add a personal dimension to students' lives. Like true immersion in a foreign culture, the students' experience of living and breathing the target language in an all-German (all-French, all-Russian) environment is exhilarating. Unlike total immersion abroad, students are not left on their own to sink or swim, but are surrounded by other learners struggling to reach the same goals. Students come to know each other and their professors on a more personal plane and gain confidence in their skills. Their realization that they can actually survive in an immersion environment is motivational, and the camaraderie that ensues creates a network of mutual support among students that carries over into the classroom (Moser & Ohnesorg, 1997).

By interacting with students in immersion events out of class, some of the most strived-after elements of modern foreign language instruction are automatically present: There is a focus on task (in most cases, having fun with other students), where the target language is always present, but secondary. Quite naturally, language is the vehicle, not the destination, and comprehensibility directs the degree to which students have to correct their utterances. Grade anxiety is also absent, and the excitement of being understood by their peers becomes self-motivating. To the typical eighteen- to twenty-two-year-old student, this peer-driven encouragement is exceptionally powerful motivation to stick with the language. At our campus, participants repeatedly express surprise when they discover there are so many students learning German. Also, we regularly welcome faculty members from other disciplines who want to brush up on their skills. This communicates to students that language learning is a lifelong process and adds to the sense of community. By the end of the weekend, students' thrill at being able to communicate in the target language is palpable ("I had my first German dream!"), and this excitement is brought back to campus with positive implications for all.[5]

Immersion weekends stretch a meager three contact hours of class into an opportunity for students to experience exponential progress in a short time. Participants have commented on the value of the cultural immersion as well, as the day-to-day life of the target culture (eating, music, traditional games and activities) brings the language alive. Other offerings with similar goals are regular coffee hours, game-playing sessions, meals where the target language is spoken, study trips to off-campus locations, or performances out of town. All small-scale activities are feasible even for small language sections. Though these activities cannot hope to replace the nuts-and-bolts learning that occurs in the classroom, they provide components that may be equally important: the motivation for students to make a long-term commitment to the foreign language and a greater level of confidence that they will be successful in the end.

Strategies

Immersion Weekends. One or two faculty members organize a 24–48-hour immersion weekend that recreates, off-campus, an all-German (all-French, all-Russian, all-Spanish) environment.[6] Simple poetry, children's books, sheet music, and posters are brought along, and exchange students are invited to add authenticity. The participants cook common meals, bake tempting desserts from recipes in the target culture, play board games, word games, and parlor games, do craft activities, sing, dance, go hiking, put on skits—all in the target language. Faculty members accompany students and serve as resources, but the students help plan and offer the activities. Advanced students are paired with beginners in activities that are language-intense, and expressive nonlanguage activities (artwork, sports, baking, etc.) are included to ensure that every participant, regardless of language level, has meaningful ways to participate. The university's Student Development Office is contacted for funding. Frequency: once per semester.

Class Trips. A language section organizes an off-campus trip to an interesting but remote location (a large city with an international atmosphere, or a former colony of speakers of the target language). Ideally, the location is connected thematically to material treated in one or more language classes. The students' language club raises funds to offset the cost. Faculty members devote a long weekend to traveling with students and coming to know them as people; students get off campus and see what they are studying reflected in life. When students are advanced learners, the target language is spoken exclusively. Frequency: annually or in alternate years.

Day Trips. Faculty members identify a museum or a performance of a play or opera off campus that is related to the target language. An excursion is organized and offered at cost. Advanced planning allows the topic (of the opera or play) or the theme of the museum to be treated in the target language in class. When students return, they write or talk about their experiences as part of class activities. Frequency: once per semester.

Conversation Tables. Faculty members, foreign exchange students, and supporters of the language from other departments meet on a regular basis outside of class for coffee and games or pizza and beer, with all conversation taking place in the target language. In advertising at all levels, students know it is acceptable to come and listen without speaking. Frequency: every two weeks.

A side benefit to sponsoring out-of-class learning opportunities for students is the degree to which faculty members come to know students' goals and aspirations for the foreign language. This automatically ensures a higher quality of academic advising for students who are considering whether to major or minor.

ADVISING AND THE ACCOUNTABILITY MODEL

With the increased focus on institutional accountability, programs marked as "unproductive" are quick to be scrutinized by the university administration. However, it is unfortunate that university student data programs have not always kept pace with the trend of today's students, who pursue double majors and multiple minors in an effort to create a professional profile. While some university statistics programs do index a second major, this is normally entered into records only in the student's senior year, rendering statistics on existing majors tenuous at best.

Foreign languages are caught in a double bind in the institutional bean-counting. Many students now choose to take Spanish instead of French or German for its perceived utility. Those students who select another language (such as French or German) and continue with it opt for a double major in the language and another subject with perceived utility (such as business). A recent survey at the University of Tennessee, Knoxville found every conceivable combination of fields as a dual major with German, including agriculture, art, biology, English, history, psychology, sociology, linguistics, prelaw, and business. However, students categorically opted to list the other field, not German, as their primary major. Ironically, this affects enrollment statistics in the less commonly taught languages most acutely, because it leaves many students—in fact, some of the most fully internationalized students on campus—fully invisible in university statistics on majors and minors.

In addition to the havoc that double-majoring wreaks on accountability statistics, the trend toward dual majors creates new challenges for advising. Students' major combinations often span two colleges with differing graduation requirements. While the advising center may work efficiently at directing a student to an advisor in her "major," which major does she choose? How does one sequence the prerequisites for two degrees at once, and how can a student plan for a semester or year abroad and still graduate on time? Ideally, students with multiple majors confer with advisors in both fields before registering each term, but the practical obstacles are significant. A departmental policy on advising with required advising for all majors and minors and a commitment on the part of language faculty to make this work are invaluable.

At the departmental level, a well-conceived advising strategy in intermediate courses counteracts deterrents to advanced classes. As in good teaching, effective advising involves keeping in mind where students are and aiming the discussion to meet them. Knowing what may discourage students from continuing in a language is key. For example, if we remember that many Americans have unrealistic expectations of how quickly they will become "fluent," we will remember to talk to students about this and acknowledge their frustrations. By considering other forces in the student's choice of courses, advising sessions open a dialogue that dispels myths (for example, that the only thing one can do with a language is to teach). Exhorting a student to continue in a language is ineffectual if others are pushing him to take only those courses that will supposedly "get him a job." Early advising allows faculty to talk about ways to combine foreign languages with other disciplines and with students' long-term career goals. In advising sessions, students can learn about study abroad programs and interesting advanced-level courses and make long-term plans for foreign internships or their job search.[7]

A well-organized departmental advising program also has an excellent side benefit for accountability, because it makes sure precise statistics on majors and minors are immediately available and up-to-date. By gathering information on the student population each year, it is possible to develop specialized advanced-level courses that incorporate the interests of students and entice them to go on. The organization required to get an advising program started is well worth the effort. As long as college administrators rely on institutional statistics to justify programs, scrupulous record-keeping in the language department is the only way one can make sure all majors and minors are reflected.

Strategies

Student Surveys. Early each spring, the department surveys all language students. Questions determine the students' major/minor combinations, who is considering continuing, who wants to study abroad and when, and what kinds of courses students would value in the future. Students' e-mail addresses and phone numbers are gathered, along with demographic information. The survey can list the names of available advisors and their specialties, giving students immediate ways to contact an advisor.

Bookkeeping. An advising coordinator prepares a master list of majors and minors with all pertinent information (major combinations, goals for foreign study, etc.). This accurate, shorthand version of the department's student clientele is a powerful tool when defending one's program to the upper administration.

Faculty Commitment to Advising. A departmental policy requires advising for all students past the third semester of language study. Faculty members receive a list of their advisees and agree to follow up on students who have not appeared for required advising. E-mail makes this easier than ever before. Especially in languages where the enrollment is small, faculty members make a commitment to follow up on each and every student.

Knowledge of Multiple Curricula. A contact person in the department learns about the degree requirements in one of the other colleges (business, communications, engineering, art, etc.) and is the advising specialist for this combination of fields. This is invaluable to students double-majoring in a foreign language and business or engineering, where the prerequisites in the first two years of study are less flexible.

With the changes in teaching methods in the last decades, today's learner-centeredness ensures that foreign language professors genuinely come to know their students in class. Extending this outside the classroom into a more beneficial advising program is an easy next step toward retaining students for advanced-level courses.

ENGAGING STUDENTS AT ADVANCED LEVELS

There is no shortage of ideas for invigorating language courses with activities that are exciting. In their work on redefining the goals of foreign language study, Kramsch (1993a, 1993b, 1995), Kern (1995), Byrnes (1998a), and Swaffar (1998, 1999) have in different ways suggested the value of teaching language as a phenomenon that is socially constructed, where language courses develop students' awareness of ways in which cultural identity manifests itself. This makes even introductory language courses compelling vehicles of culture. However, as Benseler laments, the content of the upper-division program continues to be problematic and "qualifies for designation as the most neglected area of our entire enterprise" (1991, p. 189).

In recent years, advances in content-based instruction have married foreign language study with virtually every discipline. Byrnes' ideal of "content from the onset of instruction and language to the end" (personal communication, cited in Swaffar, 1999) underscores the importance of providing ongoing linguistic development in advanced courses, regardless of the topical focus. The important issue of designing a coherent advanced-level curriculum is too broad for treatment here but invites further study (see Byrnes, 1998). Happily, in the smaller languages, our smaller size can be a strength, for it is easier to respond more fully to the specific interests of the students in our classes and to tailor language instruction to students' needs.

Strategies

Designing New Courses. A recent survey of all German students delineated two strands of students with distinctly different goals. One group was enrolled in the humanities with interests in German literature and history. The second group wanted courses directed expressly at improving their skills (conversation/composition) and those with a business focus. Armed with this knowledge, the German section added two courses in two years: a world civilization course (history) offered entirely in German for the humanities students, and a business German sequence to attract the more practically oriented learners. It was easy to advertise these courses, since we knew at the outset who had requested them. The commitment to advising and our knowledge of our students' goals ensured a strong enrollment.

Updating Existing Courses. In some cases, updating a course to reflect students' increased concern for practical language use is easy to achieve. An under-enrolled "Phonetics and Diction" course gets new energy when recrafted as "Language in Performance." Here, students master phonetics by producing small- and large-scale performances of poetry, drama, and other genres in a format where their diction matters. The performance format lets goal-directed students see their progress, and the beauty of literature is showcased to inspire the next generation of literate readers. Such a course has appeal to business students wanting to improve public speaking skills and humanities students who are more interested in literary works.

Connections with the General Curriculum. Working within the college's curricular framework, new courses are developed or existing courses modi-fied to fulfill required "slots" in the general curriculum, such as upper-level humanities or social science requirements. For example, an advanced course in French literature, Japanese culture, or Russian film can be constructed to fulfill a humanities requirement. This allows students who are double major-ing or minoring to take language courses that simultaneously complete general degree requirements. This efficacy is enticement for undecided stu-dents to continue in the language and helps overburdened double-majors graduate on time.

Flexible Exit/Entry. Advanced courses that span two semesters (for exam-ple, Composition and Conversation I and II) are designed to accommodate the inevitable fact that not all students will be able to schedule the courses in sequence. When courses flex to allow students to exit and reenter language study each semester, students lost in the fall can be reintegrated in spring. However, since students are unfamiliar with taking courses out of numerical sequence, this option must be expressly communicated when courses are advertised.

Such strategies focus on the practical need for flexibility in advanced-level courses as a key to maintaining viable programming. Programs that capitalize on the specific interests of the students in their advanced pool are better able to retain students and maintain the strong enrollment figures that keep a variety of upper-level courses on the books.

SENDING THEM OUT

Just as the time-honored lockstep curriculum with fixed contents has evolved into more modular, advanced-level courses, today's students with dual majors and minors need foreign study and internship opportunities tailored to their specific goals (see also Bräuer in this volume). Strategies for success here are a hypertext version of the bigger picture: attracting students early, advising carefully, transferring credits flexibly, and matching experience abroad to the student's combination of fields. Since we cannot assume that every student will have considered foreign study or work as a freshman, advertising of study abroad is needed repeatedly, starting from the first semester of language study.

Strategies

Flexible Study, Flexible Timing Abroad. Though the traditional year of study abroad continues to be the ideal, realities of the oversaturated curriculum for double majors may make a year away unfeasible for students in preprofessional tracks (business, engineering). Students who discovered their love of languages close to graduation also need shorter-term options for studying abroad. Rather than the convenient practice of funneling all students into a single program, the length of foreign study is matched to the student's profile.

Repeated Information on Study Abroad. Technology has made sharing information about study abroad much easier and student-friendly via sites on the World Wide Web. Encouraging students to use this information is another matter. A class project at the beginning level that sends students to web pages on study sites abroad familiarizes students with international web surfing as it publicizes available programs. Similarly, web-based lists of internship possibilities are proof that exciting jobs exist. When attractive links are connected to a central site, students can be directed there periodically each semester.

A Personal Face. Making students aware of other young people on campus who have studied abroad is a guaranteed interest-builder. Website pictures of students currently abroad, hot links to their foreign e-mail addresses, informal presentations by excited returnees—all are steps that encourage the next generation of students to consider foreign study.

Transfer Credit Advising after Study Abroad. Transfer credit continues to be key in ensuring that students can graduate on time. Faculty members must be committed to negotiating the best possible deal in transfer credits for their students who venture abroad. With our focus on internationalizing education, it is appropriate to call for deans' leadership on this. When students are juggling two majors and doing serious study in a foreign culture, it is reasonable to double-count at least a few courses. This means awarding transfer credit not only in the language but also for other courses that satisfy general degree requirements or those of a second major or minor.

On our campus, as we have transcended the boundaries of the traditional classroom to come to know our students and have added courses that speak to their specific interests and needs, students have responded with gratitude, even surprise, that it is possible to combine foreign languages with so many aspects of their lives. In some ways, developing a community of learners for foreign languages counteracts the minimalist, earnings-oriented model of education. For students considering a long-time commitment to German, Russian, French, or Japanese, it has always been the human element of language learning, the sheer thrill and transformative power of the foreign language as an entryway into a new world, that has remained constant despite the fluctuations on the enrollment landscape. Good teaching has perhaps always boiled down to a critical factor or two: discerning the realities and goals of the current population of students, and finding compelling ways to meet these students where they are.

A COMMUNITY OF SCHOLARS AND LEARNERS: OUTLOOK FOR THE FUTURE

In the ongoing debate on the role of foreign languages in the university curriculum, leaders across the country agree that "business as usual is not a viable survival strategy for the twenty-first century" (Swaffar, 1999, p. 6). Sharing our vision that a diversity of languages mirrors the needs of the world and clarifying how foreign language, especially advanced language study, internationalizes the curriculum exponentially are important starting points.

In the face of overwhelming declines in enrollment in languages other than Spanish, it would be easy to throw up our hands and resign ourselves to teaching all advanced-level courses in literature and cultural history in translation. But as specialists in foreign languages, it falls to us to show those with decision-making power how a diversity of foreign languages advances broader educational goals, ones that are inherently valuable. As in all good teaching, by keeping in mind our audience—in this case our colleagues across campus and our students—we can become effective advocates for foreign languages as an integral part of an internationalized curriculum. By forming alliances with other faculty members and communicating more visibly at all levels, we keep all languages alive and integrated into campus life. Broad-based cocurricular planning makes us accessible to all students and visible to university administrators and the broader community. By knowing our student population and their interests, advising students well, offering repeated and enjoyable chances to experience progress and to make the language a part of their lives, we come many steps closer to realizing the goal of an internationalized curriculum where foreign languages play a central role.

NOTES

1. For example, see the programs in language across the curriculum at Rice University, Emory University, Earlham College, and St. Olaf College.

2. An excellent source for providing information on career opportunities in concise, readable form (two pages) is found in Branaman, 1998.

3. At German Studies meetings at our university, this gathering is also a social function that builds community. A business meeting is held as the final component of a potluck dinner, to which foreign students and all prospective majors and minors are invited.

4. This national survey of freshmen is conducted annually by the American Council on Education and the University of California at Los Angeles Higher Education Research Institute. The figures published in fall 1999 represent students who were freshmen in fall 1998.

5. At our campus, one immersion weekend in German was so effective in moving students out of language anxiety and into language use, that students continued immersion on a smaller scale by initiating a biweekly *Stammtisch,* where they meet to speak German over dinner.

6. For detailed suggestions on how to organize an immersion weekend for students in any language, see Moser and Ohnesorg, 1997.

7. In addition to Branaham, see de Galan and Lambert and the monthly newsletter *Current Jobs International.*

REFERENCES

Benseler, D. (1991). The upper-division curriculum in foreign languages and Literatures: Obstacles to the realization of promise. In E. Silber (ed.), *Critical issues in foreign language education.* New York: Garland.

Branaman, L. (1998). Foreign languages and job opportunities. *ERIC Review* 6(1): 67–69.

Brod, R., & Huber, B. J. (1992). Foreign language enrollments in United States institutions of higher education, fall 1990. *ADFL Bulletin* 23(1): 6–10.

Byrnes, H. (1996). How visible are we now? In J. A. McCarthy & K. Schneider (eds.), *The future of Germanistik in the USA: Changing our prospects,* pp. 46–52. Nashville: Vanderbilt University Press.

Byrnes, H. (1998a). Constructing curricula in collegiate foreign language departments. In H. Byrnes (ed.), *Learning foreign languages and second languages: Perspectives in research and scholarship,* pp. 262–295. New York: Modern Language Association.

Byrnes, H. (1998b). Introduction: Steps to an ecology of foreign language departments. In H. Byrnes (ed.), *Learning foreign languages and second languages: Perspectives in research and scholarship,* pp. 1–22. New York: Modern Language Association.

Chronicle of Higher Education, Almanac Edition: 1999–2000. (1999). The nation: Attitudes and characteristics of freshmen. August 27, p. 28.

Current Jobs International. Washington: Plymouth Publishing.

de Galan, J., & Lambert, S. (1995). *Great jobs for foreign language majors.* Lincolnwood:VGM Career Horizons.

DiDonato, R. (1998). Undergraduate German programs: Strategies for success. *ADFL Bulletin* 30(1): 12–14.

García, E. (1998). Spanish, French, and German: An Edwardian pattern for a postmodern world. *ADFL Bulletin* 30(1): 9–11.

Jedan, D. (1996). Reshaping the undergraduate experience in German. In J. A. McCarthy & K. Schneider (eds.), *The future of Germanistik in the USA: Changing our prospects*, pp. 65–90. Nashville: Vanderbilt University Press.

Jedan, D. (1998). Shifting enrollment patterns: Departmental perspectives. *ADFL Bulletin* 30(1): 15–17.

Kern, R. (1995). Redefining the boundaries of foreign language literacy. In C. Kramsch (ed.), *Redefining the boundaries of language study*, pp. 61–98. Boston: Heinle and Heinle.

Knecht, M. (1999). Integrated learning and internationalized education through languages across the curriculum. *ADFL Bulletin* 30(3): 17–22.

Kramsch, C. (1993a). *Context and culture in language teaching*. Oxford: Oxford University Press.

Kramsch, C. (1993b). Foreign languages for a global age. *ADFL Bulletin* 25(1): 5–12.

Kramsch, C. (1995). *Redefining the boundaries of language study*. Boston: Heinle and Heinle.

Moser, B., & Ohnesorg, S. (1997). *A guide to language immersion weekends for undergraduates*. Cherry Hill: American Association of Teachers of German.

Rivers, W. M. (1993). *Internationalization of the university: Where are the foreign languages?* Georgetown University Roundtable on Languages and Linguistics 1992. Washington: Georgetown University Press.

Rivers, W. M. (1994). Developing international competence for a centripetal, centrifugal world. *ADFL Bulletin* 26(1): 25–34.

Roche, M. W. (1999). Strategies for enhancing the visibility and role of foreign language departments. *ADFL Bulletin* 30(2): 10–18.

Siskin, H. J, Knowles, M. A., & Davis, R. L. (1996). Le Français et mort, vive le français: Rethinking the function of French. In J. Liskin-Gasparro (ed.), *Patterns and policies: The changing demographics of foreign language instruction*, pp. 35–69. Boston: Heinle and Heinle.

Swaffar, J. (1998). Major changes: The standards project and the new foreign language curriculum. *ADFL Bulletin* 30(1): 34–37.

Swaffar, J. (1999). The case for foreign languages as a discipline. *ADFL Bulletin* 30(3): 6–12.

Van Cleve, J., & Willson, A. L. (1993). *Remarks on the needed reform of German studies in the USA*. Columbia: Camden House.

2

The Role of Beliefs, Attributions, and Perceived Goal Attainment in Students' Motivation

Christine Galbreath Jernigan

INTRODUCTION

The purpose of the study reported in this chapter was to examine university students' initial motivations for studying a less commonly taught language and their goals for the class, to find out whether these students' perceived goal attainment is related to their continued motivation for language study. The less commonly taught languages (LCTL) have received little scholarly attention in the area of student motivation, goals, and attrition and must therefore rely on studies of students of German, French, and Spanish. Given the different profile of LCTL students (Wen, 1997), however, these factors may differ for learners of different languages (McGinnis, 1994).

This study sought to analyze students' motivations through a paradigm other than the socioeducational model popular in foreign language research, a model valued for its dichotomy between integrative motivation, based on cultural interests, and instrumental motivation, based on the practical value behind language learning (Gardner, 1985). Here, value-expectancy theories prevalent in the general learning literature provided an alternative approach to conceptualizing foreign language motivation.

Participants in this study included lower-division Portuguese students, teachers, and four administrators at the University of Texas at Austin. Data sources included opening and closing surveys and interviews with students, instructors, and advisors. Qualitative and quantitative analyses were used to interpret responses.

Many participants reported reasons for studying the language that fell outside the integrative/instrumental construct. Several enrolled out of an intrinsic love of the language, while others enrolled from a desire to interact in the language with native and nonnative speakers. In factor analysis of the survey items, neither of these reasons loaded with items that would be categorized as integrative or instrumental. A new model is proposed for student motivation based on the grounded theory analysis of survey and interview data. Results indicated that continued motivational strength is affected by students' beliefs about language study and by their attributions for success or failure. This study supported the idea that beliefs and attributions interact with students' perceptions of goal importance and their expectations for goal attainment, mediating the relationship between perceived goal attainment and continued motivation. Possible teacher interventions concerning students' beliefs and attributions are offered.

THEORETICAL BACKGROUND

> The most important attitude that can be formed is that of the desire to go on learning.
>
> (Lepper & Hodell, 1989, p. 73)

As several authors of related works in this volume would testify (see Moser, Morris, and Collins in this book), a willingness to take students' interests into account when planning a language course is essential to student and program success. Knowing the reasons students have chosen to take a language course and their objectives allows for more directed instruction that should better serve students' interests.

The beliefs students hold about learning languages are also an important aspect of motivation, since the degree to which individuals feel they can accomplish a certain task will largely depend on the beliefs they hold about that task. Bandura (1981, in Schunk, 1991) posits that students' self-efficacy, or their belief about how well they can perform a task, often comes from vicarious experiences, which could result in unrealistic beliefs about learning tasks. Students may be assessing their language-learning ability based on what their parents told them about their own difficulties learning a language or on "myths" propagated by classmates. Learning more about the effects students' beliefs have on motivation could aid educators and administrators in fostering continued motivation for language study.

In examining students' reasons for taking a foreign language, most would agree that Gardner and Lambert's (1959, 1972) studies are the cornerstone of research on language learning motivation. Their research has demonstrated the effect of motivational orientation—the reasons for taking the language—on students' persistence in studying a foreign language (Gardner & Smythe, 1975b). Students' reasons could be more integrative, for those learning the language to "communicate with, interact with, or to become (in some small way) a part of the other language community" (Gardner & Smythe, 1975a, p. 219), or more instrumental, for students with pragmatic reasons for language study, including job opportunities or social recognition. These orientations are described as context and language specific (Clément & Kruidenier, 1983). If the foreign language curriculum needs to be changed to take students' motivations into account (Oxford & Shearin, 1994), it is essential to know the orientations of the specific student population before initiating change.

Though foreign language education has seen a wealth of research on students' motivations for taking Spanish, French, and German, there is little motivation research on students of less commonly taught languages (LCTL). Walton (1992) laments this state of affairs, noting that LCTL programs differ substantially from programs of more commonly taught languages.

> The LCTLs do have their own world within American foreign language education: their own . . . pedagogical traditions, financial support structures (however weak), and . . . their own problems . . . [yet] have never occupied a highly visible position in American foreign language education. (Walton, 1992, p. 2)

Unfortunately this lack of empirical focus has resulted in curricular changes based on mere supposition. A call for changes in university Portuguese courses, for example, was initiated based on the assertion that programs were not meeting the changing needs of students (Courtcau, 1996; Suárez, 1996). Though this assertion is perhaps based on educators' experiences, I have found no studies to date that support such claims. One important aspect of this study, therefore, will be to further examine the motivations and goals of students of a LCTL.

A second important aspect of this study is its application of more recent models of motivation prevalent in the general learning literature. For the past three decades, most foreign language motivation research has used as its base the integrative-instrumental constructs of Gardner's socioeducational model. His model applies primarily to the individual in a group context, generally the target culture, and therefore tends to focus on integrative motivation. Several studies have indicated, however, that although individuals may be influenced to learn a second language for social reasons—for example, to gain social recognition or to express and preserve their own culture within the target culture—they are not necessarily interested in integration (Ladousse, 1982).

It is also argued that not all motivation is tied to a group setting (Oxford & Shearin, 1994; Crookes & Schmidt, 1991). Some students take a language course merely to fulfill the language requirement, a reason that in factor analysis did not load with instrumental factors, but was instead found to be a separate orientation not accounted for in the socioeducational model (Ely, 1986; Wen, 1997). These concerns have encouraged foreign language researchers to include theories from neighboring disciplines, resulting in the following alternative views for conceptualizing motivation and spawning further theoretical (Oxford & Shearin, 1994) and empirical research (Nam Yung, 1996; Wen, 1997).

THE VALUE-EXPECTANCE MODEL
FOR STUDENT MOTIVATION

Most relevant to this study is the social-cognitive approach to conceptualizing motivation with its emphasis on students' goals and the values and expectations related to those goals. This motivational model highlights how students' beliefs and interpretations of what they are experiencing influence cognitive processes (Pintrich, Marx, & Boyle, 1993). Goal setting involves making decisions about which goals are most important. Learners' reactions to difficulties faced throughout the goal attainment process are influenced by whether or not they feel what is gained from their efforts is worthwhile (Blumenfeld, 1992). According to Atkinson's (1966, in Schunk, 1991) Expectancy Value Theory, behavior is not only a function of how much an individual values a certain goal, but how much (s)he expects to obtain that goal. In the context of the foreign language classroom, learners' expectancies of success influence their persistence in studying the language.

Misperceptions about the rate at which individuals learn a language can have obvious debilitating effects on students' persistence. Studies indicate that those who expect to be fluent in one to two years of study will be frustrated when they do not progress as they thought they would (Horwitz, 1988). Altman's (1985) review of the literature on foreign language attrition concludes that students often "grossly overestimate their own ability to perform" (Altman, 1985, p. 4) and then discontinue studying the language because the classroom experience is not what they expected (Altman, 1985; Lemke, 1992).

Changes in beliefs may be most needed for students of languages that are less commonly taught. Wen (1997) found the attrition rates of students of Chinese and Japanese to be especially high, with dropout rates in Japanese classes often as high as 80%. Saminy and Tabuse (1992, in Wen, 1997) cite as the cause the phenomenon that "learning less commonly taught languages can produce strong negative affective reactions from the students which hinder their learning motivation since they are not aware of the level of task difficulty" (Wen, 1997, p. 236). Learners enticed to take a language by its orthographic calligraphy may not realize the effort needed to learn the orthography (Wen, 1997). A similar problem may exist with students learning a language similar to one they already know. This research will examine, for example, whether Spanish-speaking learners of Portuguese have unrealistic expectations of reaching advanced levels of Portuguese within a short amount of time.

One aspect of beliefs that is integral to the value-expectancy model is that of attributions, defined in the general learning research as perceived causes for success or failure. These "perceived causes of outcomes" (Schunk, 1991, p. 246) may be interpreted by students as either independent of their own actions and thus "externally controlled" or dependent on the way they behave and thus "internally controlled" (Rotter, 1966, in Schunk, 1991). Whether students believe they have control over learning outcomes affects how much effort they expend in learning and how long they persist in their efforts (Dickinson, 1995).

STATEMENT OF THE PROBLEM

The current study attempted to answer the following questions:

1. What reasons do students give for taking Portuguese, and what are their goals for the class?
2. To what degree do students feel their goals have been attained during the semester?
3. What role if any do perceived goal attainment, students' beliefs about language learning, and their causal attributions for success and failure play in their decisions to continue or discontinue?

METHODOLOGY

To address these questions, this study employed a combination of quantitative and qualitative methods. A mixed-methods approach allows the strengths of one design to compensate for the weaknesses of another: A larger pool of participants may be surveyed while the "thicker" data obtainable from open-ended questions and interviews is also available.

PARTICIPANTS

Participants in this study included 101 lower-division Portuguese students at the University of Texas at Austin, their instructors, and 4 student advisors. Information on individual student participants was gathered through a background survey. Eighty-four students of the total 101 student participants responded to the background questionnaire. Their genders were a near perfect split, with 43 females and 41 males. The percentages of students in each category of majors included 47.6% humanities, 16.7% sciences, 13.1% business, 17.9% other, and 2.4% undeclared.

As concerns ethnicity, 2.4% were African-American, 29.8% were Hispanic, 63.1% Caucasian, 1.2% Asian-American, and 3.5% "other." In responding to a question about their first language, 77.4% were English as a first language speakers, 14.3% Spanish, 6% considered themselves English/Spanish bilinguals from childhood, and 2.4% said they spoke a language other than English or Spanish. Few students (13.1%) had not formally studied Spanish; nearly half (48.8%) had studied Spanish formally for over 2 years, 14.3% had taken it for two years or less, and 21.4% were native Spanish speakers.

Relatively few students were taking the class as freshmen (8.3%), as compared to sophomores (19%), juniors (19%), and the high percentage of seniors (25%). A large percentage (26.2%) were graduate students, and 2.4% (two students) had already graduated. A large percentage of students were not taking the class for a requirement (44.1%). Of those remaining, 33.3% were taking the class as a university requirement and 22.6% were taking it as a major, minor, or degree requirement.

INSTRUMENTS

Data sources included opening and closing surveys and interviews with students, instructors, and advisors. Prior to working with the population in the actual study, several pilot studies were performed with Portuguese students in the same university to elicit information about their reasons for taking the class, their goals, and their reasons for (dis)continued study. This information helped in formulating interview questions and in modifying previously used survey instruments to fit this specific population.

The researcher administered the first survey the first week of class. It included sections on students' backgrounds, their motivations for taking the course, their goals for the course, and their expectations for meeting those goals (see Appendix A). The second survey was administered the antepenultimate week of class and involved students' perceived goal attainment, modifications of goals, and students' reasons for (dis)continuing formal study (see Appendix B).

In addition, the researcher conducted telephone interviews with seven of the eight students who dropped the class before the end of the semester, with all six students who were auditing courses, and with five "extra" students whose survey responses merited further inquiry. In addition, thirty students taking the course for a grade were selected, using a stratified purposeful sampling technique (Mertens, 1997), to do opening and closing telephone interviews. The selection criteria were based on students' goal values and expectations ratings. Groups were formed by coding goal value and expectation sections from the first surveys (see Appendix A, Sections D and E). Using Excel, students were divided into four groups, those with a tendency to have low-valued goals paired with low expectations, those with low-valued goals paired with high expectations, and so on. Participants were separated into levels (first year, first semester; first year, second semester, etc.), and then each class was separated into the four groups. Since larger classes should have more representation in the interviews, the number of interviewees per class was based on class size. Participants' names were then randomly chosen from each group.

Interviews with teachers and administrators helped verify hypotheses emerging from student-generated data. During the last week of class, I interviewed four teachers of the lower-division classes as well as four administrators whom students mentioned as having influenced their decision to study the language.

DATA ANALYSIS

Survey data analysis was aided by the use of the statistical software SPSS and included frequencies, means, and standard deviations of background section and Likert scale responses. The reliability scales for the various sections were included, and factor analysis of responses was employed for the "Reasons for Studying Portuguese" scale.

Qualitative data included open-ended survey responses and interview responses with a grounded theory approach used for their analysis. The first stage of procedures involved the "open-coding" of interview data, defined as "breaking down . . . comparing, conceptualizing, and categorizing data" (Strauss & Corbin, 1990, p. 61). All 60 transcripts from the 30 main interviewees, along with those from the 7 "drop" and the 5 "extra" interviews, were read to see what commonalities and patterns emerged. Using a line-by-line approach to analyze each sentence, I separated data into categories relevant to the main phenomenon, students' motivation. I gave categories descriptive names like "beliefs about learning culture" and described the categories in memos. Throughout the coding process, I reread category names, their descriptions, and their coded information to ensure new information fit the categories, collapsing similar categories when needed. The categories that emerged during coding described the conditions leading students to enroll in and continue, or discontinue, studying the language.

The next step, "axial coding," made connections among the categories found in open coding. A tree-like structure contained each category, with "motivation" as the root from which branches (categories) and limbs (subcategories) emerged (see Appendix C). From this structure evolved a more general theory involving the categories' relationships to one another. Instead of examining the phenomenon in terms of only one relationship or one research question, this stage demands an overview of all the relationships relevant to the phenomenon. The qualitative research program "NUD*IST" (Non-numerical Unstructured Data: Indexing, Searching, and Theorizing) aided in the qualitative analysis, especially in expressing and validating or rejecting theories about categorical relationships.

RESULTS

Research Question One: Students' Motivations and Goals

The "Reasons for Studying Portuguese" section was employed to understand more about what motivated students to take the language class. The top fifteen ranked responses are given in Table 2.1.

The somewhat low Cronbach Alpha (.73) of the scale suggested multidimensionality within the survey items and prompted a factor analysis to see which items might be varying together. Using a Maximum Likelihood extraction method with a Promax rotation, I found that six distinct factors accounted for 45.5% of the total variance. Table 2.2 demonstrates clustered items.

One might equate the first two clusters of "Cultural Interests" and "Career/academic Advancement" with Gardner's "integrative" and "instrumental" categories respectively. However, the findings as a whole challenge these distinct categories. The item "Portuguese-speaking friends," under the "Career/academic Advancement" cluster, for example, indicates the category does not exclusively house motivations of a practical, instrumental nature. Interviews with students revealed that the "why" behind the career motives, ranked as important on the surveys, cannot be categorized as

Table 2.1 Students' Reasons for Studying Portuguese

Survey Item	Mean	SD
9. future career	2.27	.97
1. travel for pleasure	2.21	.88
27. fun	1.92	.92
7. cultural practices	1.90	.91
3. Portuguese-speaking country/countries' history	1.80	.98
8. perspectives on cultural practices	1.76	.90
2. converse with Portuguese-speakers in the United States	1.76	.90
5. cultural products	1.75	1.07
6. perspectives on cultural products	1.65	1.10
15. competitive job or grad school candidate	1.64	1.23
23. I love languages	1.62	1.09
20. sounds of Portuguese	1.61	1.12
4. major, minor, degree, or scholarship requirements	1.54	1.41
10. study abroad, research, or business travel	1.48	1.28
11. Portuguese-speaking friends	1.48	1.15

Table 2.2 Clusters of Factor Analysis of "Reasons for Studying Portuguese"

Cluster	Survey Items	Factor Loadings
1. Cultural Interests	perspectives on products	.904
	cultural practices	.881
	perspectives on practices	.828
	products	.723
	history	.549
	study in subject involving Portuguese	.487
	important language in the world	.396
2. Career/academic Advancement	study or business abroad	.697
	future career	.560
	competitive job/grad school candidate	.529
	connection to major	.503
	Portuguese-speaking friends	.475
3. Requirement Motivation	requirement university	−.658
	requirement major, minor, scholarship	−.631
	scheduling	−.472
	travel for pleasure	.457
	dissatisfied with past language course	−.347
4. Language as Hobby	languages come easy	.872
	love languages	.734
	easier given my background in Spanish	.523
5. Fun	sounds of Portuguese	.640
	something different	.558
6. Heritage	communicate with relatives	.751
	heritage	.614

instrumental, since it involves a more intrinsic rationale. The following citation from a student echoes the sentiments of many in this study: "I'm a Spanish speaker and I inherently love the (Portuguese) language and there's a trilingual fascination because of business which grew out of my love for Spanish and Brazil. So it (my reason for studying Portuguese) does have to do with love of other cultures and Brazilian friends so I love to sell Brazil" (Ricardo).

The emergence of the distinct cluster "Language as Hobby" lends support to Clément and Kruidenier's (1983) assertion that a similar cluster they titled "Acquire Knowledge" is missing from Gardner's model. Given that students learning the language outside the target country may have little exposure to the culture, they may not be integratively motivated but may still have an intrinsic, "rather distant or 'bookish'" interest in the language itself (Clément & Kruidenier, 1983, p. 288).

Finally, in keeping with more recent motivational research on language students' motivation (Ramage, 1990; Wen, 1997), "Requirement motivation" clearly loaded as a separate factor as opposed to being included with the instrumental cluster (Gardner & Lambert, 1972). Similarly, Wen (1997) and Ely (1986) found that requirement-type items clustered under "passivity towards requirements" or "requirement motivation" distinguishing themselves from "instrumental" and "integrative" factors.

As concerns students' goals, the four skills of speaking, listening, writing, and reading ranked highest among survey responses, followed by "enjoy myself" and "grade." Though students felt their desire to learn about culture influenced their decision to study the language (initial motivation), cultural items as *goals* were not highly valued. Cultural products ranked seventh, and cultural practices, perspectives on products, and perspectives on practices ranked as eleventh through thirteenth on a fourteen-item scale. The rationale behind this contradiction came to light in responding to the latter two research questions.

Research Question Two: Perceived Goal Attainment

Second-survey results indicated that students felt most of their goals were met except those involving speaking and culture. Like students of more commonly taught languages, students interviewed in this study expressed a belief that it is best to learn how to speak the language "naturally" (Wenden, 1987) in the target country rather than by taking classes. They added that the Portuguese pronunciation itself was difficult and that their speaking goals were more difficult than expected. Many reported having set unrealistic speaking goals, based on their friends' or teachers' overstated claims of the ease with which Spanish-speakers "pick up" Portuguese.

As concerns cultural beliefs, a pattern of responses indicated that students viewed learning culture as something that comes after learning the language:

> I hope to study the cultural products . . . but for the immediate present, a grasp of the language is most important (Peter).

> It was really not as important to me (learning about the culture) but later when I really get a hold of the language, then I'd really like to know what Brazilian people think and why they do what they do (Guillerme).

These students and others interviewed perceived culture as the garnish on the language-learning plate: "By taking Portuguese, sort of on the side, I'll gain the cultural stuff . . . learning the language, well, it is still most important or you don't even get that" (Landrum).

Many students also felt that culture was ill-suited to classroom learning: "I was going into the course understanding that if you're not in the society or with the group of people, you're not going to really learn much" (John). This belief stems from the view that teaching is knowledge-giving, such that the teacher imparts cultural knowledge that might be biased:

> With somebody teaching about cultural issues, they're going to filter it through their point of view so it's gonna be like a little biased on how they're presenting things and what they omit, not that they're trying to—not in a conspiracy sorta way—but what *they* think is important (Brandon).

> You really have to be in the society in order to really get a good perspective of the whole culture. . . . It could be in some way biased by the beliefs of that one person (John).

This perspective on learning underscores the need for teachers to help students realize that all information, whether in print or in the speech of a native speaker, is loaded with the "biases" of its speaker and then perceived through the hearer's cultural paradigm. Students should be instructed on how to critically view culture (Kramsch, 1993) to lessen their apprehensions of learning "inaccurate information."

Research Question Three: Factors Affecting Motivation

Interview responses supported general learning researchers' notion that students' motivation consists not only of the degree to which they value certain goals but also of the expectations they have for meeting those goals (Schunk, 1991).

> I'm interested in learning, but I haven't kicked in. . . . My attitude's not in the mood to learn. It's hard because I have the mentality that in a classroom, it's more difficult to learn the language than in the country because that's how I always saw it (Ellis).

Also supported was the assertion that students' motivation is negatively affected in circumstances in which students do not feel in control of their learning (Harackiewicz & Sansone, 1991). The citation that follows expresses many students' dissatisfaction with the text. When asked whether her frustration with the textbook influenced her decision to discontinue studying Portuguese, Pam responded,

> to an extent because maybe if it had been something I could have done after I left class, if I felt like I could have put more of my own time into it and actually understood what I was doing, but I couldn't get any feedback . . . to know what I was doing (Pam).

These sentiments support foreign language researchers (Dickinson, 1995) and researchers of motivation in general learning (Palmer & Goetz, 1988) in their assertion that whether or not students believe they have control over learning outcomes affects how much effort they expend in learning and how long they persist in their efforts. Particularly when students demonstrate vast differences in proficiency levels, the teacher's choice of a "user friendly" text could determine whether or not students can work individually to "catch up" to their peers.

DISCUSSION AND TEACHER INTERVENTIONS

The results of this study indicate students may blame their failures on and credit their successes to factors they can affect, like effort, or factors they cannot control, like their own aptitude or the difficulty of the task. Students of this study also held attributions that fell in both categories: "(I attribute not meeting my goals to) my deficiency at foreign languages. Probably I should put a lot more studying in to this class per week" (Claire). This student attributed her failure to a low aptitude for learning the language (noncontrollable) but also to her own lack of effort (controllable). In such cases and in others where students hold exclusively noncontrollable attributions, changes in these beliefs are possible and have met with success in attributional change programs in general learning (Trawick & Corno, 1995). Teachers can discuss one-on-one or as a class the beliefs students hold about language learning to deemphasize external attributions students cannot control and emphasize instead effort-based attributions that will increase students' continued motivation.

This research has also supported the work of motivation theorists in emphasizing the role of value and expectancies surrounding students' goals. Students who did not meet their speaking and culture goals demonstrated either lower goal values and expectations for meeting those objectives or, in the case of speaking, that they held overly ambitious goals based on hearsay.

In examining the reasons that students place low value on learning certain skills in the classroom, researchers in foreign language education and educational psychology agree that educators cannot ignore the role the tasks themselves play in student satisfaction and continuance (Ames, 1992; Harlow, Smith, & Garfinkel, 1980). In designing a curriculum that seeks to make students curious about learning, we should recognize that "new values must branch out from older ones" and "cannot be instated whole and unconnected" (Klinger, 1977, p. 324). Thus, tasks that have more relevance in students' lives aid in adopting goals that ensure persistence in learning (Pintrich et al., 1993).

Educators concerned about students' low expectations for success in acquiring certain skills—cultural proficiency, for example—should examine their own attitudes toward classroom learning. Only one of the four teachers interviewed mentioned culture in discussing course objectives, and his view of culture involved "every Friday having a student do a cultural presentation"

(Joshua, instructor). The "Fridays only" nature of culture's inclusion in the course only reinforced the idea of learning culture as adjunct—to be learned "secondary to learning the language" (Shawn).

In this study and others (Horwitz, 1987; Wen, 1997), many language students had a tendency to be overly efficacious as concerns their level of progress. A classroom discussion early in the semester may be warranted, since once learners form overly efficacious opinions, these notions are difficult to unlearn (Cotterall, 1995). This discussion is essential in teaching less commonly taught languages, since students have less exposure to the language before taking the class and therefore may have a more limited range of sources on which to base their expectations. Frustration and attrition should be a warning to zealous LCTL teachers and administrators tempted to use the assurance that the language is "not that difficult" as a recruitment tactic.

As a Portuguese instructor, I faced the problem of student frustration when the reality of their progress did not meet their expectations. I chose therefore to discuss a reading about Alfonso Reyes, a Mexican author and diplomat who expected to learn Portuguese quickly, but instead spent years in its mastery (Ellison, in press). The reading usually led to a lively discussion based on Reyes' frustrations, students' past learning experiences, and their preconceived notions of language learning. Students completed a journal entry about their expectations for learning Portuguese and how they were similar or different to those of Reyes. This guided introspection, followed by class discussion, gave students the opportunity—early in the semester—to modify their expectations if necessary.

Concerning students' attributions for success and failure, teachers should include language-learning strategies in the curriculum to help students become more aware of how they learn best and to combat the notion that a certain language aptitude is needed for success. Language educators should facilitate autonomous learning by offering students a "diagnosis" specific to their language-learning problems (Karlsson, Kjiski, & Nordlund, 1997). From there, teachers can offer practical guidance on how to overcome their specific difficulties and thus reach language objectives. They can also demonstrate techniques in self-evaluation so that students can monitor their own progress.

Finally, this study has implications for researchers. Through a mixed-methods approach, it appeared survey items that might be interpreted as "instrumental" in nature—for example, "because I feel it may be helpful in my future career"—were in fact based on more intrinsic motivations of wanting to live in the target country. Interviews and open-ended written questions, therefore, should accompany survey items. This allows students to clarify their responses and allows researchers, in moving beyond the techniques used by Gardner and his colleagues, to explore a broader range of student feedback and to give a more complete picture of the complexities of motivation.

NOTE

Several lengthier sections, including the background section, of the appendices' surveys have been omitted. For copies, please contact the author at cjernigan@iname.com or contact the University of Texas Curriculum and Instruction Department at (512) 471-5942.

REFERENCES

Altman, H. B. e. a. (1985). Research within reach: Research-guided responses to the concerns of foreign language teachers. Paper presented at the Southern Conference on Language Teaching [BBB29170], Valdosta, GA.

Ames, C. (1992). Classrooms: Goals, structures, and student motivation. *Journal of Educational Psychology,* 84: 261–271.

Blumenfeld, P. C. (1992). Classroom learning and motivation: Clarifying and expanding goal theory. *Journal of Educational Psychology,* 84: 272–281.

Clément, R., & Kruidenier, B. G. (1983). Orientations in second language acquisition: The effects of ethnicity, milieu, and target language on their emergence. *Language Learning,* 33(3): 273–291.

Cotterall, S. (1995). Developing a course strategy for learner autonomy. *ELT Journal,* 49(3): 219–227.

Courteau, J. (1996). *American Portuguese Studies Association Presidential Address.* American Portuguese Studies Association Inaugural Session. Amherst, MA: American Association of Teachers of Spanish and Portuguese: Portuguese Newsletter.

Crookes, G., & Schmidt, R. W. (1991). Motivation: Reopening the research agenda. *Language Learning,* 41(4): 469–512.

Dickinson, L. (1995). Autonomy and motivation: A literature review. *System,* 23(2): 165–174.

Ellison, F. (in press). *Alfonso Reyes no Brasil.* Rio de Janeiro: Topbooks Editora e Distribuidora de Livros Ltda.

Ely, C. M. (1986). Language learning motivation: A descriptive and causal analysis. *Modern Language Journal,* 70: 28–35.

Gardner, R. (1985). *Social psychology and second language learning: The role of attitude and motivation.* London: Edward Arnold.

Gardner, R. C., & Lambert, W. (1959). Motivational variables in second language acquisition. *Canadian Journal of Psychology,* 13: 266–272.

Gardner, R. C., & Lambert, W. (1972). *Attitudes and motivation in second-language learning.* Rowley, MA: Newbury House.

Gardner, R. C., & Smythe, P. C. (1975a). Motivation and second language acquisition. *Canadian Modern Language Review,* 3: 218–233.

Gardner, R. C., & Smythe, P. C. (1975b). Motivation and second-language acquisition. *Canadian Modern Language Review,* 37: 510–525.

Harackiewicz, J. M., & Sansone, C. (1991). Goals and intrinsic motivation: You can get there from here. *Advances in Motivation and Achievement,* 7: 21–40.

Harlow, L. L., Smith, W. F., & Garfinkel, A. (1980). Student-perceived communication needs: Infrastructure of the functional/notional syllabus. *Modern Language Journal,* 72: 283–294.

Horwitz, E. K. (1987). Surveying student beliefs about language learning. In A. R. Wenden, & Joan Rubin (eds.), *Learner strategies in language learning,* pp. 119–129. New York: Prentice-Hall.

Horwitz, E. K. (1988). The beliefs about language learning of beginning university foreign language students. *Modern Language Journal,* 72: 182–193.

Karlsson, L., Kjiski, F., & Nordlund, J. (1997). *From here to autonomy*. Helsinki: Helsinki University Press.

Klinger, E. (1977). Conclusions and implications for the social sciences. *Meaning and Void* (301–326). Minneapolis: University of Minnesota Press.

Kramsch, C. (1993). *Context and culture in language teaching*. Oxford: Oxford University Press.

Ladousse, G. P. (1982). From needs to wants: Motivation and the language learner. *System*, 10(1): 29–37.

Lemke, L. A. (1992). *Foreign language enrollment and the attrition rates in the Grand Blanc community schools*. Research/Technical ED 366 212. Michigan: Grand Blanc Community Schools,.

Lepper, M. R., & Hodell, M. (1989). Intrinsic motivation in the classroom. In C. Ames & R. Ames (eds.), *Research on motivation in education: Goals and cognitions*, Vol. 3, pp. 73–105. San Diego: Academic Press.

McGinnis, S. (1994). The less common alternative: A report from the task force for teacher training in the less commonly taught languages. *ADFL Bulletin*, 25(2): 17–22.

Mertens, D. M. (1997). *Research methods in education and psychology: Integrating diversity with quantitative and qualitative approaches*. London: Sage Publications.

Nam Yung, Y. S. (1996). Cultural and contextual influences on goal orientations and the relationships among goal orientations, learning strategies and achievement: A study of Korean high school students learning English. Doctoral dissertation, University of Texas at Austin.

Oxford, R., & Shearin, J. (1994). Language learning motivation: Expanding the theoretical framework. *Modern Language Journal*, 78(i): 12–28.

Palmer, D. J., & Goetz, E. T. (1988). Selection and use of study strategies: The role of the students' beliefs about self and strategies. In C. E. Weinstein, E. T. Goetz, & P. A. Alexander (eds.), *Learning and study strategies: Issues in assessment, instruction, and evaluation*, pp. 41–61. San Diego: Academic Press.

Pintrich, P., Marx, R. W., & Boyle, R. A. (1993). Beyond cold conceptual change: The role of motivational beliefs and classroom contextual factors in the process of conceptual change. *Review of Educational Research*, 63(2): 167–199.

Ramage, K. (1990). Motivational factors and persistence in foreign language study. *Language Learning*, 40(2): 189–219.

Schunk, D. H. (1991). *Learning theories: An educational perspective*. New York: Macmillan Publishing.

Strauss, A., & Corbin, J. (1990). *Basics of qualitative research: Grounded theory procedures and techniques*. Newbury Park, CA: Sage Publications.

Suárez, J. I. (1996). Maintaining a Portuguese Program II. *Portuguese Newsletter*, 6(1): 4–5.

Trawick, L., & Corno, L. (1995). Expanding the volitional resources of urban community college students. In P. Pintrich (ed.), *Understanding self-regulated learning*, Vol. 63, pp. 57–70. San Francisco: Jossey-Bass Publishers.

Walton, A. R. (1992). Expanding the vision of foreign language education: Enter the less commonly taught languages. Washington, DC, The National Foreign Language Center: 1–16.

Wen, X. (1997). Motivation and language learning with students of Chinese. *Foreign Language Annals*, 30(2): 235–251.

Wenden, A. L. (1987). How to be a successful language learner: Insights and prescriptions from L2 learners. In A. R. Wenden and Joan Rubin (eds.), *Learner strategies in language learning*, pp. 103–117. New York: Prentice-Hall.

APPENDIX A: FIRST SURVEY

Part II. Reasons for Studying Portuguese

Please rate the degree of importance the following reasons for studying Portuguese hold for you. Circle your rating using the following scale.

Not important   Slightly   Moderately   Highly important

1. because I want to use Portuguese when I travel for pleasure to a Portuguese-speaking country	Not Slight Mod High
2. because I want to able to converse with Portuguese-speakers in the U.S.	Not Slight Mod High
3. because I am interested in (a) Portuguese-speaking country/countries' history	Not Slight Mod High
4. because I need to study a foreign language as a major, minor or other specific degree requirement (including graduate degrees and scholarship or fellowship requirements)	Not Slight Mod High
5. because I am interested in (a) Portuguese-speaking country's (ies') **products** (e.g. books, art, music, political systems, etc.)	Not Slight Mod High
6. because I am interested in (a) Portuguese-speaking country's (ies') cultural perspectives on those products (attitudes explaining why certain products exist and are valued)	Not Slight Mod High
7. because I am interested in (a) Portuguese-speaking country's(ies') cultural **practices** (*how* people use cultural products; patterns of behavior like how people celebrate, dress, etc.)	Not Slight Mod High
8. because I am interested in (a) Portuguese-speaking country's (ies') cultural perspectives on those practices (i.e. the attitudes and ideas that explain why people behave as they do)	Not Slight Mod High
9. because I feel it may be helpful in my future career	Not Slight Mod High
10. because I need it for study abroad, research or business travel in a Portuguese-speaking country	Not Slight Mod High
11. because I want to be able to use it with Portuguese-speaking friends	Not Slight Mod High
12. because I need it to fulfill the university foreign language requirement	Not Slight Mod High
13. because of interest in my own heritage (Portuguese-speaking country)	Not Slight Mod High
14. because I feel the classes are less demanding than other foreign language courses at this same level	Not Slight Mod High

15. because it may make me a more competitive job candidate or graduate school candidate	Not	Slight	Mod	High
16. because I want to communicate with relatives (including spouses, in-laws, etc.) in Portuguese	Not	Slight	Mod	High
17. because I feel Portuguese is an important language in the world	Not	Slight	Mod	High
18. because Portuguese better fits my schedule than another language class	Not	Slight	Mod	High
19. because I wanted to study in some other subject that involves Portuguese	Not	Slight	Mod	High
20. because I like the sounds of Portuguese	Not	Slight	Mod	High
21. because it has a connection to my major or area of concentration	Not	Slight	Mod	High
22. because I wanted something different	Not	Slight	Mod	High
23. because I love languages	Not	Slight	Mod	High
24. because languages come easy to me	Not	Slight	Mod	High
25. because I thought Portuguese would be easier for me given my background in Spanish	Not	Slight	Mod	High
26. because I was dissatisfied with my study of another language	Not	Slight	Mod	High
27. because I thought it might be fun	Not	Slight	Mod	High
28. because my advisor encouraged me. (If you responded with slight, mod, or high, please explain their rationale for encouraging you: (space provided)	Not	Slight	Mod	High
29. because a member of the faculty other than my advisor encouraged me. (If you responded with slight, mod, or high, please explain their rationale for encouraging you:(space provided)	Not	Slight	Mod	High
30. Please list any other reason not listed above (and rate):	Not	Slight	Mod	High

Part III: Your Goals in this Class

A. What are your goals for this semester of Portuguese? Though you may also have long-range goals that differ from those you plan to accomplish in this class, please consider only your goals for the *current semester.* *(space provided)*

B. The first column below contains categories of goals that some Portuguese students have mentioned as important for them. If the goal category in Column 1 is an important area *you* want to work on in your Portuguese class this semester, write what specifically you hope to accomplish in that area on the blanks in Column 2. You may write more than one specific goal if you like (see example). If the goal category in Column 1 is *not* something that is your goal this semester, write "*none*" on the blank in Column 2.

Example:

Column 1: Goal Category	Column 2: **Specific** goals you hope to accomplish this semester
Writing	*write e-mails to friends, write business letters*
To compare Portuguese to other languages I know	(To which language(s)?) _ *none* _
Cultural products (e.g. books, art, music, political systems, etc.)	*learn lyrics to Música Popular Brasileira*
Cultural perspectives on those products (attitudes explaining why certain products exist and are valued)	*learn about why MPB is so popular in Brazil*
Cultural practices (how people use cultural products; patterns of behavior like how people celebrate, dress, etc.)	*learn etiquette about conducting business like how to act and dress for a business lunch*
To enjoy myself	(What does this mean to you?) *to meet people with my same interests, have fun in class*

*Please complete only Column 2 below—Column 3 requires further instructions.

Column 1: Goal Category	Column 2: **Specific** goals you hope to accomplish this semester	Column 3
1. Writing	_(space provided)_	N S M H
2. Listening	_____	N S M H
3. Reading	_____	N S M H
4. Speaking	_____	N S M H
5. Cultural **products** (e.g. books, art, music, political systems, etc.)	(specifically...)_____ _____	N S M H
6. Cultural perspectives on those products (attitudes explaining why certain products exist and are valued)	(specifically...)_____ _____ _____ _____	N S M H
7. Cultural **practices** (how people use cultural products; patterns of behavior like how people celebrate, dress, etc.)	(specifically...)_____ _____ _____ _____	N S M H
8. Cultural perspectives on those practices (i.e. the attitudes and ideas that explain why people behave as they do)	(specifically...)_____ _____ _____ _____ _____	N S M H

9. To compare Portuguese to another language I know	(To which language(s)?)_____ _____	N S M H
10. Accent	_____	N S M H
11. Translating	(To and from which languages and what would you like to translate?) *(space provided)*	N S M H
12. Earn a certain grade	(What grade?)_____	N S M H
13. To enjoy myself	(What does this mean to you?) _____	N S M H
14. To complete a language requirement	(Which requirement?)_____ _____	N S M H
15. Other	(Describe goals not under mentioned categories)_____ _____	N S M H

C. Please look back over Column 2 in Part B. If you wrote more than one specific goal for a category, circle the one that is most important to you. An example is given at the bottom of this page.

D. Look back again to Part B and rate your estimate of the importance for each specific goal you wrote. Circle your rating in Column 3 using the scale below (put "N" for "Not important" if you put "none" in Column 2). If you had more than one specific goal for a certain category, do your rating for the goal you circled. An example is given below.

Not important Slightly important   Moderately important Highly important

Column 1: Goal Category	Column 2: Specific goals you hope to accomplish this semester	Column 3
Writing	*write e-mails to friends, write business letters*	N S (M) H
To compare Portuguese to other languages I know	(To which language(s)?) *none*	(N) S M H

E. What would you estimate is the probability that during the course of this semester you will achieve your specific goals you rated as slight, moderately, or highly important in Part D? Below are written only the goal categories ("Writing," for example) but please answer based on the specific goals you listed for each category in Column 2. If you listed more than one specific goal for a category, do your probability rating for the one you circled. Circle the expected probability for each outcome. (Please circle only one number per item.)

	no probability 0%							100% probability		
1. Writing	0	10	20	30	40	50	60	70	80	90	100
2. Listening	0	10	20	30	40	50	60	70	80	90	100
3. Reading	0	10	20	30	40	50	60	70	80	90	100
4. Speaking	0	10	20	30	40	50	60	70	80	90	100
5. Cultural **products** (e.g. books, art, music, political systems, etc.)	0	10	20	30	40	50	60	70	80	90	100
6. Cultural perspectives on those products (attitudes explaining why certain products exist and are valued)	0	10	20	30	40	50	60	70	80	90	100
7. Cultural **practices** (how people use cultural products; patterns of behavior like how people celebrate, dress, etc.)	0	10	20	30	40	50	60	70	80	90	100
8. Cultural perspectives on those practices (i.e. the attitudes and ideas that explain why people behave as they do)	0	10	20	30	40	50	60	70	80	90	100
9. To compare Portuguese to another language I know	0	10	20	30	40	50	60	70	80	90	100
10. Accent	0	10	20	30	40	50	60	70	80	90	100
11. Translating	0	10	20	30	40	50	60	70	80	90	100
12. Earn a certain grade	0	10	20	30	40	50	60	70	80	90	100
13. To enjoy myself	0	10	20	30	40	50	60	70	80	90	100
14. To complete a language requirement	0	10	20	30	40	50	60	70	80	90	100
15. Other	0	10	20	30	40	50	60	70	80	90	100

APPENDIX B: SECOND SURVEY

Part II: Goal Attainment This Semester

A. Goal Attainment Ratings

Below are handwritten the specific goals you listed on the first survey. (If you listed more than one goal per box, only your circled goal appears below). In Column 4, please rate the degree to which you feel your **specific goal in Column 2** was attained this semester.

0%	20%	40%	60%	80%	100%
not at all attained	attained	attained	attained	attained	completely attained

• You will use Column 3 in Part **B** only.

Column 1: Goal Categories	Column 2: **Specific Goals you hope to accomplish this semester**	Column 3	Column 4: Percentage of Goal Attainment: 0%= not at all attained 100%= completely attained
1. Writing	*(The specific goals students entered in the First Survey were handwritten here and the ratings for goal value were handwritten in column 3→)*	H	0 20 40 60 80 100
2. Listening			0 20 40 60 80 100
3. Reading			0 20 40 60 80 100
4. Speaking			0 20 40 60 80 100
5. Cultural **products** (e.g. books, art, music, political systems, etc.)			0 20 40 60 80 100
6. Cultural perspectives on those products (attitudes explaining why certain products exist and are valued)			0 20 40 60 80 100
7. Cultural **practices** (how people use cultural products; patterns of behavior like how people celebrate, dress, etc.)			0 20 40 60 80 100

			0 20 40 60 80 100
8. Cultural perspectives on those practices (i.e. the attitudes and ideas that explain why people behave as they do)			0 20 40 60 80 100
9. To compare Portuguese to another language I know			0 20 40 60 80 100
10. Accent			0 20 40 60 80 100
11. Translating			0 20 40 60 80 100
12. Earn a certain grade			0 20 40 60 80 100
13. To enjoy myself			0 20 40 60 80 100
14. Fulfill language requirement			0 20 40 60 80 100
15. Other			0 20 40 60 80 100

16. For goals you feel were **attained**, to what do you attribute the success? *(space provided)*

17. For goals you feel were **not** attained or were attained **to a lesser degree,** to what do you attribute that lack of success? *(space provided)*

APPENDIX C: EXAMPLE OF CATEGORIZATION
PROCESS AND DESCRIPTIONS

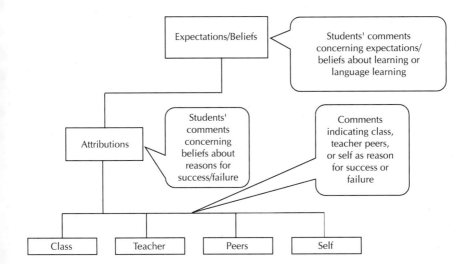

3

Enhancing Motivation and Promoting Positive Attitudes Toward Second Language Learning Through Community Experience

Frank A. Morris

INTRODUCTION

There has always been an attempt by foreign language educators and researchers to positively influence learners' attitudes and motivation toward foreign language learning and culture. For example, it has been suggested that foreign language instructors should become aware of students' motivations and attitudes in the classroom, of why they pursue foreign language and why they studied the language. In order to promote a stronger commitment, the development of all learners' attitudes and motivations should be incorporated and encouraged in the classroom. In addition, it has been suggested that through the course of study students should be given feedback and could be asked to evaluate their own progress relative to their goals. The goals of the class set up by the instructors should be specific, achievable, accepted by the students, and accompanied by feedback about progress (see also Jernigan in this book).

Why is it important to take into account language learners' attitudes and motivation? Research has demonstrated that there is a positive correlation between language learning attitudes and motivation and their foreign language achievement (Gardner, 1992, 1988, 1985, 1979; Gardner and Lambert, 1975, 1972, 1959). Therefore, fostering learners' attitudes may enhance their attitudes and motivation toward second language learning and as a result ensure language achievement (Tremblay and Gardner, 1995; Oxford and Shearin, 1994; Ely, 1986). Gardner and Tremblay (1995) have suggested that educators and researchers should now focus on investigating pedagogical tools that may enhance attitudes and motivation and to what extent motivational behavior in the classroom can be positively affected.

How can educators nurture positive attitudes and increase motivation toward foreign language learning? It is possible that the incorporation of service-learning programs in university and college campuses across the United States may further enhance foreign language education by positively affecting learners' attitudes and motivation towards foreign language learning and culture.

Recently, colleges and universities have been working to incorporate in their college curricula what is known as "service-learning," or community based learning (CBL). The goal of these programs has been to create a shift in undergraduate education from an emphasis in teaching to one of active learning (Corporation for National Service, 1996). Service-learning has been used to further enhance academic learning, not to undermine it (see also Bräuer in this volume).

What is "service-learning"? For the purpose of this chapter, the definition provided by Jacoby (1996) was adopted: "Service-learning is a form of experimental education in which students engage in activities that address human condition and community needs together with structured opportunities intentionally designed to promote student learning and development" (5).

Service-learning, then, is a program of experiential learning that engages students in responsible and challenging actions both inside and outside the classroom. The programs allow students to work in their communities with people of diverse language, racial, economic, and religious backgrounds. At the same time, students spend time in the classroom engaged in academic readings that address issues such as diversity, poverty, education, gender, and sexuality. Students then relate such topics to their community experience.

Because service-learning is a form of experiential education and learning, Kolb's (1981) experiential learning model is particularly useful for service-learning educators. The core of Kolb's model is a learning cycle that represents how experience is translated into concepts, which, in turn, are "used as guides in the choice of new experiences" (1981). An individual can enter the cycle at any of the four points in the process but must complete the entire cycle in order for effective learning to occur. The four points are the following:

- Concrete Experience (CE) abilities
- Reflective Observation (RO) abilities
- Abstract Conceptualization (AC) abilities
- Active Experimentation (AE) abilities

According to Kolb, the learning cycle is as follows: Immediate concrete experience is the basis for observations and reflection. An individual uses these observations to build an idea, generalization, or theory from which new applications for action can be deduced. These implications or hypotheses then serve as guides in acting to create new experiences (235). Kolb further argues that learners must "be able to involve themselves fully, openly, and without bias in new experiences (CE); they must be able to observe and reflect on these experiences from many perspectives (RO); they must be able to create concepts that integrate their observations into logical sound theories (AC); and they must be able to use these theories to make decisions and solve problems (AE)" (236).

Kolb's model suggests that effective learning can occur through active experience. While service-learning presents students with multiple opportunities to engage in concrete experiences that can lead to individual reflection and peer discussions, service-learning can be used as a teaching tool to enhance learning.

Because service-learning programs have been successful, researchers and educators have argued that they should be incorporated into second and foreign language curricula (Overfield, 1997). It is believed that service-learning could have a positive effect on learners' motivation and attitudes toward second language learning and culture. Research should then assess the effect of service-learning on second and foreign language learners' motivation and attitudes.

The study presented in this chapter attempted to advance the research that examines pedagogical tools that may enhance learners' attitudes and motivation. The study sought to examine whether participation in the Service Learning for the Chicano/Latino Community (SLCLC) class affected students' motivation and attitudes toward learning Spanish and studying Spanish speakers and their cultures. The research question asked was: Do students exhibit a change in motivation and attitudes after completing the Service-Learning for the Chicano-Latino Community Class?

THE SLCLC CLASS

The Service-Learning for the Chicano/Latino Community Class, Spanish 3401, at the University of Minnesota allows students to participate in Spanish-speaking organizations in the Minneapolis/Saint Paul area. To be allowed to register for the course, students must have completed 2 years of college Spanish. Students are placed in numerous organizations throughout the Twin Cities where they spend a minimum of 3 hours per week volunteering their time. Their duties are, for example, to tutor or teach ESL to Hispanic immigrants; to serve as interpreters; to act as counselors at women's shelters, day cares, law firms, and employment agencies; and to act as liaisons between government and Hispanic communities in the Twin Cities.

An important component of the course is class meetings, which are held once a week. In class, students analyze academic materials dealing with race, class, gender, current patterns of power in the United States, and roles of citizens within the system and relate such issues to their community experience. For example, as part of the Spanish 3104 class at the U of M, students were asked to read an article titled "Getting and Spending" that appeared in the *Business Week* Special 1994 Bonus Edition "21st Century Capitalism." The article discussed the possibility that as privatization in Latin America takes place, wealth and the opportunity for education are readily available. As a result, a new middle class is emerging in Latin America. After discussing the article in class, students were asked to interview at least 3 immigrants from Spanish-speaking countries who had recently arrived in the Twin Cities, and ask them their opinions regarding privatization in Latin America and how they were affected (i.e., negatively or positively) by it. Students were asked to write a 3–5 page journal reflecting on the points made by the article and the interviews. A student, for instance, learned that although free enterprise in Latin America has allowed for the development of a middle class, many do not benefit from it. A number of individuals do not have the opportunity to be a part of the wealth and growth and are excluded by those who benefit.

RESEARCH DESIGN

Participants

All students (a total of 54) registered for the Service-Learning for the Chicano/Latino Community Class during the summer and fall of 1998 at the University of Minnesota were selected to participate in the study. Eighteen were eliminated because they either dropped the course or did not complete the post survey. In the end, 36 students participated in the study: 11 males and 25 females. A biographical survey revealed a median age of 20.6 and that all participants were pursuing a bachelor's degree with a concentration in Spanish. Twenty-one of the 36 participants reported double majors; second majors included business (11 students), international relations (7 students), and Portuguese (3 students). English was reported as the native language for all but 3 participants (2 Korean and 1 Swedish).

Participants claimed to have spent a number of years studying Spanish (mean = 6.1 years). All indicated that they began language studies in high school because it was a requirement. Spanish was chosen because it was the only language offered at the high school they attended. When asked why they wish to continue studying Spanish, 11% (4 participants) indicated that they do so because they think it is fun, 19% (7 participants) like learning languages, 39% (14 participants) do it for professional purposes, and 31% (11 participants) have an interest in Spanish speakers and their cultures. When asked why they registered for the class, 8% (3 participants) revealed an interest in developing a better worldview, 25% (9 participants) wished to fulfill a class requirement, 42% (15 participants) wanted to enhance their career/professional potential, and 25% (9 participants) have an interest in Spanish speakers and their culture. Overall, participants did not seem to hold hostile attitudes toward learning Spanish or about the culture and its speakers.

Instrumentation

Three instruments were used to gather data: a biographical survey, a pre-survey, and a post-survey. The biographical survey recorded demographic data and required the participants to indicate the reasons why they began Spanish language learning, why they continued to study it, and why they registered for the Service Learning for the Chicano/Latino Community class. The pre-survey, consisting of 11 items, elicited the participants' motivation and attitude toward the study of Spanish and Spanish-speaking people and their culture. The post-survey included two parts. The first part required students to answer questions similar to the pre-survey. The second part of the post-survey, or the post-survey-only questions, asked participants to comment on the value of the class and their experience while participating in the class. The scale for both the pre-survey and the post-survey was numbered one through six: 1 - Disagree Strongly, 2 - Disagree Moderately, 3 - Disagree Slightly, 4 - Agree Slightly, 5 - Agree Moderately, 6 - Agree Strongly.

Data Collection Procedures

The biographical survey, the pre-survey, and the post-survey were administered by the researcher, with the help of the course instructor. The biographical survey and pre-survey were administered the first day of class. Students were assigned a code to maintain anonymity and to match and compare individuals' responses to the pre-survey and post-survey items. However, while most participants lost or forgot their code number, their responses to the pre-survey and post-survey items could not be matched and individually compared. Instead of comparing individuals' responses, the researcher compared all the responses for each pre-survey item with all the responses for each post-survey item. The post-survey was administered after completion of the course on the last day of class. On both occasions, participants were told that the survey was voluntary. They were instructed to give only one answer per question and to be as accurate and honest as possible in their answers. They were also told to give their first reactions after reading each item, but not to rush the process, as it was important to express their true opinions. The participants were told that the results would be recorded by an assigned number and not by names.

Data Analysis Procedures

To answer the research question, Do students exhibit a change in motivation and attitudes after completing the Service-Learning for the Chicano-Latino Community Class?, data was analyzed by examining and comparing means, standard deviations, frequencies, and percentages for each pre-survey and post-survey item. A *t* test was also used to establish whether there was a significant change between each pre-survey and post-survey item. To find the difference significant, the *p* value must be below .05. The *t* test would establish whether the results occurred by chance alone. In addition, participants' responses to the post-survey-only questions were examined.

RESULTS

Before we answer the research questions posed at the beginning of the study, the results of the pre-survey and the post-survey are discussed here.

Pre-Survey and Post-Survey Results

Results for the pre-survey and the post-survey are shown in Table 3.1. For each item in the surveys, the percentages, frequency, means, and standard deviations were calculated. Pre-survey and post-survey item responses differ. The mean for each post-survey item is higher than the mean for each pre-survey item. Hence, the number of participants who agreed with each post-survey item is higher than the number of participants who agreed with each pre-survey item.

Overall, results suggest that there is a substantial positive change between each pre-survey and post-survey item. Table 3.2 presents the results of a *t* test ($p < .05$) of the difference between the pre-survey and post-survey items. Results indicate a significant positive change between each pre-survey and post-survey item ($p < .001$ for all items, but $p < .003$ for item #5). Therefore, the results did not occur by chance alone.

Post-Survey-Only Questions

The qualitative findings obtained from the participants' written answers to the post-survey-only questions further support the quantitative results of this study. None of the participants responded negatively to the open-ended post-survey questions. What follows is a summary of respones, with examples of the participants' individual responses. A detailed look at the qualitative responses indicates that participants seemed to have examined their national (American) culture and the way it treats Hispanics. Many participants declared that Americans are too ethnocentric; they treat Hispanics as second-

Table 3.1 Comparison of Pre-Survey and Post-Survey Results (frequencies, percentages, means, and standard deviations for each pre-survey and post-survey item)

	1	2	3	4	5	6*	n	m	sd
1. Spanish will help me make more Spanish-speaking friends.									
Pre-Survey									
Frequency	0	6	5	10	7	8	36	4.16	1.38
Percentage	0%	17%	14%	28%	19%	22%	100%		
Post-Survey									
Frequency	0	0	0	17	10	9	36	4.77	.83
Percentage	0%	0%	0%	39%	28%	33%	100%		
2. A language requirement should be a necessary prerequisite to obtain an undergraduate degree.									
Pre-Survey									
Frequency	6	5	3	10	8	4	36	3.58	1.64
Percentage	17%	14%	8%	28%	22%	11%	100%		
Post-Survey									
Frequency	0	1	4	16	9	6	36	4.42	1.00
Percentage	0%	3%	11%	44%	25%	17%	100%		
3. Learning Spanish allows me to have a better view of Hispanic people and their cultures.									
Pre-Survey									
Frequency	1	7	8	9	5	6	36	3.77	1.43
Percentage	3%	19%	22%	25%	14%	17%	100%		
Post-Survey									
Frequency	0	0	2	16	11	7	36	4.64	.87
Percentage	0%	0%	6%	44%	31%	19%	100%		
4. Being proficient in Spanish will increase my income potential.									
Pre-Survey									
Frequency	3	2	6	18	4	3	36	3.75	1.25
Percentage	8%	6%	17%	50%	11%	8%	100%		
Post-Survey									
Frequency	0	1	4	21	7	3	36	4.19	.86
Percentage	0%	3%	11%	58%	19%	8%	100%		

Table 3.1 (continued)

	1	2	3	4	5	6*	n	m	sd

5. To learn Spanish, it is important to speak it outside of the class.

Pre-Survey

	1	2	3	4	5	6*	n	m	sd
Frequency	0	0	2	18	9	7	36	4.58	.87
Percentage	0%	0%	6%	50%	25%	19%	100%		

Post-Survey

	1	2	3	4	5	6*	n	m	sd
Frequency	0	0	0	15	13	8	36	4.81	.79
Percentage	0%	0%	0%	42%	36%	22%	100%		

6. It is necessary to know the foreign culture in order to speak the foreign language.

Pre-Survey

	1	2	3	4	5	6*	n	m	sd
Frequency	3	5	8	16	4	0	36	3.36	1.13
Percentage	8%	14%	22%	44%	11%	0%	100%		

Post-Survey

	1	2	3	4	5	6*	n	m	sd
Frequency	0	0	7	12	11	6	36	4.44	1.00
Percentage	0%	0%	19%	33%	31%	17%	100%		

7. Every student who declares Spanish as a major should be required to take this course.

Pre-Survey

	1	2	3	4	5	6*	n	m	sd
Frequency	4	6	5	12	8	1	36	3.47	1.38
Percentage	11%	17%	14%	33%	22%	3%	100%		

Post-Survey

	1	2	3	4	5	6*	n	m	sd
Frequency	0	0	1	17	10	8	36	4.70	.86
Percentage	0%	0%	3%	47%	28%	22%	100%		

8. I feel comfortable with the level of Spanish that I have achieved.

Pre-Survey

	1	2	3	4	5	6*	n	m	sd
Frequency	4	3	5	5	11	8	36	4.11	1.65
Percentage	11%	8%	14%	14%	31%	22%	100%		

Post-Survey

	1	2	3	4	5	6*	n	m	sd
Frequency	0	1	3	10	13	9	36	4.72	1.03
Percentage	0%	3%	8%	28%	36%	25%	100%		

Table 3.1 (continued)

	1	2	3	4	5	6*	n	m	sd
9. I am highly motivated to learn Spanish.									
Pre-Survey									
Frequency	0	3	5	12	14	2	36	4.19	1.04
Percentage	0%	8%	14%	33%	39%	6%	100%		
Post-Survey									
Frequency	0	0	0	9	22	5	36	4.89	.62
Percentage	0%	0%	0%	25%	61%	14%	100%		

10. I try to speak Spanish outside of class, with Spanish speakers, as often as I can.

	1	2	3	4	5	6*	n	m	sd
Pre-Survey									
Frequency	5	4	7	10	5	5	36	3.58	1.57
Percentage	14%	11%	19%	28%	14%	14%	100%		
Post-Survey									
Frequency	0	0	2	14	16	4	36	4.61	.77
Percentage	0%	0%	6%	39%	44%	11%	100%		

11. I will continue to study Spanish beyond the requirements.

	1	2	3	4	5	6*	n	m	sd
Pre-Survey									
Frequency	3	4	2	17	9	1	36	3.77	1.27
Percentage	8%	11%	6%	47%	25%	3%	100%		
Post-Survey									
Frequency	0	0	1	20	8	7	36	4.58	.84
Percentage	0%	0%	3%	56%	22%	19%	100%		

*Scale: 1 - Disagree Strongly, 2 - Disagree Moderately, 3 - Disagree Slightly, 4 - Agree Slightly, 5 - Agree Moderately, 6 - Agree Strongly.

class citizens and do not make an effort to get to know Hispanics. For example, one student commented,

> I realized that there are a few Americans out there making the effort at welcoming people of different cultures into America; some are just neutral (not doing anything) but some are rude, selfish and do their best to make Hispanics feel uncomfortable. We have white privilege whether we like it or not. We are ethnocentric.

Table 3.2   Results of Significance
Comparison of means and standard deviations for each pre-survey and
post-survey item

Survey Item	Pre-Survey Number	Mean	Standard Deviation	Post-Survey Number	Mean	Standard Deviation	T-test $p < .05$
1	36	4.16	1.38	36	4.77	.83	$p < .001$*
2	36	3.58	1.64	36	4.42	1.00	$p < .001$*
3	36	3.77	1.43	36	4.64	.87	$p < .001$*
4	36	3.75	1.25	36	4.19	.86	$p < .001$*
5	36	4.58	.87	36	4.81	.79	$p < .003$*
6	36	3.36	1.13	36	4.44	1.00	$p < .001$*
7	36	3.47	1.38	36	4.70	.86	$p < .001$*
8	36	4.11	1.65	36	4.72	1.03	$p < .001$*
9	36	4.19	1.04	36	4.89	.62	$p < .001$*
10	36	3.58	1.57	36	4.61	.77	$p < .001$*
11	36	3.77	1.27	36	4.58	.84	$p < .001$*

*Shows significance

In addition, participants assessed their own preconceived notions with regard to Hispanics; they were able to put aside such notions as they learned about the Hispanic cultures to which they were exposed. As the following example demonstrates, a student claimed to have believed that Hispanics came to the United States because of its welfare system. However, exposure to Hispanic groups informed the participant that Hispanics came to seek better employment opportunity and success.

> I feel that my opinions regarding Hispanics, which before were not so developed, have grown significantly. For example, I used to think that they came to Minnesota because they were somewhat lazy and to get welfare. But the reality is that they are not lazy and do not come to this country simply because they want welfare.

In the process of reexamining and modifying their notions regarding American and Hispanic cultures, many participants expressed that they found themselves sharing many traits with Hispanics they helped and with whom they worked. For instance, they were both attempting to learn a second language and be accepted by the second-language culture. A student stated,

> We are all struggling to understand each other and learn from each other's cultures. Ironically we both had generalizations in our minds about other

peoples' cultures. As I got to know Hispanics in Minnesota, we shared a lot of experiences and personal opinions which allowed us to realize that our old ideas were wrong. We are studying a different language and in the process we both struggle.

The cross-cultural interaction with the target language group provoked a change of attitudes and motivation, as many participants alluded to wishing to continue language learning, to working with the community, and to wanting to learn more about Hispanic culture, including literature. A number of participants pointed to being more comfortable around Hispanics and not being afraid to speak with them. One of the participants indicated,

> My desire [to learn Spanish] has always been high, but now it is even higher. I actually look forward to talking in Spanish. The best part is that I am no longer afraid to get close to Hispanics and start talking. In fact, I will change my minor to major because I want to go to grad school and learn more about Hispanic literature, since, as the class showed me, so much of their culture has been transmitted through literature.

Overall, participants believed that the class was a worthwhile experience. For instance, one student stated, "This class was very helpful and very valuable. It motivated me to volunteer in the community, and served as an eye opener to the Spanish-speaking community."

It is now possible to answer the research question posed at the beginning of the study: Do students exhibit a change in motivation and attitudes after completing the Service-Learning for the Chicano-Latino Community Class? The answer is "yes." First, a significant positive change was found between each pre-survey and post-survey item. In addition, responses to the post-survey-only questions suggest that participants became more receptive to the language and the speakers of the target language. We conclude that participation in the Service-Learning for the Chicano/Latino Community class positively affected students' motivation and attitudes toward studying Spanish, Spanish speakers, and their culture.

DISCUSSION AND CONCLUSIONS

When students are exposed to foreign language learning, they are often exposed to the second language culture through teachers and texts. Teachers spend time teaching about the second language culture and expect students to become curious about the culture and more motivated to learn the language. However, sometimes a change of motivation and attitudes does not occur. Teachers have reported that students often develop negative attitudes about the L2 language learning process and the target language culture. A possible reason might be that students are being exposed to culture through a book or video or through the eyes of a language teacher, all which approaches could be too constructed. Culture is often approached by giving learners facts to be learned and stored. Such an approach to teaching culture places culture as a static product.

This study suggests that attitudes toward language learning and toward speakers of the target language can improve by allowing learners to negotiate meaning with target language speakers and by understanding the communicative and cultural contexts in which language is used. Attitudinal change occurs through social contact and social practice. Motivation and attitudes can be enhanced by fostering access to, and possibly membership in, the target language community. This study, in particular, demonstrates that face-to-face contact with local native-Spanish speakers had a positive effect on the participants' motivation and attitudes toward learning Spanish and toward Spanish speakers and their culture. In addition, the current study offers instruction required by many foreign language curricula today (see Bräuer in this book).

Limitations

First, the number of participants in this study was limited to thirty-six students. Thus, it cannot be assumed that the course would have a positive effect on the overall population. Further, the participants' responses to the pre-survey and post-survey may show a desire not to be too negative. Because verbal reports were not done to assess the participants' responses, it is not known, for instance, whether a rating of "4" was considered a bit negative by respondents.

In addition, geographical location may have affected the results. In the Twin Cities, the economic and political situation of Hispanics is different than in many other states. Antagonism toward Hispanics, which exists strongly elsewhere, may not be as strong in the Twin Cities. Thus, it is not known whether the same results would be obtained in regions where students hold negative attitudes toward Spanish and Hispanics. It must be noted that participants in this study held somewhat high levels of motivation and positive attitudes toward learning about Spanish, its culture, and its speakers when they registered for the course. Although a positive trend did become even more positive after the ten-week program, it cannot be assumed that participation in the class will have the same effect on learners who lack motivation and hold negative attitudes at the moment of registration.

Another limitation is that research did not assess the long-term effects of the course on learners' motivation and attitudes. Will their motivation and attitudes change over time or remain the same? Also, it is not known whether any factors other than the course influenced the change in participants' motivation and attitudes. In addition, the study cannot conclude whether the learners' foreign language knowledge improved. From personal observation, the researcher can indicate that, after participation in the service-learning course, learners spoke the foreign language (Spanish) with less apprehension. Finally, it would have been useful to look at individual responses to the pre-survey and post-survey and to assess individual attitudinal changes. Unfortunately, because participants either lost or forgot their code numbers, the pre-survey and post-survey could not be matched by individual.

Future Research

The study should be replicated using participants who possess low motivation and negative attitudes. It would be beneficial to also assess the effect of participation in the SLCLC class on learners' language development. The long-term effects of participation in the SLCLC class on learners' motivation and attitudes should also be investigated. In addition, the effects of negative cultural experiences or intercultural communication on learners' motivation and attitudes needs to be examined. Finally, researchers should continue to look at pedagogical tools that may help students integrate socially and cognitively in the L2 community (see Lee and Bräuer in this volume). In particular, researchers should attempt to ascertain which tools are best used in areas where there is no access to native-Spanish speakers or a Spanish community.

Pedagogical Implications

Participation in the Service-Learning for the Chicano/Latino Community class positively affected students' motivation and attitudes toward learning about Spanish, Spanish speakers, and their culture. Therefore, providing a foreign language curriculum with courses and activities that force learners to socially and cognitively engage with native speakers of the target language may prove to positively change their motivation and attitudes. This study offers an example of the type of process-oriented culture instruction that is needed in many foreign language curricula today. Culture in most language classes is communicated through products and practices, but the goal of the foreign language instructors and researchers is to move culture instruction beyond products and practices and into philosophical perspectives such as meaning, attitudes, values, and ideas. The service-learning class described in this chapter does precisely that.

NOTE

I am grateful to Kathleen Ganley, the course instructor, for her valuable help in the process of conducting this study. I am also thankful to Professor Andrew Cohen for his helpful comments and insight in the development of this paper.

REFERENCES

Corporation for National Service. (1996). *Learn and serve America: Higher education program descriptions.* Washington, DC.

Ely, C. M. (1986). Language learning motivation: A descriptive and casual analysis. *Modern Language Journal* 70: 28–35.

Gardner, Robert C. (1979). Social psychological aspects of second language acquisition. In Howard Giles and R. St. Clair (eds.), *Language and social psychology,* pp. 193–220. Oxford: Blackwell.

Gardner, Robert C. (1985). *Social psychology and second language learning: The role of attitudes and motivation.* London: Arnold.

Gardner, Robert C. (1988). Attitudes and motivation. *Annual Review of Applied Linguistics* 9: 135–148.

Gardner, Robert C. (1992). Second language learning in adults: Correlates of proficiency. *Applied Language Learning* 2: 1–28.

Gardner, Robert C., and Lambert, W. E. (1959). Motivational variables in second language acquisition. *Canadian Journal of Psychology,* 13: 266–272.

Gardner, Robert C., and Lambert, W. E. (1972). *Attitudes and motivation in second language learning.* Rowley, MA: Newbury House.

Gardner, Robert C., and Lambert, W. E. (1975). Second language acquisition: A social psychology approach. *University of Western Ontario Research Bulletin,* 332.

Jacoby, Barbara. (1996). Service learning in today's higher education. In Barbara Jacoby (ed.), *Service-learning in higher education: Concepts and practices,* pp. 3–25. San Francisco: Jossey-Bass Publishers.

Kolb, D. A. (1981). Learning styles and disciplinary disciplines. In A. W. Chickering and associates, *The modern American college.* San Francisco: Jossey-Bass.

Overfield, D. (1997). From the margins to the mainstreams: Foreign language education and community-based learning. *Foreign Language Annals,* 30: 485–491.

Oxford, R., and Shearin, J. (1994). Language learning motivation: Expanding the theoretical framework. *Modern Language Journal,* 78: 12–26.

Tremblay, Paul F., and Gardner, R. C. (1995). Expanding the motivation construct in language learning. *Modern Language Journal,* 79: 505–518.

4

(Re)Considering L1 Use in Adult ESL Classrooms

Effects on Learner Motivation

Timothy G. Collins

BACKGROUND TO THE STUDY

One of the most deeply held beliefs among many ESL/EFL teachers is that the monolingual, English-only classroom is the preferable environment in which to learn English. This belief, a tenet in methods as diverse as the audiolingual method, the silent way, total physical response, and the natural approach (Phillipson, 1992), has been justified on a variety of grounds.

The audiolingual method, for example, discouraged L1 use because the L1 was thought to be a source of interference with learning the new language (Brumfit & Roberts, 1983). Audiolinguists believed that avoiding exposure to the L1 reduced the chances of further "contaminating" the learners' new language with features of the L1 (Irujo, 1998). Instead, learners could focus on forming good habits in the new L2. Though the audiolingual method has few defenders these days, this single tenet still has remarkable staying power. As recently as 1982, Dulay, Burt, and Krashen argued that the second language is a new and independent system and that the L1 is a source of interference. As a consequence, the authors urged teachers to discourage L1 use in their classes.

The exclusive or near-exclusive use of the L2 has also been justified under what has come to be called a "maximum exposure" hypothesis—that is, learners need as much exposure as possible to the target language because the greater the amount of input, the greater the gains in the new language (Cummins & Swain, 1986). In the 1950s and early 1960s, L1 use was discouraged because bilingual children's performance on standardized tests was lower than monolingual (English-speaking) children's performance. Not until more cognitive approaches to language learning were introduced, starting in the 1970s, did people begin to reject the purported association between bilingualism and poor test performance and to look for other sociological factors that explained the poor performance of minority children on standardized measures (Hakuta, 1985).

As a result of these beliefs, learners in many teachers' classrooms are expected to leave their L1s at the classroom door and to listen, speak, read, and write only in the new language. In order to enforce the L1-only policy, teachers have often converted themselves into linguistic police officers, listening for sounds of learners speaking their first language and reminding them to speak English. In the past, some programs for young children even directed teachers to punish students who used their native language at school (Baron, 1990). Today, many teachers continue to discourage learners from speaking their L1 through less coercive means. In some classrooms for older learners, teachers impose small fines, such as five or ten cents, each time they catch learners using their first language. At a state TESOL conference a few years ago, a presenter suggested that teachers hold up a "penalty card" like the ones used in soccer each time they observe a learner making a grammatical error or speaking in his or her L1. These repressive policies, though well intentioned, ignore possible negative implications for classroom rapport and learner motivation. Studies such as Auerbach (1993) have pointed out negative implications of discouraging or repressing the L1. This practice has the unintended result of undermining students' self-esteem because an important part of their selfhood, their language, is excluded from the classroom discourse community. Thus learners, especially those at lower levels, are left unable to express themselves, to collaborate with their peers, and to use their other adult skills in the L2 learning task and as a result experience a decrease of motivation or, at times, anger and hostility toward the school and the teacher. Measures that equate a well-formed L1 sentence with an error in the L2 have the effect of devaluing the learner as well as his or her L1 and culture.

Furthermore, according to Phillipson (1992), the English-only policy has the effect of devaluing teachers. Many highly effective nonnative teachers lack the ability to develop entire lessons exclusively in the L2, and many talented native speaker teachers have found that they need recourse to the learners' L1 in order to make their lessons comprehensible to the learners.

The insistence on exclusive use of the L2 has the effect of making both groups' lessons methodologically suspect.

A number of studies of both child and adult L2 acquisition offer compelling evidence that the exclusion of learners' L1 is not empirically motivated from a pedagogical point of view. In a review of several studies of bilingual education with young children, Cummins and Swain (1986) conclude that the maximum exposure hypothesis has been refuted in every study of bilingual education and that the highest gains in L2 proficiency occurred in programs in which children got instruction in both the L1 and the L2. Skutnabb-Kangas (1981) reached similar conclusions. Young children's L2 gains were highest when they had instruction in both systems. Legarreta (1979) reports that children in bilingual programs had significantly higher gains in L2 proficiency than those in monolingual (English-only) programs. Auerbach (1993) summarized a number of studies of adult education programs that deliberately incorporated learners' L1 in the instruction with very positive results. In fact, the learners were often more successful than when the same programs used L2-only models. Samash (1990) reported, in a study conducted at the Invergarry Learning Center, near Vancouver, Canada, that learners first wrote compositions about themselves in their L1, transitioned into writing in a mixture of the L1 and the L2, and then moved into writing in the L2 exclusively. This process allowed learners to transition into the new language when they were ready and in the meantime provided meaningful language development in their L1. D'Annunzio (1991) reported on a study in which untrained bilingual tutors worked with adult Hmong learners of ESL. According to D'Annunzio, the learners' gains in English were much more dramatic than when the same program used an English-only instructional model. According to Auerbach,

> These findings concerning the use of the L1 are congruent with current theories of second language acquisition. They show that its use reduces anxiety and enhances the affective environment for learning, takes into account sociocultural factors, facilitates incorporation of learners' life experiences, and allows for learner-centered curriculum development. Most importantly, it allows for language to be used as a meaning-making tool and for language learning to become a means of communicating ideas rather than an end in itself. (Auerbach, 1993, 20)

The studies in support of L1 use have one element in common: The programs incorporated the L1 into the instructional model by design. The present chapter, a product of a participant-observation study conducted in a beginning ESL class at an adult education center in central Texas, reports on a situation in which the instructional model initially did not encourage L1 use, but was later revised to allow limited interaction in the L1—a change that greatly enhanced the learning environment. This study will first discuss how the data was gathered—including details on the center, teachers, and adult learners—and then discuss ways the learners' L1 was used to enhance their learning process.

THE STUDY

The Site

This research was conducted at River City Adult Learning Council, a not-for-profit organization, located in a small city in central Texas,[1] that provides instruction in language and literacy to both L1 and ESL learners. The council serves several hundred adult learners each week, in learners' and tutors' homes and workplaces as well as in its 3,000-square-foot facility. This rented space consists of a large open area in which learners gather and work with tutors, three classrooms, a large auditorium-style room for meetings and volunteer training, and office space for the Center's staff. The physical setup of classrooms includes a large table with several chairs and a white board.

The Center generally uses one-on-one tutoring, though when ESL learners enter the program, they first study in a class for several weeks before being assigned to tutors. The purpose of the class is to accustom the new students to the language learning process and to keep them involved until tutors become available. The Center offers two classes, one on the beginning and one on the intermediate level. Both classes meet from 7:00 P.M. to 9:00 P.M. on Tuesdays and Thursdays.

Participants

The key informants in this study were volunteer instructors and learners enrolled in the Center's beginning ESL class and one of the Center's assistant directors.

Learners. The group of beginners in the class I observed was highly fluid. Attendance ranged from three to eight. While I was observing the class, at least three new students entered the class, and one left when he was assigned a tutor. Attendance varied based on learners' work schedules, health, and access to child care. All the learners were immigrants to the United States from Mexico. However, the Center's staff said that usually the classes include a few learners from other countries, particularly Korea, Vietnam, and China, reflecting the overall immigration to the area. According to the staff members, it was unusual that the class consisted entirely of Mexicans, though they agreed that Mexicans always constituted the majority. The following six learners were the primary informants in this study:

Tony Vasquez. A 24-year-old single shrink-wrap operator in a software factory, Tony has been in the United States for five years, but he has not learned much English despite a previous brief attempt at another literacy program in the city. In Mexico he dropped out of high school in his last year. He has fairly well developed literacy skills in Spanish.

Victoria Vasquez. Tony's sister, Victoria, came to class about half the time. She also dropped out of high school in Mexico. She demonstrated a knowledge of traditional grammar terms in Spanish and had well-developed study skills. She was the only key informant I was unable to interview, a result of her sporadic attendance.

Mayra Gomez. From Mexico City, Mayra had been in the United States for less than six months and joined the class in the last few sessions I attended. She came to the United States in order to care for an ill friend. In Mexico, Mayra was a bill collector for a department store and also a talented mariachi performer. She has a high school education and is the mother of five children, three of whom are already adults. The younger two are in Mexico, being cared for by relatives. She works full-time at a minimum-wage job at a printing plant and is constantly looking for more remunerative employment.

Ariel Escondido. A factory worker, Ariel has been in the United States for over 15 years but has never learned English. He only attended elementary school in Mexico. He is married and has a son. He has lived in Florida, Mexico, New York, and Texas. He joined the class after I had attended the first few sessions.

Maria Dolores de los Santos. A 25-year-old housewife and mother of two elementary-school–age children, Maria came to class the most regularly, but with only a primary school education, she had the least well developed literacy skills in Spanish of all the learners. She had great trouble taking notes or even repeating single words after the teacher. She attended class with her husband, Eduardo Mata.

Eduardo Mata. The husband of Maria Dolores, Eduardo dropped out of secondary school and is now an auto mechanic. He earns enough on his job that Maria Dolores can stay at home to look after their two children. He has been in the United States for five years.

In interviews, the students revealed that their motivation in learning English was intrinsic and integrative: They wanted to be able to participate in their children's education (Maria Dolores, Eduardo, and Ariel), feel comfortable interacting with Americans they encountered while shopping or at work (Tony and Victoria), socialize with Americans (Tony, Victoria, and Mayra), and complete their high school educations in order to feel better about themselves and provide good role models for their children (Eduardo). In fact, all the learners agreed that their extrinsic needs were already met: All had jobs; all had homes; and all were able to meet their basic daily needs for shopping, health care, and recreation.

Teachers and Staff. All teachers and tutors at the River City Adult Learning Center are volunteers from the local community. All the tutors I observed were single, young adults, but the Center's staff indicated that many of the other tutors were older adults, often retirees, who were interested in involving themselves in community service. All volunteers at the Center go through an eighteen-hour training program in L1 literacy and ESL instruction that is supervised by a professor of educational psychology at a local university who is also a member of the Center's board of directors. During the short time I observed this class, it had three different teachers, as follows.

Martin Schmidt. The first teacher, an undergraduate at a local college, was a highly proficient German-English bilingual who had learned ESL in the United States as a child. I observed two of his classes before he stopped coming to class for reasons I was not able to clarify.

John Sullivan. The second teacher was an electrical engineer who agreed as a favor to the assistant director of the Center to substitute for Martin until she could find a permanent teacher for the class. John said that he usually taught L1 learners and did not feel comfortable teaching the ESL class.

Diane Miller. The third teacher was a quality assurance analyst at a small software company. She had tutored learners of L1 literacy at the Center for several years, but reported that recently she had felt a need for a change and asked to be assigned an ESL class.

The Center also had a small salaried administrative staff, a director and two assistants, one of whom played a role in the study:

Rosina Martinez. An administrative assistant, Rosina was in charge of the Center's operations at night. She coordinated schedules, placed students, and organized the classes. Organizing the classes was one of her most important duties, as the composition of classes could shift from day to day based on learner and teacher attendance. She was the daughter of immigrants from Mexico and grew up speaking Spanish at home. She did not learn English until she enrolled in elementary school. She had a high school education, but no special training in ESL or education. In fact, she had come to the Center as a clerical temp and had stayed on in a staff position because she found the Center's work important and fulfilling.

Data Collection

Participant-observation and one-on-one interviews were the principal means of data collection. Each methodology had distinct advantages and disadvantages. Here, I will first discuss the observations and then the interviews.

Participant-Observation. Using participant-observation to study learning strategies has a number of advantages and disadvantages. Participant-observation allows direct observation of learner behavior. However, as Cohen (1998) observed, participant observation allows access only to observable behavior and not to internal, mentalistic strategies and (for the most part) gives access to extroverted learners' behavior. To compensate for this weakness, I used oral interviews and gained access to selected learners' notebooks to gather complementary data. Cohen (1998) warns that for participant-observation to be effective as a data collection technique, observations have to be fairly frequent in order to notice strategies in use. I visited the beginning ESL class for a total of 36 hours over a twelve-week period from September 1997 to December 1997, an amount of time I judged sufficient to get an overview of learners' use of strategies. Because I have knowledge of Spanish, gained through a master's degree program in Spanish linguistics and prolonged residence in Spain, I was in an ideal position to actively follow the learners' L1 communications. On the first night, Rosina, administrative assistant for the night courses, briefly introduced me to the teacher prior to the start of class. Then she introduced me to the class in Spanish. She told them that I was from a local university and was observing classes at the Center for one of my projects. I sat with the students throughout the observations.

As I became acquainted with the Center and its operations, I noticed that the teachers' and learners' interactions prior to class were also important. During this time, Rosina organized the classes and one-on-one tutoring based on who was present. The learners' and teachers' interactions in English and Spanish during this time gave insight into the groups' overall motivation and learning and teaching styles. Consequently, I began to make an effort to get to the Center well before the start of class in order to observe these interactions. I took notes during class (including lesson topics, description of activities, all sentences on the board, and key notes the learners took). I received copies of all handouts and recorded my data in extensive field notes that I typed shortly after returning home from each observation.

Interviews. I interviewed each of the learners and teachers individually during the course of the study. I could not schedule the interviews ahead of time because of the informants' erratic attendance. Instead, I interviewed them whenever their attendance in class presented an opportunity for an interview. Interviews took place before or after class, lasted about twenty to thirty minutes, and were conducted in either Spanish or English. I asked the students to choose the language of the interview. Most of the learners decided to be interviewed in Spanish, except Tony, who deliberately chose English. I used a semistructured interview format and took care to cover all the following topics in each interview:

- learners' and teachers' motivation
- their preferred learning and teaching styles
- learners' attitudes toward their teachers and the instruction they received

I also asked individuals very specific questions about strategies I observed in the class sessions, such as the reasons learners used translation, the reasons teachers allowed or discouraged translation, the ways learners helped one another, and their reasons for doing so (etc.). In each interview I also asked if they believed that using Spanish facilitated or hindered the L2 learning process. Because, as Cohen (1998) warns, semistructured interviews can lead to very cursory answers, I took care to ask follow-up questions to ensure that informants backed up their answers with reasons and explanations. During the interviews I took notes, which I transcribed in more detail shortly afterward.

FINDINGS

Both instructors, Martin and John, adopted the exclusive use of L2 in their lessons. On my first day of class, when Martin found out that I knew Spanish, he expressly requested that I would not interact with the learners in Spanish, so that the whole class would be in English. When I spoke with Martin about this privately, he told me that he felt this was the best way to ensure that learners had maximum exposure to English and practiced the phonics skills he had taught them. John told me that he did not use Spanish in class because he did not know it. Because learners frequently did not understand, they spoke among themselves in Spanish, used bilingual dictionaries, asked me questions when the teacher's back was turned, and wrote down unclear language for clarification after class.

The attitude of Diane (the third instructor) toward L1 use was different from Martin's and John's. She told me that she had studied Spanish in college and from time to time used her knowledge to translate into Spanish words and phrases that the students did not understand. In her opinion, if learners did not understand, there seemed no harm in using the Spanish she knew to help them. Diane frequently translated individual words either from English or Spanish upon a learners' request. In addition, she sometimes gave brief explanations of grammar points or an exercise in Spanish to make sure everyone had understood the English explanation she had provided first.

The mood in the class brightened after Diane began teaching the class. Learners liked her approach, and the amount of side discussion in Spanish decreased both because content was taught more clearly and because the learners could raise translation issues directly with Diane. The first time Diane used Spanish, the learners looked surprised and pleased. The learners I interviewed after Diane's arrival felt that the class had really improved a lot and cited Diane's use of Spanish as an example. When I asked these learners whether they felt that using Spanish was interfering with the amount of English they were speaking, all of them agreed that Diane's knowledge of Spanish was not a hindrance, but rather made the instruction clearer. Indeed, because of Diane's overall approach, the amount of L2 use by the participants increased even as she and the others translated to and from Spanish. I also noted that class participation increased and learners with irregular attendance came to class more often.

However, despite the advantages of Diane's approach, her teaching shared at least one feature with her predecessors': The instruction was not reflective of the students' purposes for learning English (such as reading to their children, socializing with Americans, or continuing their education), perhaps because all three teachers never took the time to talk with the students about their purposes for learning English. All three teaching approaches were heavily grammar- or phonics-based and included few opportunities for purposeful, learner-centered use of the new language, such as interpreting a paycheck, using social language, or reading a child's report card.

After I realized that John's and Martin's lessons were not pedagogically sound and that Diane's improved instruction still failed to meet many of the learners' needs, I resolved to discover why such a seemingly dysfunctional situation was, oddly enough, working. When I talked to the students, it became clear that one of the reasons they continued to attend was because they were deeply interested in learning English and saw the class as a good, or sometimes their sole, opportunity to do so. Studying at the Council offered several advantages: The classes were free (Tony), they were offered at a time the students didn't have to work and could arrange child care (Maria Dolores and Eduardo, Mayra, and Tony), and they took place in a convenient location (Tony, Maria Dolores and Eduardo, and Ariel). As I followed interactions in Spanish during class, I noted close attention and a use of Spanish only to clarify and improve the instruction. In fact, many of the learners' interactions in their native language involved what Oxford (1990) calls "learning strategies." Oxford (1990) defines learning strategies as "specific actions taken by learners to make learning easier, faster, more enjoyable, more self-directed, more effective, and more transferable to new situations" (p. 8). I observed that the learners paid careful attention, took notes, and used prior and real-world knowledge to make sense of the instruction.

Oxford (1992, 8–10) provides a typology of five kinds of learning strategies, which is useful for discussing the L1-mediated strategies these learners used:

Metacognitive Strategies: Strategies helping learners regulate their own cognition

Cognitive Strategies: Strategies involving the mental processes of learning, such as generalizing or drawing conclusions

Compensation Strategies: Strategies learners use to overcome lack of knowledge of the target language, such as circumlocution

Social Strategies: Strategies learners use to get increased interaction in the target language

Affective Strategies: Strategies that learners use to help themselves feel better about their learning

The students of the class I observed used their L1 to accomplish strategies in all of the five groups. Some representative examples follow.

Among metacognitive strategies, all the learners used notebooks in which they wrote English words, phrases, and sentences the teachers taught them. They also copied sentences from the board and wrote down informal language that came up incidentally throughout the lesson. In addition to recording the English words, learners also translated everything into Spanish and wrote transcriptions of the pronunciation in English using Spanish spelling. For example, when Eduardo entered the room a few minutes after class began and the teacher said, "Have a seat," Victoria stopped the lesson to ask the teacher to clarify the meaning of this expression. Then she and the other learners recorded it in their notebooks. In this way, the students created a resource they could use to review at home and to refresh their memories during class. Thus, when Ariel entered the room shortly after the first latecomer, Victoria looked back at her notes and invited the new arrival, "Have a seat." The learners seemed to particularly value these examples of idiomatic, conversational English, and they took great pains to figure out the meaning in order to write it down, often to the teacher's surprise. Probably, the learners recognized that the expressions' conversational value related to their desire to "fit in" and to comfortably interact with Americans.

It is important to indicate that all learners stated in the interviews that notetaking was not a strategy any of the teachers at the Center had taught them, but instead was a transfer of training from previous instruction in Mexico, which offered an effective means for them to gain control over their learning.

A chief cognitive strategy was translation. For example, during Martin's unsuccessful phonics reading activity, the learners made it successful by using their own prior knowledge and a bilingual dictionary one of them carried to figure out the meaning of the unfamiliar words they were trying to sound out. When a student was struggling to say a word, another learner would quietly say the translation in Spanish or a learner would look up the word.

Learners also used their L1 and related cognitive strategies to understand new grammar. For example, after having seen several examples of the future-indicating structures *going to* and *will,* the learners asked the teacher to contrast the structures' meaning. The instructor looked at the examples and helplessly scratched his head while Victoria used the examples and her knowledge of Spanish grammar to figure out herself that *going to* indicates an event that is scheduled or planned, while *will* usually represents a promise to be fulfilled in the future, and explained all this to her peers in Spanish. Afterwards the teacher exclaimed that there was no difference between the structures. At that point, Victoria stood her ground and repeated her explanation in Spanish, which, to me, is a striking example of a self-confident adult using prior knowledge of Spanish grammar and her skills of inference and deduction to define the meaning of an unfamiliar structure in a new language, even though it meant contradicting the teacher in front of her peers, albeit in a language that the teacher did not understand.

The learners' chief compensation strategy was codeswitching. Whenever the learners did not know a word they needed, they merely said the word or phrase in Spanish in the middle of an English sentence in order to help their peers. The participants entered the new word or phrase into their notebooks. In this way, the student speaking, but also any other student who wished, could learn the new piece of language. If there was any unclarity or contradiction in regard to the English words supplied, for example, *garbage* and *trash* for one Spanish word, *basura,* the learners would ask the teacher for clarification and also discuss the words in Spanish among themselves in order to resolve the confusion.

As for social strategies, though using Spanish did not directly increase the actual amount learners spoke in English, the learners did use Spanish to strategize ways to increase their interaction in English. For example, when John was presenting his list of sample sentences in various verb tenses, Victoria asked the other learners if they felt they should be speaking more. When they agreed, she proposed that they each say one of the sentences written on the board, which everybody agreed to do. She then interrupted the teacher to ask if learners could go around the room repeating aloud the sentences on the board. This activity "broke the ice" for the teacher, who realized that the learners were ready for more interaction, and he then began to provide more opportunities for oral drill.

In the area of affective strategies, students used their L1 to great advantage. In interviews I conducted in Spanish, all of the learners voiced frustration about activities they were unable to do successfully because of their level of English, such as talking to their children's teachers, reading a story in English to their children, talking to a cashier or another shopper in a store, or getting to know English-speaking coworkers. They also expressed frustration because they felt under time pressure and believed they were not progressing fast enough in learning English. The learners compensated for these frustrations by creating a collaborative, mutually supportive classroom environment. As noted earlier, everyone supported each other by supplying translations and grammar explanations in the L1. In addition, they gave each other language-learning tips. For example, when Ariel joined the class for the first time, Tony noticed that Ariel did not have a notebook and tore off a sheet of paper, handed it to him, and said in Spanish, "If you take notes, you'll learn faster." When Ariel had trouble taking notes at first, Tony let him copy from his notebook. At the next session, Ariel had a notebook of his own. When I asked Tony why the students assisted each other so much, he said, "Well, we're all friends, and the class is more enjoyable when we help each other."

The learners also took care to greet each other in Spanish at the beginning of class and also quietly greeted each latecomer in Spanish, thus making sure everybody felt welcomed and valued. In addition, when Mayra and Maria

Dolores had trouble understanding the teacher or difficulty in repeating or saying a word accurately, the others would help that student by modeling the pronunciation for the learners to repeat. Interestingly, the two women were often more successful when a fellow student modeled pronunciation, rather than the teacher. This might be because students had a lower affective filter when peers helped them. Students never demonstrated impatience when a peer had difficulty. They waited patiently as the student struggled to pronounce or to get the correct answer.

Finally, students also comforted one another at times of emotional stress. For example, on one occasion Mayra became overwhelmed when she could not understand the lesson and ran from the room in tears. In a prior interview, Mayra had expressed extreme frustration that she was not learning English as quickly as she had hoped, and I believe that this frustration led to the outburst of emotion. The other students looked puzzled, but continued the lesson. When the student returned a few minutes later, one of the female students comfortingly patted her hand, and all the others gave her smiles or nods. Then, at the break, several of the female students in the class hugged the student and reassured her that English was difficult for all of them. In subsequent classes, Mayra demonstrated more self-confidence and seemed less frustrated.

The students made very deliberate decisions to use Spanish at some times and English at others, depending on the situation. For example, even though they greeted each other in Spanish, they also made efforts to use English to greet each other, particularly when they arrived at the Center early for class. The students who arrived first would jokingly greet students who entered after them first in English and then in Spanish. The students also took every opportunity to increase their interaction in English with native speakers. Thus, students who were early would frequently approach their teacher, other teachers, or me, greet us, and initiate brief conversations in English. In addition, when I interviewed the students, all of them made an effort to use English as much as they could, even though they could express themselves much more completely in their L1. For example, during her interview, Mayra struggled to say in English the simple sentences, "I'm a singer. I want to sing in English." After doing so, learners clearly felt great satisfaction. Mayra, for instance, smiled broadly and happily each time she managed to speak in English during class and the interview. At the end of his interview, Tony called out joyfully to the assistant director of the Center, "Rosina, Rosina, we spoke, we spoke in English!" Finally, although the students used Spanish to comfort and motivate each other, they used English to motivate their teacher. A very dramatic example occurred after Diane's first lesson, which was considerably more successful than the teaching of her two predecessors. Victoria announced in a clear voice in English, loud enough for everyone in the room to hear, "At last we have a good teacher." Clearly, the learners' use of the L1 was not a kind of avoidance strategy or a disruption, but rather part of a series of deliberate decisions students were making to enhance their learning process.

DISCUSSION AND CONCLUSIONS

A number of conclusions can be drawn from the present study. First, the learners definitely used their L1 interactions to improve instruction. Notably, during all the class sessions I observed, the students always used the L1 in ways that were related to the instruction—they were never off topic.

Second, the transformed classroom atmosphere after Diane's arrival is clear replication of the studies in favor of L1 use cited by Auerbach (1993). In this study, ironically, the amount of communication in the L2 increased during Diane's more interactive lessons, thus belying teachers' long-held belief that L1 use reduces learners' use of the L2. Therefore, rather than suppressing all use of L1, teachers need to decide if learners are talking because they are, in fact, off topic, need help or clarification, or are collaborating in their L1. Teachers may need to conference with learners to find out why instruction may not be clear, not be supplying sufficient practice, or not be meeting the students' needs. In addition, teachers should plan carefully how to structure L1 use in classes of mixed native languages. Teachers can use multiple groupings to ensure students have opportunities to interact with speakers of their own L1 as well as speakers of other languages in order to avoid polarization in the class. Teachers also must take extreme care when they have only one learner of a particular L1 in their class. In this situation, the teacher needs to help the learner develop L1 strategies without having the benefit of assistance from other native speakers and also to take measures so that this student does not feel isolated when other learners are interacting in their native languages. Teachers also need to be aware that learners in such a situation will not have the built-in affective support in the L1 that the other learners might have.

Third, in this study, all three teachers did not understand the learners' needs, interests, and motivation. This failure to communicate is somehow related to their unwillingness or inability to communicate with the students in their L1. Teachers therefore need to devise systems to communicate with learners, even when the teachers do not know the learners' L1. It is crucial to find out learners' motivation, to discuss their learning difficulties, and to talk about their feelings and emotions about learning another language. Moreover, teachers need to let students use adult learning strategies, which are often available to them only in the L1. For example, instead of instituting a blanket prohibition of the L1 in small-group activities out of fear that learners will chat among themselves instead of completing the assignment, teachers need to structure activities so that the participants can use their L1 while staying on task. Finally, teachers need to find ways to instruct the effective usage of

L1 strategies in English so that these strategies are available to students when interacting in monolingual environments outside the ESL classroom.

To sum up, the present study provides considerable support for Auerbach's contention that learners' L1 should be included in ESL instruction. Clearly, the English-only classroom is a notion that needs further investigation. Additional studies of both English-only classrooms and different kinds of classrooms that deliberately incorporate the L1 in a variety of ways are needed in order to provide instructional designers and practitioners with additional data they can use to build alternative instructional models. More generally, the present study is a clear-cut example of the power of a positive attitude. The participants of this study, because they were so highly motivated to learn English and because they believed that this class was their best opportunity for doing so, took affirmative steps to make the experience as beneficial as possible, instead of merely complaining and dropping out. This positive attitude enabled them to help each other learn, to provide clarification, and to increase their motivation, even in the face of the considerable difficulties faced by immigrants to the United States. Particularly dramatic were the instances in which learners took initiative to redirect classroom focus to items of interest to them, such as idiomatic expressions; collaborated to gain more interaction in English; and provided clarification of grammatical concepts when their teacher was unable to do so. This study, then, reminds teachers, not only those of adults, that one of their greatest resources is already in their classrooms: their students, who bring to the learning process a wealth of experience, ideas, and motivation.

NOTE

1. The names of the people and places have been changed as necessary to protect the anonymity of the participants.

REFERENCES

Auerbach, E. R. (1993). Reexamining English only in the ESL classroom. *TESOL Quarterly,* 27(1): 9–32.

Baron, D. (1990). *The English-only question: An official language for Americans.* New Haven: Yale University Press.

Brown, H. (1994). *Principles of language learning and language teaching,* 3rd edition. Englewood Cliffs, NJ: Prentice-Hall Regents.

Brumfit, C., & Roberts, J. (1983). *An introduction to language and to language teaching.* London: Batsford.

Cohen, A. (1998). *Strategies in learning and using a second language.* London: Longman.

Cummins, J., & Swain, M. (1986). *Bilingualism in Education.* London: Longman.

D'Annunzio, A. (1991). Using bilingual tutors and non-directive approaches in ESL: A follow-up report. *Connections: A Journal of Adult Literacy,* 4: 51–52.

Dulay, H., Burt, M., & Krashen, S. (1982). *Language 2.* New York: Oxford University Press.

Hakuta, K. (1985). Cognitive development in bilingual instruction. *Issues in English language development.* Washington: National Clearinghouse for Bilingual Education.

Irujo, S. (1998). *Teaching bilingual children: Beliefs and behaviors.* Boston: Heinle & Heinle.

Judd, E. (1987). The English language amendment: A case study on language and politics. *TESOL Quarterly,* 21(1): 113–135.

Kloss, H. (1977). *The American bilingual tradition.* Rowley, MA: Newbury House.

Legarreta, D. (1979). The effects of program models on language acquisition by Spanish-speaking children. *TESOL Quarterly,* 13(4): 521–534.

Oxford, R. L. (1990). *Language learning strategies: What every teacher needs to know.* New York: Newbury House Publishers.

Phillipson, R. (1992). *Linguistic imperialism.* London: Oxford University Press.

Rivera, K. (1990, October). Developing native language in language minority adult learners. *ERIC Digest.* Washington, DC: National Clearinghouse on Literacy Education, Center for Applied Linguistics.

Samash, Y. (1990). Learning in translation: Beyond language experience in ESL. *Voices,* 2(2): 71–75.

Skutnabb-Kangas, T. (1981). *Bilingualism or not: The education of minorities.* Clevedon, England: Multilingual Matters.

Part II

Classroom Environments

5

Performance and Creativity in the Language Classroom

Kathleen N. March

Perhaps it was the repetition of the same methods and results over a number of years that led me to rethink the classroom environment for beginning and intermediate Spanish.[1] Or perhaps it was a need to make something happen differently in the adult learners' class. Whatever the reason, the feeling gradually came to me that today's mature or post-secondary students ought to have a different learning environment than they have traditionally encountered. Most college-level language teachers realize that the old reliance on familiarity with grammatical terms and sensitivity to linguistic features has become virtually ineffective for a growing portion of students. This fact alone is a stimulus to seek new approaches to the adult setting.

When children, especially the youngest ones, are taught a second language, teachers inevitably think in terms of the personal. They also will generally say they strive to make language learning fun, just as they do with all the primary school subjects. "Fun" usually translates into playing games, singing songs, and interacting with videos, to name a few of the school activities. Field trips to connect with and get to know the nearby communities are also a favored method for the natural promotion of learning. For obvious reasons, reading out of a textbook may be conceived of as less central to the actual classroom environment, although not to the overall learning process. The well-known adage of Lao-tse is widely accepted and practiced: "I hear and I forget. I see and I remember. I do and I understand."

In the area of second language learning, speaking and physically carrying out matching movements—that is, performing—are active applications of linguistic skills. Through audiovisual materials, the passive skill of listening is developed as well. Younger language learners are not expected to write a great deal in the target language, although they do manipulate objects that serve to connect words and meaning fairly directly. Also important is the amount of repetition younger children do in learning. While the reasoning may be erroneous—that is, they can indeed handle large amounts of linguistic information—the effect is to create fluency and a sense of security in the usage of the second language.

On the other hand, adult L2 learners are usually confronted with a textbook that has suitably mature topics, organized grammatical explanations, and considerable reading and vocabulary. All of these are designed to enable the acquisition of a large amount of material so that students can communicate as adults, on adult matters. Although it would be impossible to pin down, it has been observed that at least part of the time the "adult" mode of instruction in a foreign language can begin in middle school. The use of metalanguage to talk *about* Spanish rather than *in* it may begin as soon as it is felt that the students can recognize the parts of speech (which, ironically, are being taught less and less in language arts classes). Perhaps this is the starting point for the formation of beliefs on how one "ought to" go about learning a foreign language, as well as for beliefs that one is either talented or useless at doing so.

There is still considerable disagreement as to whether the age factor in language learning is of little or large consequence (Singleton and Lengyel, 1995). This chapter does not propose to enter that vast field of linguistic study, but instead offers the perspective that adults, like children, can greatly benefit from the sort of classroom environment in which performance and creativity are strongly emphasized (see also Schultz, Gonglewski, and Bräuer in this volume). Yet, because we see maturity as closely tied to literacy, we expect that adult learners will take notes, summarize content, write out exercises, or produce compositions and papers, regardless of the subject. Thus, somewhere between the active, playing child and the focused, more logical adult the concept of how a language is actually acquired gets lost. Hausner and Schlosberg (1998, p. 29) point out that there are differences in manner of thinking between children and adults, which they summarize as follows:

- Logical thinking: Adults need thoughts to "make sense" or "fit." Creative adults must make an effort to temporarily "suspend disbelief." Children will jump about more with their ideas, while play gradually forces them into the recognition of rules.

- Prior knowledge and the imagination: Children have less prior knowledge and thus their imaginations have "more room to flourish."
- Freedom from embarrassment: Children are less concerned than adults about the impression they cause by what they say or do. (The implication is that this frees them to experiment with new ideas, words, and other representations of their thought processes.)
- Differing objectives: Children think more for pleasure; adults think in order to reach a conclusion and achieve some result.

It may be particularly because of the fourth point that we think logical, structured presentations of the material will suffice and may spend a goodly amount of class time with these presentations, with small portions of the time devoted to actual production of language by students. We welcome questions from motivated students about how the new language is put together and how it becomes a flowing entity. Yet as long as we do this, we allow the students to remain mentally on the stage of their first language and are not enticing them to occupy the roles of native Spanish (or French or Portuguese, etc.) speakers (see Collins in this volume for a different perspective). Fuller's encouraging little book (1987) for the layperson, *How to Learn a Foreign Language*, may state the obvious for the specialist, yet his observations may be very enlightening for learners to whom language, even their own linguistic system, is transparent: They can't feel its presence. He calls it "learning to think all over again" and explains:

> When you were a child, you didn't know what a tree was at first. Somebody had to tell you. . . . Your parents probably had to repeat the word to you on several different occasions before you finally got the hang of it. You had to learn to associate the sound of the word "tree" with the big green leafy thing you saw in front of you.
>
> That's what you must learn to do again. Only this time, since you're grown up, you will be able to get the hang of it much faster. You'll know why somebody is pointing to a tree, or to a picture of a tree, and saying a strange word. But you'll still have to learn the new word. You may even have to relearn it many times before you finally actually learn it. (29–30)

Fuller's Sausserian simplicity is to the point: "To learn a foreign language you must get away from the idea of translating words. Translating takes too much time and mental energy. You will never learn to really speak and understand a foreign language if you have to translate everything" (30). We all hear this but we less often practice it, as students or instructors. Adults instinctively turn to the linguistic system they already have in place to represent their world and attempt to proceed from within that comfort zone. The translation process is, in fact, a serious short-circuiting of comprehension and fluency. We can think of the flawed learning process as potentially occurring in the following manner:

- The learner hears Spanish and does not understand. He or she compares the utterance to English, trying to make it "fit" what is already in his or her linguistic repertoire.
- If comprehension does not take place, the natural response is to ask (frequently in the native tongue) what the linguistic input from Spanish means.
- The response tends to be given, automatically, in the form of a translation from Spanish to English.
- Unless there is enough context and flow of Spanish input—and in beginning/intermediate levels especially, there often is not enough of this—the learner remains focused on the English sound and meaning. This literally constitutes a break in the production/comprehension of the target language. In other words, the flow of Spanish has been stopped.

Fuller reminds his readers yet again: "The challenge of new thinking will not be limited merely to the area of new words; it is going to go much deeper than that. You will be learning new paths through the woods of the mind" (30–31).

Why refer to the observations of a non-specialized book for the general public in a chapter for specialists in language instruction? Perhaps because people like Fuller have successful experiences to build their observations upon, and they state the essentials in a very direct way. In the previous observation, the contrast between words and paths is a valid one. It distinguishes between the mistaken belief that making lists of vocabulary and short phrases constitutes an effective study habit and the theoretical knowledge that native speakers develop their competence for all aspects of their language, including the syntax or "paths" along which that language is connected. Let's take the use of flash cards, which is one of the most favored practices. This study method actually reinforces the fragmentation of linguistic phrases into isolated chunks, definitely not placing information in any discursive framework. It also forces the student to continuously flip-flop between the two codes, a process that (I suspect) requires greater effort in the early learning period. The only way to avoid this with flash cards is if no English translation is used, or if the meaning of the Spanish is represented by a graphic item rather than a written one. The constant breakage of the L2 production process, its mediation by or diversion toward English, is both wearisome and undermining of linguistic flow.[2] If nothing else, the attention to English structures and lexicon takes time out from the space occupied by Spanish during the class or study intervals.

I strongly believe that approaching second language study as performance and as a creative activity will result in a higher success level for students. How else do children internalize grammar when they enter another linguistic environment? Whatever the exact process that occurs in the brain, we all know that they are able to learn without conscious grammar study. If exposure is sufficient, children will acquire what Chomsky calls native-speaker competence. In the first place, they have spent almost no time being distracted from the focus on the language in which they are immersed. Again, Fuller's self-help description of language learning has appeal as an apt summary of what children do in natural settings, even though his audience is adult learners:

1. You can never really learn to speak a foreign language, or understand it when it is spoken, unless you can learn to think in the language. You can actually start to think in the language from virtually the first day.
2. Learning to think in a new language means learning to associate an initially meaningless new sound with the idea or image of what it means. You practice to the point where the new sound takes on meaning for you. (33)

It may be precisely because of the classroom environment that adults, even those less sophisticated in terms of linguistic sensitivity, frequently affirm they cannot learn a foreign language unless they travel to the country where it is spoken. Overlooking the fact that they could always just be looking for an excuse for poor performance (ours or theirs?), we can also surmise that they are rightfully telling us they still need to perform the language. In other words, they know that in many ways they are still just like children, in terms of the initial approach of human beings to language acquisition. These adult learners are, in addition, telling us that they also desire and require meaningful, contextualized communication. Why do language instructors so often agree with them, then proceed to organize the adult classroom in the usual way?

Even the adult learners sense that a language should be used for "real" communication and not merely for constructing appropriate utterances for an examination grade, despite the penchant for dividing the syllabus up in different categories and percentages. The very concept of studying material "for the (written) test" is a fragmenting factor that distracts from the concept of language as a flowing process. The second language, if it is to be acquired and used with fluency, still needs to "happen." It still must be, in a word, performed or spoken in one form or another. What they may not easily perceive is what constitutes performance of an effective sort. Farber's (1991) glib but realistic and hard-hitting style of advice is:

> You can't just push a button and let the language you want to learn roll over you. Expecting to learn a language by laid-back listening is like expecting to build a magnificent body by going to the gym, sitting in the steam room, chugging a glass of carrot juice and then bragging about your 'workout.' (38)

For the purpose of achieving the level of fluency that will encourage people to flex their linguistics muscles with confidence, I propose that the promotion of a creative flow in L2 production is one of the most desirable objectives for the adult classroom. Before going any further, it will be helpful to present a definition of what we mean by performance and performing. The American Heritage Dictionary of the English Language provides the following entries:

> **Performance:** 1. The act of performing; or the state of being performed. 2. The act or style of performing a work or role before an audience. 3. The way in which someone or something functions. 4. A presentation, especially a theatrical one, before an audience. 5. Something performed; an accomplishment; a deed.

> **Perform:** (tr.) 1. To begin and carry through to completion, do. . . . 2. To take action in accordance with the requirements of; fulfill (a promise or duty, for example). 3.a. To enact (a feat or role) before an audience. b. To give a public presentation of. (intr.) 1. To carry on, function. 2. To fulfill an obligation or requirement; accomplish something as promised or expected. 3. To portray a role or demonstrate some skill before an audience. 4. To present a dramatic or musical work or other entertainment before an audience.

Surprisingly, second language learning, despite Searle's long-familiar classifications of all language in terms of speech acts or utterances, was not, until fairly recently, viewed as a performance when practiced in the classroom. Instructors may refer to the need to promote skill-building, but the methods employed may not ultimately be conducive to this end. Nor is the part about skills often taken into account by students, who hear this the first day and still head for the flash cards or vocabulary list at the end of each chapter. In contrast, nobody would expect to reach proficiency in performing on a musical instrument without long hours of practice. Even the best music teacher cannot produce musicians if the students' contact with music is limited to talking about the notes and finger placement. Musicians also must listen to the music of others in order to gain comprehension and insight into the production of their own music, yet language students so often view work outside the classroom, particularly with audio materials, as something beyond the call of duty. They have difficulty seeing that the development of linguistic skills depends at least partially on sheer repetition, as does typing or any keyboard activity, in order to become automatic and fluid. They do not have a sense of the time investment required for skills or of the active nature of the activity this entails.

To use another comparison, nobody would expect a coach by himself or herself to have a winning team; the players themselves must invest a great deal of time developing the necessary physical and mental combination. No one can do it for them, just as the grammar explanations in the L2 class may clarify the language to some extent, but do not equate subsequently with correct student usage. If this were so, the basic explanation about, for example, the agreement in person, number, and gender in Spanish would be effective.[3] Practice (i.e., performance) proves otherwise, and the errors persist for some time. The language teacher can only aspire to being a good coach.

Similar situations to those of the athlete and the musician can be seen for the dancer and the actor, both of whom are undoubtedly aided by theoretical explanations, but who—logically, obviously—must practice if they are to perform. This is the "do" part of the definition cited earlier. There are any number of human activities that improve with sheer practice, time spent in doing and observing rather than articulating rules and their prescribed applications, until one's own performance is more automatic.

Returning to the title of this paper, we ask specifically how the emphasis on second language learning as performance would differ from the traditional classroom in which, after all, the target language is widely used. How can creativity, itself an elusive concept for the average person, contribute to the flow of class time as well as to individual learners' performance? To answer these questions, we first propose the following five practices. The set could be larger or smaller, but for our present purposes this arbitrary set of classifications will suffice:

1. Present and perform material at the appropriate level
2. Present material in an organized manner
3. Invite engagement with the material on a personal level
4. Use language creatively and expect/require the same of students
5. Include task-based, problem-solving performance for assessment

Points 3 and 4 are most closely related to creativity, a concept that merits definition. Csikszentmihalyi (1996) states that creativity "is a process by which a symbolic domain [i.e., a set of rules and procedures] in the culture is changed" (8). He goes on to assert that creativity requires the availability of surplus attention and that "centers of creativity tend to be at the intersection of different cultures, where beliefs, lifestyles, and knowledge mingle and allow individuals to see new combinations of ideas with greater ease" (8–9). The element of surplus attention would appear to argue in favor of more repetition in the L2 classroom, whether the students are children or adults. The more automatically the learners can manipulate the material, the abler they are to produce personalized, true responses. They also experience a confidence in the setting (or stage) in which they are performing, and they take more risks.

From the perspective of foreign language study, we can agree that "[i]n cultures [i.e., classrooms] that are uniform and rigid, it takes a greater investment of attention to achieve new ways of thinking" (9). If students are truly performing their language, it is likely that their attention will be more fully focused. Stevick (1983), in "Interpreting and Adapting Lozanov's Philosophy," discusses applications of the Suggestopedia method and describes his theatrical performing of a Swahili monologue for a class (= audience) through words, gestures, and overall tone. The feedback Stevick got indicated that much communication could be accomplished without the conscious articulation beforehand of linguistic rules. This in turn links with Csikszentmihalyi's statement that "[c]reativity occurs when a person, using the symbols of a given domain . . . has a new idea or sees a new pattern" (1996, p. 28).

APPROPRIATE LEVEL

If we have previously stated that adults think differently but also that children are more creative, what do we mean by appropriate level? It is easy to overlook this aspect for the adult L2 learner. While adults may have greater awareness that they use a linguistic medium for verbal communication, if they are attempting to communicate in a new language there are enough different elements to require multiple moments of practice. This is particularly true if they have not previously studied a language other than their own. Fuller notes that the strictly linguistic data is as new for the child as for the adult, and this should not be forgotten. The beginning levels are almost the same as far as the range of structures and lexicon that can be acquired. The adults may be able to focus longer on form and content, but can ultimately learn to speak only if they speak. In other words, they too need to jump in the pool and swim their laps if they are not to sink. *Una mesa* is just as newly *una mesa* for the adult as for the child as *cantar* is *cantar* for both age groups. The less time spent talking about *mesa* or *cantar* or filtering the Spanish input through the L1, the sooner the language muscles of brain and body perform the plays as required. The key here can be *flow*, a concept to which we will return.

ORGANIZED PRESENTATION

An organized presentation is not a lecture and may sound contrary to the concepts of creativity and flow, but in the long run it contributes to greater fluency at a faster rate. In fact, through the application of carefully organized information or input, the use of metalanguage, or using the L1 to talk about the target language, can be reduced or eliminated in the classroom. Moreover, even very basic patterns can be practiced in such a way as to leave room for an elementary sort of creativity from day 1. The performance of basic syntactic structures can incorporate humor and thus motivate and sustain participation. The desire to produce original, meaningful utterances—the desire to be creative—leads to greater concentration and to retention of material because it has been produced within a context. This context may either exist within the classroom or be one that is vividly imagined by the performer in response to appropriate stimuli/cues. The idea of vividness brings up the question of the instructor's role as performer as well. We shall return to this idea later.

PERSONAL ENGAGEMENT

By focusing on truthful individual responses (or on blatant lies, if the occasion requires), the classroom is opened up to creative exchanges. Here, the truth aspect should not require exchanges that seriously exceed the students' level, nor should it disrupt the practice (flow) of important patterns. The instructor has to control the questions in such a way as to elicit accessible information and must also know the students well enough to predict which answers can safely be elicited. A simple, early example from the beginning weeks of most Spanish 101 classes is the verb *gustar*, which easily can serve as the basis of brief, realistic, personalized questions with slight variation to test comprehension.

CREATIVE LANGUAGE USAGE

The creative production of language can be stimulated by the use of new, surprising, even audacious materials and activities. These may support silly content as well as content of a serious nature and both engage and encourage responses. Having students create their own materials further promotes L2 output that is focused and appropriate (see also Gonglewski and Schultz in this volume). Even with children, the encouragement of creativity does not imply total freedom from rules, and certain types of behavior can be expected within a range of potential participation in communication (Hausner and Schlosberg, 1998).

Hausner and Schlosberg have their own focus on the concept of creativity. It is worthwhile to list a few of their points:

> (1) Creative people have a powerful drive to make things better. . . . They are good at [it] not only because they are open to new answers but also because they are good at changing around the questions. (2) Creativity can be taught. (3) Creativity leads to innovation, and innovation leads to progress. (4) Companies are now teaching grown-ups to reconnect with their creative selves. (5) One of the biggest factors in successful, creative, productive people is that they believe they can solve problems and . . . make change for the better.

The fact that creativity can be taught can help encourage those who say, "but I'm not creative," just as we try to encourage those who, as noted previously, insist they are "not good at languages."

The foreign language instructor who wants motivated, participating students (and who doesn't? See also Part I of this volume) must be creative, as well as a performer of the target language. In the *NEA Advocate*, Morris Burris

(1999) looks at the teacher as actor. Although he is a professor of theater, the author does not limit his attention to drama classes. After providing an example from a veterinary class, he ends with the affirmation that what professors do visually can help imprint ideas in the memories of their students (8). Actors, Burris also notes, keep their performances fresh by listening and adjusting to their audiences. The acting or performance connections between the foreign language classroom (we want our students to understand and remember the material presented) and creativity are further strengthened when we think that actors are generally considered to be very creative people. When we consider the four parts to Hausner and Schlosberg's definition of creativity[4] and the four ways in which creative people act,[5] we discover an almost exact description of the perfect second language classroom. We can equate the new ideas in general to new ideas about how one articulates one's reality through a new language. The abundance of ideas, also called "fluency" or "ideaphoria," could be viewed as paralleling the ability to see how new linguistic elements organize in such a way as to create new modes of communication. The instructor, then, not only must perform along with the students but must also provide numerous opportunities for them to do so and must be consistently encouraging. Even adults need a sense of security when taking risks.

TASK-BASED ENVIRONMENT

A task oriented toward a meaningful, realistic context naturally links the individual to someone other than the instructor. Within the classroom, it aids in the development of a classroom community. Furthermore, if creativity and the commitment to a task usually stimulate one another, we can expect greater motivation to practice or make use of the foreign language outside the classroom if students are engaged in creative tasks. Problem-based service learning, or PBSL, is one of my personal preferences, because it even more strongly enhances the potential for meaningful language usage and lends transcendence to the activity in which students are engaged.

For children, performance in the second language classroom may take the form of participating in a game. Older learners still learn from and willingly take part in games (why not play bingo, for example, to practice numbers, since adults seem to play this?), but they are also able to focus more easily than children on extended projects. Both games and projects, it is important to emphasize, require the active, motivated production of speech. As long as there is a community that expects and motivates communication in the foreign language, production will occur. Moreover, when the foreign language is performed creatively, with the motivation to do so originating in the learner, it becomes in a sense its own encouragement and reward. The sense that a thing or an activity has value in and of itself, while not very pragmatic, is an accepted tenet for experts in the field of creativity (Csikszentmihalyi; Hausner and Schlosberg).

By concentrating on the promotion of creative activity or performing in the target language, the goal is for the "doing" to become a distracting force, leading the learner away from the conscious contemplation of the mechanics of the foreign structures. At the same time, the language production points self-referentially back to itself, is its own insertion point into the flow of its own syntactic patterns. It becomes its own stage and speaks its own lines, generating a connected and motivated energy that leaves less time for contrasting the input/output with English, (or *la lengua barbara*, as I call it in my classes, pretending not to understand it [cf. Stevick]). It is the loss of self-consciousness and distancing from the metalinguistic focus that likewise frees learners to focus on creating their own acts of speech, whether unpolished and a bit flawed or (nearly) perfect. Just as with children, when the learner is less concerned with making mistakes and more concerned with the pleasure of performing, a certain freedom from the fear of risk is achieved. It is easy to see how this is conducive to better results. We encourage children to experiment and explore, so why do we expect adults to "do it right" so quickly? And so uncreatively?

The early advances made in second language learning by adults are no less baby steps than those taken by young children. A similar statement was made earlier in this chapter, but it merits repetition, for in fact the greater awareness of mature students may result in the inability to take any steps at all, not even baby ones.[6] After all, psychoanalytic theory indicates that the self or identity is intimately embedded in language. If we are forced, in what is perceived to be a risky setting, to give up that language, less learning is likely to occur. Some of the activities and games from part 2 in Hausner and Schlosberg's *Teaching Your Child Creativity* (1998) can actually be adapted to adult foreign language learning with little difficulty.

The overuse of reading and writing, if the format is not natural or truly communicative, may serve as crutch (at best) or as hurdle or barrier (at worst). This does not mean that I am suggesting the total elimination of writing. For one thing, there are the workbooks that test rule application, when they are most functional and, when not, at least provide constant opportunities for consulting vocabulary lists. Do workbooks promote flow? Almost never, in the ones I've used for Spanish. Creativity? Perhaps in its most tenuous form, but even then students frequently resist creating the more open kind. They are intimidated, not willing to take risks, even privately, perhaps especially because they are working without a supportive community to motivate them into creative performance. On the other hand, writing out exercises does signify language production of some sort. Csikszentmihalyi (1997) observes that "[c]reative people are especially good at ordering their lives so that what they do, when, and with whom will enable them to do their best work" (41).

The simple act of making space to sit down and write or listen can create a rhythm of contact and a personal workout that will be profitable.

Perhaps, however, writing and reading are most effective when they support the classroom activities or a project, as in shared experiences such as the group-generated skit or narrative. Even written work, when directed at the appropriate level, can promote "the spontaneity state" (Mann, 1970, cited in Stern, 1983, p. 214). Stern, after citing Mann on this state, observes regarding the use of psychodrama in the language classroom, "Also of relevance is the free-flowing creativity that is unleashed" (214). Students can easily be instructed to use the written medium to generate their psychodramas (see also Schultz in this volume).

Working alone at writing in the foreign language, and especially achieving flow, can be a challenge. At the beginning level, it may not be a reasonable goal, because flow in writing even in one's own language takes at least fifteen minutes to be achieved at each sitting. Maybe this flow can still be fostered, as suggested by the writers Perry (1999) interviewed for *Writing in Flow*, by rituals and routines, (un)cluttered work space, timing, "just doing it," silence (or music), going back (i.e., reviewing) to go forward, and/or eating/drinking (161, ff). But in the long run, it may be that the best perspective we can come up with is that all students must have a reason to write, just as professional creative writers need one, if they are to enter flow (Perry, 1999, p. 37).

The majority of this chapter has focused on the oral production of a foreign language, on performance on the stage that is the classroom, with creativity of performance one of the most desirable aspects, if not the most desirable aspect, of the class. This does not mean that writing is of no importance in the learning process, but rather that it invariably needs to be, once and for all, a means for learning to speak, not an end in itself. Is this not ultimately the primary objective of our students when they enter a modern language class?

NOTES

1. Even when not directly stated, references in this paper are to Spanish and English, with English as the L1 or native language, and Spanish as the L2 or target/foreign language.

2. It is tempting here to relate this fragmentation to the current media practice of sound bites, where it is felt that brevity can convey the whole meaning. The disruption of cognitive flow is also painfully obvious in MTV and music videos in general. Hausner and Schlosberg, for their part, link the decline in creativity among children—perhaps also a decline in memory and certainly in ability to articulate thoughts—to passive television viewing that is not accompanied by the need to perform or produce ideas themselves.

3. Farber has a lot to say against grammar in his chapter "Psych Up." Here are two of his remarks: "Grammar, I again protest, is usually presented in American classrooms as a kind of obstacle course designed to leave you gasping facedown on the Astroturf somewhere between the pluperfect and the subjunctive. Grammar can do that to you if you insist on attacking it the old way: frontally, rule by rule, exception by exception, with no fun en route

and never feeling the joy of progress" (42). And, "You don't have to know grammar to obey grammar. If you obey grammar from the outset, when you turn around later and learn why you should say things the way you're already saying them, each grammatical rule will then become not an instrument of abstract torture disconnected from anything you've experienced but rather an old friend who now wants you to have his home address and private phone number" (43).

4. "(1) the desire to IMPROVE things; (2) the tendency to undertake such improvements by looking at situations from a new point of view or REDEFINING a problem; (3) being OPEN to many new ideas or possible solutions, even those that seem 'all wrong' at first; (4) ACTING on those fresh perspectives to CREATE novel solutions" (15–16).

5. "(1) almost always show desire, or need, to improve things; have self-esteem to know they can; (2) have the ability to think outside the box; (3) have an open mind when challenged with new ideas; allow themselves to have lots and lots of ideas if highly creative; (4) driven by the need to implement their ideas; willing to take risks, in thought and action" (19-20).

6. Consider one of my students, who came, very concerned, to tell me that he simply could not put words together in sentences and showed me some samples from his growing stack of flash cards. He was clearly stuck in the translating mode when he could not understand the error of "*Su llama es* ___," although we had never used "*Su nombre es* ____" in the classroom and had always stressed *Me llamo, te llamas, se llama* as the way to introduce a person. This same student, when in class shortly afterward and in the performing mode, could be heard giving consistently accurate responses to a simple, dramatic activity in which flow and repetition were utilized.

REFERENCES

Brown, H. Douglas. (1993). *Principles of language learning and teaching*, 3rd edition. Englewood Cliffs, NJ: Prentice-Hall.

Burris, Morris. (October, 1999). All the world's a stage! An actor's method enlivens the classroom. *National Education Association Advocate*, 17(1): 5–8.

Collins, Mary Ann, and Amabile, Teresa M. (1999). Motivation and creativity. In Robert J. Sternberg (ed.), *Handbook of creativity*, pp. 297–312. Cambridge: Cambridge University Press.

Csikszentmihalyi, Mihaly. (1990). *Flow: The psychology of optimal experience*. New York: Harper & Row.

Csikszentmihalyi, Mihaly. (1996). *Creativity: Flow and the psychology of discovery and invention*. New York: HarperCollins Publishers.

Csikszentmihalyi, Mihaly. (1997). *Finding flow: The psychology of engagement with everyday life*. New York: Basic Books.

Farber, Barry. (1991). *How to learn any language*. New York: Citadel Press.

Fuller, Graham E. (1987). *How to learn a foreign language*. Washington, DC: Storm King Press.

Hausner, Lee, and Schlosberg, Jeremy. (1998). *Teaching your child creativity*. Washington: Lifeline Press.

Lubart, Todd I. (1999). Creativity across cultures. In Robert J. Sternberg (ed.), *Handbook of creativity*, pp. 339–350. Cambridge: Cambridge University Press.

Mann, J. (1970). The present state of psychodramatic research. Paper presented at the American Psychological Association Convention, Miami Beach, 1970. ERIC ED 043 055.

Moskowitz, Gertrude. (1978). *Caring and sharing in the foreign language class: A sourcebook on humanistic techniques*. Boston: Heinle & Heinle.

Oller, John W., and Richard-Amato, Patricia A. (eds.). (1983). *Methods that work: A smorgasbord of ideas for language teachers.* Boston: Heinle & Heinle.

Omaggio, Hadley A. (1993). *Teaching language in context,* 2nd edition. Boston: Heinle & Heinle.

Perry, Susan K. (1999). *Writing in flow: Keys to enhanced creativity.* Cincinnati: Writer's Digest Books.

Singleton, David, and Lengyel, Zsolt (eds.). (1995). *The age factor in second language acquisition.* Clevedon, England: Multilingual Matters Ltd.

Stern, Susan L. (1983). Why drama works: A psycholinguistic perspective. In John W. Oller and Patricia A. Richard-Amato (eds.), *Methods that work: A smorgasbord of ideas for language teachers,* pp. 207–225. Boston: Heinle & Heinle.

Sternberg, Robert J. (ed.). (1999). *Handbook of creativity.* Cambridge: Cambridge University Press.

Stevick, Earl. (1983). Interpreting and adapting Lozanov's philosophy. In John W. Oller and Patricia A. Richard-Amato (eds.), *Methods that work: A smorgasbord of ideas for language teachers,* pp. 115–145. Boston: Heinle & Heinle.

6

Toward a Pedagogy of Creative Writing in a Foreign Language

Jean Marie Schultz

INTRODUCTION

Throughout their foreign language education American students are asked to practice various forms of writing. On the most elementary level, students may simply fill in the blanks on grammar exercises or compose discrete sentences illustrating a specific grammatical concept. In response to learners' needs to express themselves more fully using their emerging language skills, most foreign language work also requires written composition. At the elementary and intermediate levels, writing is, appropriately, personal in nature, with students typically asked to describe their hometowns or family members, to tell what they did on a vacation, or to summarize a film they recently saw. Students thus draw on what they know from personal experience for the content of their writing, practicing fairly easily generated *knowledge-telling* forms of composition (Bereiter & Scardamalia, 1987). In advanced reading and composition courses (see Gonglewski in this volume) and in upper-division courses, students begin practicing *knowledge-transforming* types of writing: analyzing literary or cultural materials (see Lee in this volume) and producing academic essays, where interpretative and organizational skills play a prominent role.

Writing at elementary and intermediate levels, the subject of which is often determined by the grammar point to be practiced, can be viewed fundamentally as a kind of advanced language exercise, a view reinforced by the relative ease with which students can generate the content. Writing at upper-division levels continues the focus on language skill development, but moves students into a more objective realm where critical thinking becomes increasingly important, requiring greater sophistication of linguistic mastery. Moreover, in upper-division writing particularly, students must begin to master the set of genre conventions appropriate to academic assignments (see Swales, 1990, and Büker in this volume). At both levels, however, writing tasks are determined by a *specific set of goals* defined by the teacher or the textbook. Linguistic and academic utility, no matter how defined and no matter at what level, is the hallmark of the vast majority of writing required of students enrolled in language courses. Within the goal-driven context of foreign language programs, therefore, students are rarely afforded the opportunity simply to write from their imaginations, practicing their language skills in formats that they define for themselves. Although students may occasionally be asked to write a poem or perhaps even a short story, these activities are generally seen as peripheral to the course goals, which are largely determined by a specified set of language functions to be covered. Creative writing may prove a nice diversion, but it rarely figures prominently into foreign language courses. Even more rarely do language department offerings include an entire course devoted solely to creative writing.

The preference accorded to carefully defined academic forms of writing has a long history and its own set of justifications. Various fields require certain types of written presentations where high levels of abstraction and generalization are the hallmarks of subject mastery and therefore of excellence in writing (Geisler, 1994). Moreover, there is a deep-seated belief within writing programs that progress cannot be made without an eventual abandonment of the personal in favor of a rigorous attention to the detached, impersonal, and objective (Britton et al., 1975). Within foreign language programs the progression determined for writing tasks is driven not only by these beliefs but also by the need to cover specific language functions, as suggested earlier. The American Council of Teachers of Foreign Languages (ACTFL)'s work on language acquisition sequencing, particularly in proficiency-based curricula, bolsters the effort by foreign language educators to lay out a carefully determined series of writing tasks that will move students into the realm of the increasingly abstract and hypothetical characteristic of superior language skills (ACTFL, 1999; Omaggio, 1993). In short, given the looser requirements of creative writing, there seems to be little time within foreign language curricula for this luxury, particularly when one of the perceptions associated with the form is that language issues risk becoming more problematic than in standard courses.[1]

Although the privileging of academic over creative writing is entirely tenable within its context, what such assignments fail to take into account is the significant degree to which personal commitment to a given task can shape writing in a positive way. As the work of both James Britton et al. (1975) and James Moffett (1981) has shown, the more personally involved developing authors are in their writing projects, the more compelling are their products. According to Britton's research,

> When involved, the writer made the task his own and began to write to satisfy himself as well as his teacher; in perfunctory writing he seemed to satisfy only the minimum demands of the task. When a writer wrote to satisfy himself as well as to fulfill the task, he seemed better able to bring the full force of his knowledge, attitudes and language experience to bear on the writing, which was carried to a conclusion on some sort of "rising tide." (7)

In his work on the transition from personal, creative writing to impersonal, academic writing, James Moffett (1981) has found that constraining writing to conform to a set of specified, sequential tasks, with one task to be executed before moving on to the next, can, in fact, short-circuit the expressive potential and progress of an individual student (9). As both of these researchers demonstrate, creative writing can indeed play an important and productive role in academic curricula.

GENERAL BENEFITS OF CREATIVE WRITING

Within the foreign language classroom, creative writing can feed positively into the language learning experience in multiple ways. Creative writing, first of all, invites students to begin their writing experience from a personal stance, which, as suggested earlier, can be more easily generated than can the objective and analytical (see Bereiter & Scardamalia, 1987; Flower, 1988, pp. 4–5). However, unlike the textbook-generated personal narrative and descriptive essay topics designed to provide students specific grammar and vocabulary practice, creative writing urges students to form and shape the raw material of experience into an artistic and compellingly executed format. This creative process thus encourages students to reach beyond relatively simple tasks that end when the assignment has been turned in and continue their work in more complex forms that take into account multiple constraints, including audience, character development, description, plot development, and, of course, language. The individualized orientation of creative writing can potentially have a positive reverberative impact on students' other language skills, notably their reading skills and their oral proficiency[2]; one of the criteria for determining whether a student is minimally at the intermediate level in speaking competence is the ability "to create with the language" (ACTFL, 1999, pp. 9, 15, 86–87).

The creative aspect of foreign language acquisition derives in part from the liberating effect that imaginative writing can provide. For many students, writing creatively in a foreign language can be a linguistically freeing experience. Approximately half of the students who enroll in the creative writing courses at the University of California at Berkeley have never before tried to write their own short stories or poems in their native language.[3] When asked why not, many respond that they are afraid of not having talent and of sounding silly. Writing in a foreign language can help alleviate these concerns for a number of reasons. There is, first of all, the benefit of using a language that is not one's own. Although this might initially seem to be a potential source of anxiety, students expect, in fact, that a greater degree of tolerance will be shown toward their creative efforts in a foreign language than if they were writing in their native language. The tacit assumption among students is that teachers expect them to be able to manipulate vocabulary, grammar, syntax, and a range of registers appropriately and without error in the native language, whereas in a foreign language, writers can make mistakes that will be taken into account in a liberal manner. Consequently, creative writing in a foreign language actually lowers the affective filter, thus fostering an atmosphere conducive to language acquisition (Krashen, 1982). This linguistic liberation is accompanied, moreover, by a psychological freedom students experience from the feeling that they are developing a new identity in the process of studying a foreign language. Alice Kaplan (1993) puts it very well when she discusses her own relationship to French. She says, "I am grateful to French . . . for teaching me that there is more than one way to speak, for giving me a role, for being the home I've made from my own will and my own imagination" (216). Writing creatively in a foreign language thus provides students with a distancing from themselves that allows them to dare and to try new things, something they often will not do in the concretized identity associated with their native language.

A third benefit of creative writing is that it maximizes students' personal commitment to the task, a function that Britton et al. (1975) sees as crucial to the development of effective writing skills. Because students must fundamentally generate the content of their writing from their own experiences, they must by definition do so from a committed position. They must draw on, and therefore progress toward mastering, the grammatical structures most appropriate to their authorial intentions and goals. Likewise, students must activate an individualized vocabulary to communicate their meaning. In creative writing the intensity of the commitment to the specifics of the foreign language goes well beyond that elicited by writing assignments where students are instructed to use the vocabulary from a textbook list or the grammar from a given lesson. In the five upper-division creative writing courses that have been taught at Berkeley, fully 90 percent of the students enrolled specified on their preliminary questionnaire the wish to improve their French in an individualized context as a primary goal in the course. As one student states, "The most important reason that I chose this course is to improve my French. . . . I hope that this course will allow me to spend more time on the complex structure of the French language in saying what I want."[4] More significant, however, are the student responses on the final course-assessment questionnaire. In answer to the question concerning improvement of language skills, the following typify the range of student responses:

- "I believe that the course helped me a lot to write in French. You use a vocabulary and style very different from when you write analyses, etc. And I like very much to write in a more personal style. In writing freely, it helped me to be less rigorous and more open to the language itself."
- "I think my writing improved very much—it was definitely a new experience. It allowed me to write in a manner that I had never written in before—I could experiment with style, etc. I tried to be very concrete with the grammar."
- "The exercise of writing, sharing (what you have written), and then revising has been extremely effective. The best concrete evidence of this that I can find is the *visible* improvement in my writing that occurred."
- "I liked being able to choose my subjects. I was much more personally interested in the writing and this both helped and hindered me. Once I settled upon a subject, I was more dedicated to perfecting it. However, because of the personal nature of the subject matter, I occasionally wished for more direction, or more distance between my feelings and my subject matter."

All of these students specify the perceived improvement of their French in terms of grammar, vocabulary, and style as a direct benefit of creative writing in a foreign language, a benefit clearly tied to their freedom of choice in terms of topic and consequent personal commitment to the writing (see Moffett, 1981; Britton et al., 1975). However, the last student cited mentions one problematic area in creative writing that moves more into the realm of the psychological. Despite the appreciation of greater freedom of expression, the student feels the need nevertheless for a certain degree of control over the very personal subject matter. In the rest of article, I will discuss the overall structure of the creative writing program in French at Berkeley and how such courses can be designed to overcome the challenges of creative writing and to help students develop their linguistic, reading, and writing skills as they advance in their foreign language study.

THE STRUCTURE OF CREATIVE WRITING COURSES

Berkeley offers three distinct courses in creative writing in French: (1) Autobiographies and Diaries, (2) Short Stories, and (3) Detective Stories. Although the courses can be taken in any order, ideally they are organized sequentially in terms of the ease with which each distinct genre can be produced. In the first course students begin by writing their own personal, authentic autobiographies and diaries, which, because they are the most directly tied to personal experience and fundamentally expressive in nature (Britton, p. 89), allow students to generate content more readily than moving directly into the realm of fiction. Eventually, these first experiential efforts will become the basis for fictionalized versions of the diary and autobiography. The course on short stories is more technically based, encouraging students to practice a wide variety of authorial devices, including writing from different points of view, using a variety of types of narrators, and practicing monologues and dialogues. The progression of writing exercises is structured loosely according to principles in James Moffett's work (1981), to which I will refer later in detail. The final course designed thus far in the sequence focuses on a very specific subgenre of the short story, detective fiction. All the techniques employed in the writing of diaries, autobiographies, and the short story are obviously also brought to bear in writing detective fiction. However, plot requirements render the writing more rigorous in terms of advance planning.

One of the primary foundational threads of all three courses is to treat creative writing like any other form of artistic expression. Aspiring artists and musicians, for instance, attend school where they learn about the evolutionary development of various artistic and musical traditions, about the different mediums or instruments they may be working with, and an entire repertoire of techniques by great artists or composers, which they also practice. Taking its cue from these other expressive domains, the academic aspect of the creative writing courses is grounded in these same artistic precepts: (1) the study of models representative of specific genres and organized so as to impart to students a sense of literary tradition, (2) the analysis of the narrative techniques illustrated in literary models, and (3) the practice of those techniques in a series of well-defined exercises. At the same time that students are engaged in a detailed study of the literature and practicing the targeted techniques in short exercises, they also are involved in writing their own creative texts. The students' own work is not constrained by any external demands imposed by the instructor. However, because students are actively involved in the analysis of potential models, they do naturally draw inspiration from them and learn techniques for shaping better the content of their stories.

There are clear pedagogical reasons for basing part of the approach to creative writing on models written by important authors. The use of models for the instruction of writing dates at least from the ancient Greeks. Wisdom had it that in order to learn to write well themselves, students should study examples of good writing, analyzing specifically the features that define it as such (Hillocks, 1987, p. 76). Up until the early twentieth century, such an approach to writing dominated not only composition instruction (see Bain, 1875) but also the writing of poetry, prose, and drama. As Ulrich Weisstein

(1973) points out, authors do not write in a void, generating their texts solely from their own imaginations. Rather, they write in response to their own repertoire of literary predecessors, defining themselves within a context of distinct traditions (29–47). As old-fashioned as this may seem, research in writing reveals that, indeed, writers need to have internalized literary models of the desired genre in order to produce their own versions of that genre (Hillocks, 1987, p. 76; Swales, 1990). In all of the creative writing courses, therefore, there is a specific reading list of works by major French authors carefully selected according to two criteria: (1) The text must be representative of the targeted genre, and (2) it must highlight specific narrative techniques. Students read the texts and discuss them in class, focusing particularly on the ways in which authors create the effects their texts produce. In the Autobiography and Diary course, for example, students read Jean-Paul Sartre's autobiography (1964), *Les mots*, studying his use of chronology, his characterization of significant family members, and his analysis of his own development as a writer. Students then read Sartre's fictional diary (1938), *La nausée*, looking at the ways in which the author communicates through another solipsistic genre the philosophical underpinnings of the novel, at his use of chronology here, at the characterization of the narrator, who is himself a writer struggling with his own identity as such, and at the other characters as presented by that narrator. Although many of these issues may be treated in other French department courses, the basis of class discussion is different from that of a traditional literature class. Students here are attentive not only to the textual features themselves, how they figure into specific literary traditions, and how they typify a given author, but also to how they might adapt these literary techniques and features to their own writing concerns.

The practicum component of the courses is carried out through a very specific sequence of brief writing exercises with which students experiment in a daily journal. The writing exercises are essentially indexed against the short stories discussed in class for that day and according to a predominant feature of those texts. For example, when reading Flaubert's (1965) *Un coeur simple*, a major focus of discussion is this author's use of *indirect free style*—or the representation of a character's thoughts directly without the narrator's apparent mediation—in order to tap into the psychology of the main character while maintaining the illusion of a purely objective, fundamentally absent third-person narrator.[5] After studying this technique, students are asked to practice it themselves, beginning from the position of a third-person impersonal narrator, who presents a character as neutrally as possible, and then moving into the mind of that character, allowing him or her to express his or her thoughts. This particular advanced exercise is executed only with a great deal of preliminary preparation, however. There are eight distinct writing exercises, sequenced in terms of difficulty, that students practice before attempting *indirect free style*. They are first of all instructed to imagine a character about whom they will be writing for the next two to three weeks and told that they must know this fictional character intimately. For the first exercise, students are asked to present a physical description of their character, paying close attention to the details of his or her appearance and their relationship to the character's personality. In the next exercise the students move inside their character's head, presenting his or her thoughts without regard to any precise organization. In exercise three, students use this raw material to practice a stream-of-consciousness technique. In exercise four, students focus the thoughts using internal monologue; and for the next exercise they create a silent imaginary listener in order to produce an external monologue. With the character now better defined, he or she is given his or her own voice, telling his or her story as a first-person narrator. In the seventh exercise, students create a narrator-witness who recounts the same events, but from the point of view of an observer, who may nevertheless have a very definite opinion as to the character. From this exercise students move into use of the third-person omniscient narrator. In the last exercise, students incorporate this penultimate rendition into the character's thoughts through the *indirect free style* technique. The sequencing of the exercises thus moves from the stance of an observer of the character's external appearance into the psychological realm, moving from a rendition of inner to external speech (see Vygotsky, 1986), and then finally to a synthesis of both objective and subjective points of view through the use of indirect free style and third-person omniscient narration. As can be seen from this description, there is a constant recycling of the same core material, but from different angles and with increasingly sophisticated elaboration. Students are thus continually rewriting the content and in the process also perfecting the linguistic aspects of their work.

Much of the inspiration for this particular exercise sequence was drawn from the work of James Moffett (1981), who created a series of writing exercises designed both to encourage high school students to write creatively and eventually to move them into the effective analytical writing they would need in college. Drawing partially upon Vygotsky's work on inner and external speech, Moffett experimented with writing assignments that would move his students from the personal to the objective. He summarizes some of the main lines of progression as follows:

- From vocal speech and unuttered speech to private writing to public writing.
- From dialogues and monologues to letters and diaries to first-person narratives to third-person narratives to essays of generalization to essays of logical operation.
- From an intimate to a remote audience.
- From perception to memory to ratiocination. (12)

Although Moffett's writing sequence is controversial for academic writing, it does provide a solid point of departure for a program in creative writing, which is essential for the smooth functioning of such a course. A poorly organized creative writing class can too easily degenerate into an amorphous free-for-all with little actual guidance in writing. A course organization based on models and on the constant practice of genres and writing techniques sequenced according to difficulty, moving most often from inner-directed, more solipsistic modes toward outer-directed, audience-sensitive modes, assures that students will be offered tangible writing help. In addition, it facilitates the targeting of specific language issues, which is particularly important in foreign language writing.

As crucial as the study of models and the practice of writing techniques is, it is equally important that creative writing take place in a safe environment. Because students may have self-doubts as to their talents and abilities, an essential foundational principle of such courses is that students feel confident that their efforts will not be met with ridicule. The implementation of a process approach to writing and of collaborative formats among peers are among the best techniques for creating just such an environment. Over the past twenty years, a great deal has been written about the benefits of such methods in the foreign language classroom (Barnett, 1989; Gaudiani, 1981). A process approach first of all places the emphasis on the dynamic, evolving nature of the writing experience. Rarely do professional writers produce a satisfactory piece upon their first effort. Several drafts are often created. Friends and colleagues are consulted. Once the editorial process begins, still more changes are made to the draft before it is finalized. The dynamics of multiple drafting and of sharing one's work are often very different from many students' academic writing experience, where they produce a single draft seen only by the teacher to whom it is submitted. This end-product approach is, in fact, partly responsible for students' mistaken impression that writers are born with innate genius and that they can produce a great work the first time they put pen to paper. Within the creative writing classroom, therefore, a process approach emphasizes to students that writing is, indeed, an evolving process and that their first effort will most likely not result in a masterpiece.

The process approach does more than create a less stressful writing environment by lowering students' anxiety in terms of their immediate self-expectations, however. Sharing their writing with classmates also contributes positively to the course atmosphere of trust by placing everyone on the same level of vulnerability. Precisely because all students will eventually share their writing with their classmates, they tend to be more receptive to having their own work critiqued and to offering positive suggestions for improvement to their peers. This collective sense of exposure to critique thus significantly mitigates the possibility of any harsh or negative criticism that might occur in a creative writing course.[6] In order to ensure further that a counterproductive critical atmosphere not emerge in the course, however, the instructor may lay specific ground rules for peer response, namely, that suggestions for improvement always tap into the positive potential of the writing.

A third way in which a collaborative, process approach contributes to the creation of a safe writing environment is by first restricting the public presentation of writing to a small group of peers. Students in the creative writing courses at Berkeley typically begin by sharing both their daily journals and their first creative efforts in small groups of three, which is far less intimidating than presenting one's drafts immediately to an entire class. As students build up a rapport of trust with the members of their small group and confidence in their own abilities, they feel more comfortable in eventually sharing a finished piece with the other students. In fact, once the course dynamics are well established, the instructor can then implement an "author's chair" format. Here a portion of each class is devoted to one or two individual students who read their finished pieces to the entire class. At the end of the reading, all students then write a brief, paragraph-long appreciation to the author. Receiving positive written feedback from the class members further increases the students' confidence in their work at the same time that all class members are invited to partake in a peer's literary experience. In creative writing, sharing one's work is, in fact, a primary motivator for writing at all and for taking care with one's work.

Thus far the discussion of the benefits of collaborative text-editing formats has addressed the psychological aspects of the creative writing course. Of greater academic interest, however, are the benefits to writing skills and to language acquisition. Here, too, a process approach contributes significantly to improvement in these areas. By rewriting their drafts, students must pay attention not only to the content and its impact on the reader but also to style and the language basics of grammar and vocabulary in a more conscientious way than in a course organized according to an end-product approach. In the practice of sharing multiple drafts with peers, students must focus on their grammar and vocabulary and progressively eliminate any errors for their final drafts. Moreover, they must develop sensitivity to issues of register and style, particularly as they attempt to create fictional characters who use language in a particular way. Finally, the fact that students share their writing orally with other students and discuss it frequently in French in their small groups fosters the development of students' oral proficiency, giving them valuable conversational practice on topics that are significant to them.

An additional benefit of a process approach is thus the development of students' sense of readership. In an end-product approach, the only outside reader of students' work is the teacher who serves as sole evaluator and grader. Often in such courses, students admit that they try to connect with the teacher's psychology and to anticipate his or her expectations in writing, adopting what Britton et al. (1975) calls a "pupil to teacher" stance, which is a feature of less mature writing (120). Once the audience has been extended to include the teacher and a small group of peers, students' sense of readership radically changes. No longer does their writing move unidirectionally from author to teacher/reader, falling into a readership void after the assignment has been completed and graded. Now students must write for others, and significantly for readers who are much like themselves. Eventually this circle of readers will be extended to include the entire class; and in that students' work will ultimately be "published" and made available to an unknown and generalized readership, as will be described later, students' are encouraged to develop an increasingly ubiquitous sense of readership, which ultimately contributes to writing improvement, not only in mechanics but also in organization, content, and style. In fact, in Britton's study on writing development, he specifies sense of audience as crucial to excellence and uses this feature as one of the salient criteria for evaluating student writing (72).

As a final step in the collaborative format of the creative writing courses, students are asked to produce their own class anthology of their best writing, which is handled as an in-house publication. For the preparation of the final manuscript, each student is assigned a specific role, from that of artist for the cover design to the writer of the table of contents to the pagination. The first step in the process is the election of an editorial board of peers to which student authors submit the finished piece of writing that they feel represents their best effort. The board members review the writing and advise each author of any final improvements to be made. Students then polish their work one final time, put it into the format decided upon for the anthology, and turn it in again to the board. At this point, other board members prepare the manuscript for the anthology, deciding upon an order for the different texts. The manuscript then goes to the person responsible for the table of contents. Another student writes a preface; a cover design is settled upon, and the final copy is prepared and submitted for photocopy "publication." Throughout the publication process the instructor moves into the capacity of advisor rather than teacher, offering help on any language difficulties or suggestions on last-minute content changes and generally facilitating production. This final course project thus provides students with experience in the various phases of publication, bolsters their feelings of accomplishment in that they have a published volume of their work, and lends additional significance to their efforts. This latter effect is enhanced at Berkeley, since a copy of every anthology produced in the creative writing courses is kept as a permanent part of the departmental library's collection.

CONCLUSION

Because of the experimental nature of the creative writing courses at Berkeley, students' reactions to them and their impact on writing, reading, and language skills have been systematically assessed via a final questionnaire (see Appendix). All iterations of the creative writing courses have proved to be very successful in terms of student satisfaction on multiple dimensions—personal growth, creativity, enjoyment of the literature read, and improvement in their own writing skills and in the development of their reading skills. Students attributed many of these positive effects to the open atmosphere of the class. As the description of the course organization outlined earlier indicates, however, this atmosphere is not created at the expense of rigor in approach. On the contrary, students read extensively (minimally one or even two short stories per class meeting), and they write copiously in their journals in response to specific exercises indexed against the assigned readings. Although the journals themselves are not graded, thus providing a forum wherein students can dare to fail without negative repercussions in their writing experiments, they do receive two types of feedback in terms of peer and teacher response. Moreover, students work diligently on their own short stories and fictional prose, producing at least three drafts before handing in their final versions for a grade. In a typical fifteen-week semester, students generally write three such finished pieces of fictional prose, one of which is eventually submitted to the class anthology. The relaxed atmosphere of the class is thus created rather by the receptiveness accorded to students' efforts at creative writing and most important by the lack of constraints imposed upon their writing and interpretative reading.

In their standard language and literature courses, students themselves note that their reading and writing is directed toward the clearly defined and specific academic goals presented at the beginning of this discussion. It is not that students object to these demands, recognizing their importance and appreciating greatly what they learn; but they do need to tailor their approach to reading and writing according to the academic underpinnings of the courses. The overriding advantage of the creative writing courses is that they provide students a context in which they can simply enjoy the literature, not feeling compelled to analyze it objectively according to criteria imposed by the conventions of literary analysis, but rather considering it in terms of what it can do for them personally and for their writing. Likewise, writing in these courses does not need to conform to the genre expectations of the academic paper. Instead students are free simply to experiment with imaginative writing. The pure pleasure of reading and writing were, in fact, among the primary goals of the first experimental version of the creative writing courses. What was unexpected in the first iteration of the course, and confirmed in all subsequent iterations, were the marked benefits to reading, writing, and linguistic mastery directly attributable to the very different academic constraints. One student described these benefits very clearly on his questionnaire:

It is certain that in the creative writing course I read the literary works very differently than in another type of course. There is less stress put on me in this course, and I find that I can let myself appreciate the works on a stylistic level. I don't always have to be in the process of looking for symbols, metaphors, etc. And, in fact, by letting my mind go a little, I see elements in the stories that I would never have seen in another course.... As many of the authors we have read have indicated, [writing] helps one to organize one's thoughts and therefore to understand life a little better. This course also gave me confidence because in trying to use my own metaphors, I see that in fact I have learned something about the authors whom I have studied. After having studied them, it is interesting to try their literary techniques in my own work.

Rather than being a peripheral course that could potentially detract from standard literature or language courses, creative writing draws on everything students learn in these other courses, but it shifts the context of the learning and language acquisition experience. In studying literature in traditional formats, students acquire analytical skills, internalize genre specifics, and focus on literary traditions. In language courses, students learn grammar, vocabulary, and stylistics. All of this is necessary for successful creative writing, where students must now synthesize this knowledge in order to create their own meanings. At the same time, the loose external constraints of creative writing encourage students to work this material in a new, different, and more personal way. This very experience produces a positive reverberative effect on students' overall language skills in terms of acquisition and appreciation, making creative writing a positive complement to standard foreign language and literature courses. Moreover, creative writing supports for the foreign language writing curriculum what researchers have learned about native language writing, namely, that a different type of writing experience, one that begins from a position of personal commitment and with fewer genre constraints, encourages students simply to enjoy the reading and writing in a low-stress situation with its own kind of rigor without risk. As a result of their experiences in the creative writing courses, students begin to see literature in a different light, appreciating more than previously the craft of writing.

NOTES

1. As the recent publication of *National standards for foreign language learning* indicates, language departments are increasingly being held accountable for students' progress in language acquisition. The fact that language progress seems somewhat unpredictable in creative writing can contribute to teachers' hesitation to incorporate it into the curriculum.

2. The development of students' oral proficiency through writing can be significantly enhanced through the implementation of a process approach, where students share their work in small-group formats, presenting their writing orally and discussing their efforts with their peers.

3. All students taking the creative writing courses complete two assessment questionnaires: one at the beginning of the course and one at the end. Sample questionnaires are provided in the Appendix to this chapter.

4. "La raison la plus importante pour laquelle j'ai choisi ce cours, c'est pour améliorer mon français. ... J'espère que ce cours me permettra de passer plus de temps sur la structure complexe de la langue française pour dire ce que je veux" (my translation).

5. According to Maingueneau (1990, pp. 95–101), indirect free style is a complex discourse device that mixes two voices—the voice of the narrator and the voice of the character—blending direct and indirect discourse to create a unique enunciative act.

6. In the creative writing courses in many English departments, peer criticism can become very pointed. The underlying assumptions are often quite different, however. In many cases, acceptance into the program is very competitive, with students first having to submit a portfolio of their creative work. Moreover, language acquisition is not as salient an issue as in foreign language courses.

REFERENCES

ACTFL oral proficiency interview tester training manual. (1999). Yonkers, NY: American Council of Teachers of Foreign Languages.

Bain, A. (1875). *Rhetoric: A manual*. New York: Appleton.

Barnett, M. (1989). Writing as process. *French Review* 63: 31–44.

Bereiter, C., & Scardamalia, M. (1987). *The psychology of written composition*. Hillsdale, NJ: Lawrence Erlbaum Associates.

Britton, J., et al. (1975). *The development of writing abilities*. Urbana, IL: National Council of Teachers of English.

Flaubert, G. (1965) (1877). *Les trois contes*. Paris: Garnier-Flammarion.

Flower, L. (1988). The construction of purpose in writing and reading. *Occasional Paper 4*. Berkeley: Center for the Study of Writing.

Gaudiani, C. (1981). Teaching writing in the foreign language curriculum. *Language in Education: Theory and Practice, 43*. Washington, DC: CAL.

Geisler, C. (1994). *Academic literacy and the nature of expertise*. Hillsdale, NJ: Lawrence Erlbaum Associates.

Hillocks, G. (1987, May). Synthesis of research on teaching writing. *Educational Leadership, 44*: 71–82.

Kaplan, A. (1993). *French lessons*. Chicago: University of Chicago Press.

Krashen, S. (1982). *Principles and practice in second language acquisition*. New York: Pergamon Press.

Maingueneau, Dominique. (1990). *Eléments de linguistique pour le texte littéraire*. Paris: Bordas.

Moffett, J. (1981). *Active voice*. Portsmouth, NH: Boynton/Cook Publishers.

Omaggio, Hadley A. (1993). *Teaching language in context*. Boston: Heinle & Heinle.

Sartre, J.-P. (1938). *La nausée*. Paris: Gallimard.

Sartre, J.-P. (1964). *Les mots*. Paris: Gallimard.

Standards for foreign language learning: Preparing for the 21st century. (1999). Yonkers, NY: National Standards in Foreign Language Project.

Swales, J. (1990). *Genre analysis*. Cambridge: Cambridge University Press.

Vygotsky, L. S. (1986). *Thought and language,* translated by A. Kozulin. Cambridge, MA: MIT Press.

Weisstein, Ulrich. (1973). *Comparative literature and literary theory*. Bloomington: Indiana University Press.

APPENDIX

Initial Questionnaire

1. Have you ever done any creative writing previous to this course? In what languages? If yes, please describe your experiences in these courses. If no, why not?

2. Why did you decide to enroll in this course in creative writing?
3. What are your expectations for this course?

Final Questionnaire

1. Please describe your experience in this course.
2. Please describe the effect this course had on your writing ability in French. Did this course help you improve your written French? Why or why not? How?
3. Describe the effect of this course on your reading ability. On your reading experience. Do you read in the same way as in a course devoted solely to the study of literature? Do you prefer one approach to another? Which one? Why?
4. Does this course tie in with other courses you have taken in French? Which ones? How?
5. Has this course contributed to your appreciation of literature and of the authors we read? How?
6. What are the personal and academic benefits of a course in creative writing?
7. Would you like to see other courses in creative writing offered during the academic year? Would you enroll in such courses?
8. For this course, did you find the progression in writing exercises and creative writing assignments logical and beneficial? Did this progression help you express yourself more easily than if you had tried to write without as much preparation?
9. How useful was working in small groups of peers and receiving feedback on each draft of your work? Is there an aspect of the small group organization that you would modify?
10. Do you have any other comments? Are there aspects of the course that you would change?

Writing Exercises for the Short Story Creative Writing Course

1. Free observation: go to a public place and write down what you see and hear without regard to any type of logical presentation.
2. Organize your observations from #1 as if you were telling them to yourself.
3. Define a reader for yourself (someone like you, a friend, a teacher, an imaginary reader) and tell him/her the "story" in #2.
4. Tell about a supernatural experience that happened to you or to someone you know.
5. Use the form of a diary to tell the same story.
6. Create a narrative frame and tell the same story.

7. Review the different descriptions we have studied and using them for inspiration, describe a place of your choosing.
8. Give the physical description of a character you create.
9. Present the character's (#8) thoughts without regard for organization. What would he or she think about?
10. Use a stream of consciousness technique to present the character's thoughts.
11. Now present the character's thoughts using an internal monologue, i.e. the character is consciously reflecting to him/herself on a specific issue.
12. Define a specific but silent interlocutor for your character and have him/her express his/her thoughts as a first-person narrator in external monologue form.
13. Create a narrator-witness who tells what happens to the character. (The narrator may reveal something about him/herself in the process of telling the story of your character).
14. Use a third-person omniscient narrator to tell what happens to your character.
15. Use a third-person narrator to tell what happens to your character, but this time incorporate some *indirect free style* in order to reveal the character's own thoughts.
16. Create two distinct characters and write a dialogue that lets the two different voices come through.
17. Present the portrait of a psychologically troubled character.
18. Begin a story about this character using any of the techniques we have practiced.
19. Write a fable.
20. Write a legend.

7

Hypermedia

Enriching L2 Compositions

Margaret Gonglewski

INTRODUCTION

Why all the hype about hypermedia in the second language (L2) classroom? Much of the zeal stems from a blind faith in the power of technology. However, the enthusiasm also stems from the outcome of legitimate investigations into hypermedia's application in L2 learning and teaching. For example, research has shown that the World Wide Web enhances L2 learning mainly by increasing learners' access to and interaction with authentic texts, leading them to gain L2 reading and cultural proficiency (Armstrong & Yetter-Vassot, 1994; Lafford & Lafford, 1997; Lee, 1997, 1998; Oliva & Pollastrini, 1995; Osuna & Meskill, 1998). While we have seen an increase in research on the Web as a navigational tool, we know little about the use of the Web (or hypermedia[1]) for L2 composition. Yet according to Pennington (1996), this multifaceted electronic medium has the potential to create an excellent environment for communicative L2 composing because it "encourages a view of writing as being about communication, the making of meaning, and the creative exploration and synthesis of ideas and aesthetic resources such as sound and pictures, rather than about production of printed words and sentences" (p. 96). Indeed, through its online, networked, and linked nature as well as its multimedia capabilities, the Web can afford a learner-centered, context-rich setting to support meaningful communication with an authentic audience—factors linked to successful L2 writing (Chávez, 1997; Cononelos & Oliva, 1993; Greenia, 1992). Such a promising tool warrants investigation for its suitable application, particularly in the advanced L2 composition classroom.

In an effort to identify how L2 writers can profit from writing in this new technological medium, I implemented a pilot project in which advanced learners of German composed hypermedia documents (Web pages) for their final writing assignment. This study provides a qualitative examination of students' hypermedia compositions in the three clearly observable features of text organization, external links, and multimedia components, particularly as compared with their conventional text versions of the same task. Input from surveys and interviews conducted after completion of the course provides further data about the writers' composing processes. By investigating how these writers utilized features of the Web medium, I gain insight into both the successes and the pitfalls of this technology for L2 composition. Based on the results of this project, I offer suggestions for implementing hypermedia composition in L2 courses, providing teachers with strategies to help L2 writers cope with the demands of this new technology as well as maximize its capabilities for their communicative needs.

HYPERMEDIA: ITS FEATURES AND POTENTIAL BENEFITS TO THE L2 COMPOSER

Hypermedia is a technological tool that allows users to create or navigate nonsequential blocks of text or multimedia in a document linked (potentially) to hypermedia documents on other computers via an electronic network such as the World Wide Web. A good way to characterize hypermedia is to contrast several of its fundamental features with those of traditional print text,[2] the medium typically used for L2 composition, as shown in Table 7.1.

In this section, I provide a review of the basic features of hypermedia, paying particular attention to the three features that relate to the categories I have chosen for analysis in the students' compositions, that is, text organization, external links, and multimedia components. Aside from clarifying how hypertext features differ from the print text environment, the review of features that follows describes projects using hypermedia writing in L2 classes and draws on insight from second language acquisition theory to elucidate the value of the features for L2 learning and writing.

Hypermedia exists online. Hypermedia documents exist only online—a dynamic, ever-changing and changeable setting. In print text, the author's aim

Table 7.1 Differences between hypermedia and traditional print texts.

Hypermedia (Web) Documents	Traditional Print Texts
exist online, a fluid environment.	exist on paper, a fixed environment.
are networked and available to a wide audience.	are not networked and reach a smaller audience.
are nonsequential and nonlinear.	are sequential and linear.
can link to countless other texts, images.	can reference other texts but not provide them.
have multimedia capability.	cannot typically incorporate multimedia.

is to produce a final product meant to be printed on paper or in a book that cannot be changed without great trouble (Slatin, 1990), whereas in hypertext, the text is more "fluid and customizable, updatable and expandable" (Bernhardt, 1993, p. 173). The flexibility of the online text can also help "allay the non-native student writer's fear of making errors" (Pennington, 1996, p. 20) and may make L2 writers more willing to revise drafts both in local editing and in reconceptualizing ideas.

Hypermedia documents are networked and thus available to a wide audience. Networking compositions makes writers more conscious of their audience and hence of the primacy of communicating a message while writing in the L2. In traditional writing assignments, where the teacher is the sole recipient of the writing, students often concentrate on the formal aspects of their writing, as does the teacher. However, posting compositions to a networked system extends the audience from teacher-only to classmates and potentially all Web users. As Greenia (1992) and Chávez (1997) found in networked settings, writers are not only inclined to focus on their message, they also are more likely to correct grammar errors on their own when these errors impede communication with their audience. The possibility for feedback from others online thus fosters the need to negotiate meaning with another party, and writers work "toward the delivery of a message that is not only conveyed but that is conveyed precisely, coherently, and appropriately" (Swain, 1985, p. 249). The networked nature of hypermedia, then, can help L2 writers "improve in communicative ability both by taking in comprehensible input and by striving to produce comprehensible output—in both cases causing them to achieve at an 'i+1 level' that is just beyond their current ability" (Pennington, 1996, p. 7).

Several Web publishing projects underscore the importance of the expanded audience for the L2 learner. Kern (1995), Meloni (1995), and Vilmi (1995) provide short summaries of collaborative projects in which students created cultural pages including aspects of their own culture or present surroundings or contributed to an online class newsletter (Jor, 1995). The instructors' evaluations of these projects address the satisfaction and pride learners gained from displaying their work for all to see.

Hypermedia documents are nonsequential and nonlinear. To say hypertext is nonsequential is to say that there is no single linear sequence that must be followed in reading or composing the document (Nielson, 1995). Bernhardt (1993) has likened nonsequential writing in hypertext to "Chinese boxes," meaning text can be "nested within text, and huge texts can reside within tiny fragments" (p. 164). As such, hyperdocuments have "multiple points of entry, multiple exit points and multiple pathways between points of entry and exit points," in contrast to print text, which is highly stable and has a comparatively clear point of departure and way of proceeding throughout (Slatin, 1990, p. 871). Of course, hypermedia writers are not denied linear presentation, because the flexibility of the medium allows for multiple organizational styles: "With the combination of both hierarchical subordination and lateral links from any point to any point, hypertext offers greatly expanded possibilities for new structures characterized by layering and flexibility" (Bernhardt, 1993, p. 164). By offering learners the opportunity to approach a topic through "associative" rather than through traditional linear organizational structures, hypermedia composition lends students more control over their learning, thus providing teachers a way to individualize instruction and reach a wider range of individual learning styles (Bush, 1997).

Hypermedia documents can be linked to countless other texts and images. Associativity describes the feature of hypermedia that permits authors to link their text to other texts (e.g., documents, images, sites) created by other authors on the Web. The L2 learner-writer can benefit from the linking feature of composing in hypermedia in two ways: First, the Web places the writer in the center of an environment rich with comprehensible linguistic and cultural input, and second, it compels learners to engage with that input, not only to read and comprehend it but also to connect it to their own knowledge base via links to their document.

As part of composing in hypermedia, authors make links to other Web documents that relate to information on their own pages. Making those links, students become immersed in an enriched environment mediated by the computer, exposing them to the target language and culture "with high frequency and efficiency" (Liu, 1994, p. 303). In composing hypertexts, writers must engage in similar processes readers do in "reading the Web": They must find, evaluate, and make use of a wide variety of information sources (Warschauer, 1999, p. 158). Thus, *composing* in hypermedia, students become part of an environment rich with comprehensible input, which Krashen (1982) has asserted is one of the elements of successful language learning.

With a multitude of target language writing and images in a variety of contexts, the Web offers students models for language *in use*, an important key to understanding sociolinguistic matters of linguistic and cultural appropriateness. Cultural input available in abundance through online text, graphics, and especially video has also been touted as an important resource for teaching students language in context (Kramsch & Andersen, 1999). Several researchers have noted that online reading of L2 cultural products (e.g., newspapers, bulletin boards) exposes learners to authentic, up-to-date cultural information in the target language and thereby increases learners' understanding of contemporary cultural values (Kost, 1997; Lee, 1997, 1998; Lafford & Lafford, 1997; Osuna & Meskill, 1998; Walz, 1998; see Warschauer, 1995, for synopses of several projects using online resources for cultural input). Steeped in this context-rich setting, L2 writers not only acquire L2 language and cultural knowledge, they also begin to formulate their own voice in their L2 writing by placing it among the many other voices in the new discourse community.

Yet reading and selecting texts (and images) to link to their own is only half the battle. Beyond exposing learners to L2 and C2 input, the Web compels hypermedia writers to show through linkages how their own thoughts and ideas connect with the greater body of knowledge, information, and ideas in the world (available on the Web). Perhaps more than with traditional print writing, hypermedia authors engage in a process of reading and critical thinking and constructing knowledge from information as they select, organize, and connect subject matter from many diverse sources (Snyder, 1997). Although this is also possible in print text through footnotes, the Web makes it much more efficient by placing millions of documents literally at the writer's fingertips, which may make online authors more willing and likely to connect to these sources (Slatin, 1990).

Hypermedia has multimedia capability. Not only does Hypermedia allow for graphics, pictures, video, and sound, but the medium itself virtually demands these elements, whereas in traditional print essays in the L2 classroom, they are virtually absent. Observing Hawaiian language learners compose Web pages, Warschauer (1999) noted students incorporated multimedia "to communicate in as effective a fashion as possible in order to have a positive impact on their readers" (p. 109). Warschauer (1999) points out that using a combination of media in a learning setting is simply a principle of good education "because it allows educators to reach out to learners no matter what their preferred learning medium or style is" (p. 109). Indeed, when writers have more than just print media at their disposal, the "learning process becomes more varied, more interesting, and even more individualized" (Armstrong & Yetter-Vassot, 1994, p. 479). Giving learners more control over how they present their knowledge makes them more responsible for their learning and supports the student-centered environment that L2 teachers today strive for (Patrikis, 1995).

Similarly, the multimedia capabilities of hypermedia composition comprise an effective approach to reaching the student body in the era of high technology (Warschauer, 1999; Blake, 1998). Many of today's students "respond well to the medium of images" (Blake, 1998, p. 213), because they have grown up surrounded by visual and aural stimuli from multimedia input such as video (television, movies), items that in their day-to-day environment have been used to convey messages; students themselves have either become proficient using these same modes to communicate their own meaning or recognize such technology "as an important component of their education" (LeLoup & Ponterio, 1996, p. 27). By embracing these communicative modes, teachers afford students a chance to express themselves in a manner perhaps more fitting to their talents as well as to the hypertext medium itself. Thus, hypermedia composing encourages new forms of literacy such as visual or multimedia literacies and helps students to experience the foreign language through a variety of different media, giving the language itself additional texture, color, and context (Armstrong & Yetter-Vassot, 1994, p. 479). Teachers who assimilate multimedia modes in L2 composition courses validate learners with strong affinities toward these nonverbal literacies and thereby provide curricula less biased toward strictly verbal, that is, print-based, literacy (Herron & Moos, 1993; Kellner, 1998).

ADVANCED GERMAN LEARNERS' HYPERMEDIA (WEB PAGE) COMPOSING: A PILOT PROJECT

Synopsis of the Course

The third-year German course at The George Washington University utilizes Internet resources in two ways: First, e-mail via the class listserv is the principal form of communication outside class. Second, course materials are taken from the Web, such as articles found in online versions of German language newspapers, and other texts from educational, government, and commercial sites. These media provide learners with communicative contexts to practice language skills, with a particular focus on reading and writing. Despite the fact that students were both producing (via e-mail) and accessing (via the Web) much of their work/language during the semester online, longer writing assignments still comprised typical, traditional print text assignments composed for the teacher only. In light of the potential benefits to L2 learners in Web composition, discussed earlier, I initiated a pilot project giving students the opportunity to produce their final writing assignment in hypermedia for publication as a Web page. Topic choice was left open, and most students chose to write on themes covered in class, ranging from

National Socialism to Germany in the European Union. Students then turned in both a regular print version and the hypertextualized version of the same assignment.[3]

Because technical training has been implicated as an important factor in the success of integrating technology into the curriculum (Barnes, 1994), a brief training session was made available to familiarize students with Web-page composing tools such as *Netscape Composer,*[4] as well as copyright issues. Beyond that, students received no specific instructions on site design. The intent was to provide students with the fundamentals of hypermedia composing while allowing them the freedom to create their own unique sites.

Text Organization

All the students' print text versions were linear documents with a clear starting point and direction in which to read (from page one to the final page). However, in their hyperdocuments, many students explored a number of different organizational patterns. Specifically, four students maximized the nonlinearity feature of the hypertext composition process by writing one main page with several additional pages holding other portions of their documents. Susan's page on National Socialism is a good illustration of the elaborate network students produced through the creation of *internal* links. Her main page presents merely the title, a bold graphic of a Nazi propaganda poster and a number of terms in an outline, linked to pages of her own text (segments that in the printed version follow each other on the pages in consecutive order). In her view, this organizational structure matched more closely what she hoped to get across: "It helped me organize my thoughts and changed the way I wanted to present this topic. The different parts of the outline aren't necessarily in one particular order, and putting them on the Web page this way makes that clear. I wanted that to get across to the reader, so I organized it as links." To Susan, the internal links are choices she has made in the conception of the presentation—choices she wants the reader to have as well.

In contrast to such multiple-paged documents, eleven students posted their documents as a single Web page with links mostly to outside pages rather than to further internal documents they themselves had written. Their hyperdocuments appear more sequential than Susan's, since they were con-ceived as one longer page, viewable by scrolling down. However, use of a singular page in presentation does not necessarily indicate sequential text. Through the "named anchor" (or "target" feature), which allows students to create links to specified points within their own document, three students lent a greater nonlinear texture to their Web documents, giving readers greater choice in both *what* they would read and *in what sequence*. Steven's page on the problems in German reunification is a good example of target links application. Like Susan, he composed a list of terms addressed in his paper that readers are free to follow at will. Instead of creating a new page for each link, he linked them to the appropriate spots on his single page, thereby giving the feel of nonlinearity even within a more linear online structure; more important to Steven, "people reading it can get to what they want to see right away."

Two students noted ways in which they explicitly changed their document for the Web medium by devising internal links. Laura, who authored a Cinderella story set in Boston with Ted Kennedy as the fairy godfather, felt it fitting to provide her readers with an English translation of her fairytale on the Web page, since many German Web pages offer English versions. Karl linked to his e-mail address so that readers could contact him and ask questions or make comments on his work. He emphasized that the nature of the Web promotes such interaction and the nature of the hypertext medium allows him to continue the composing process:

> I see writing a Web essay as a long-term process. It's not finished yet, because I can change it at any time, and I would if someone wrote to me and told me something wasn't right, or if some new information would come to light then I would add that. But after I turn in my written essay, it's finished and I'm lucky if I ever look at it again.

I have noted that some students chose to apply nonlinear organizational patterns in presenting their ideas; however, the majority organized their Web documents using the more linear and sequential text organization characteristic of traditional print text. Students gave several reasons for conceiving their hyperdocuments as one single page rather than as multiple pages. One felt that his document was not long enough to warrant "dividing it up" into more pages; another believed the coherence of her document remained intact only when posted as a single document. Their comments revealed that these writers resorted to a linear presentation in the Web setting because they did not compose in this setting, but rather composed the text as a regular print document and afterward worked with it in the hypermedia environment. Because they conceived their text prior to working in hypermedia, they were not easily able to transfer their preconceived organizational structure to the new medium; as a result, they were not able to take full advantage of this feature.

External Links

Using the hypermedia feature of linking, students could include a greater amount of information in their hyperdocuments than in their print versions, and most chose to do so. In all printed versions, students marked references to other works where necessary, whereas in their hyperdocuments, they literally connected to references available on the Web. Comparing links to footnotes, Alex noted that the Web allowed him to "essentially footnote everything. These footnotes or links are far more convenient and open doors to all new information." Although these documents were not text that students themselves had created, they became potentially part of their overall message the moment students linked to them, adding literal layers that arguably cannot exist in the printed version. Likewise the texts became part of the students' writing process as they read and selected them for their own document links.

Through links students supplemented their own documents with other information in an efficient manner. All students included within their own hyperdocuments links to outside sources providing further information on their topic or a subtopic therein. An example is Rob's paper, in which he illustrates Hitler's rise to power. Rob addresses briefly the role of propaganda, mentioning director Leni Riefenstahl: "Regisseur wie <u>Leni Riefenstahl</u> drehten Filmen, die Deutschland, den Führer (Hitler) und das deutsche Volk verherrlichten. (*Directors like <u>Leni Riefenstahl</u> made films that glorified Germany, the Führer (Hitler) and the German people.*)" Here he links the name "Leni Riefenstahl" to an article on her role in the propaganda ministry. He selected this text among other Web sources to supplement his topic and "to give readers the opportunity to learn more about different points I raised, even if they're not my own main points." At the same time that he has enriched his essay by making the article available to readers, he has enriched his own composing experience as he engaged in the process of selecting this text— among many others available on the Web—to link to his own.

In the surveys, students did in fact note an increase in time spent reading as they searched documents to link to their own. One student exclaimed: "I never had to read so much German in my life! It sometimes helped me find words or phrases that I wanted to use but didn't know how to say." The students' self-reported intensified interaction with other texts underlines the notion that Web composition affords language learners increased comprehensible input in a meaningful context, thereby enriching the environment for composing in the L2.

Connecting to external sources allowed not only for additional information in the text but also for a wider variety of kinds of information. In her Web page on National Socialism, Josie includes links providing further historical information on Hitler, but she also provides links to the Shoah Project and a site on political resistance during the Third Reich. In her words, she has provided "more information" about Hitler and the NSDAP while providing "alternate perspectives" in the hypertext version. In the process of writing the hyperdocument, as opposed to the print version, Josie felt that she expanded her own knowledge and presentation of that knowledge rather than merely supplementing her own text.

Most students viewed adding external links as the biggest plus in the composition process and one that most perceptibly differentiated the printed from the Web versions, aside from the obvious physical changes through the addition of graphical components. One student commented specifically on how the process of selecting links enhanced her composing experience as contrasted with producing the print version.

> There's only so much you can do in a paper. The links expanded the depth of my paper. First I had to choose them which means I had to read a ton of other stuff, because I wanted to select the best links, the ones that fit best into what I was trying to get across in my paper. Then I had to incorporate all of that into my essay. It made my Web paper multidimensional. It felt like it made my thinking multidimensional when I was choosing the sources of the links.

While the Web's strongest point may be the plethora of authentic L2 materials and resources it makes available, this strength can also be the biggest hazard for the composer. Selecting what to link to one's own document is a potentially limitless task and can be daunting. Nearly all students viewed that task with enthusiasm, claiming for example that "there is a lot of material on the Web just waiting to be used" and incorporating those links help make the project "more complete" than the traditional print version. Still, in the process of searching and reading, authors can easily get "lost in cyberspace" and lose track of their own objective not to mention quickly reach cognitive overload (Charney, 1994; Slatin, 1990). One student voiced frustration that with so much to read through and evaluate, he paid less attention to his own writing. The Web's surfeit of linkage potential made some writers feel disadvantaged rather than empowered.

Integrating this additional material into their own work proved equally challenging for some students. Specifically, some writers' links were vague or ambiguous because of an imprecise choice of word or phrase to be linked on their document, making it difficult to gauge where a link might lead. Tom's page on Germany's reunification provides links to terms less than self-explanatory in this context: "Die Dame könne nicht ihre Miete bezahlen, weil sie nicht genug Geld habe. (*The woman claimed she could not pay her rent because she did not have enough money*.)" Neither the underlined text (Geld habe) nor the site to which it is linked (a page with scanty information on pension insurance in the former East German states) has a clear-cut connection to Tom's document. Furthermore, several writers added links that could either sidetrack both composer and reader from the topic at hand or, worse, lead the reader to a page providing mismatched information for the paper's content. In her Web page on Hitler's rise to power, Barbara created a link from the word "government": "Die Wirtschaft brauchte viel von die Regierung. (*The economy needed much from the government*.)" When clicked, this link brings the reader to the official page of today's democratic German government (www.bundesregierung.de), which, other than containing the word "-regierung," has no connection to the content of the sentence. In the print text version, vague or inappropriate links are not explicit, since they lie perhaps beneath the surface rather than in explicit linkages made to other Web documents.

Multimedia Components

The majority of the students incorporated graphical components such as photographs and pictures into their Web pages, taking advantage of a feature that was potentially available to them in the traditional print version yet was not present in it. This stemmed at least partially from students' understanding of the two different types of media. Alex, who included a number of graphical images on his Web page, noted: "When I wrote the regular [print] essay, it didn't even occur to me to put in pictures. It would make it seem more like a magazine article than an essay. When I wrote the Web page, it never occurred to me that I wouldn't use pictures. I mean, why even bother doing it as a Web page if you don't take advantage of that?" Similarly, Steven noted the value of graphics to enrich his message. In fact, this very aspect inspired him to compose his essay on German reunification as a Web page. According to him, providing pictures of East and West German towns at the time of reunification "gives a better feel for the differences between East and West at the time of reunification" than words could.

One graphical component visible in the Web versions that provides a stark contrast to the texture of the print versions is the use of backgrounds. Using colors or textured backgrounds, students transformed their texts into a visually changed product compared with the white paper printouts. Josie, who used no graphics in her hyperdocument, chose instead to use the graphical background "firecloud," rolling reddish storm clouds, to supply a suitable setting to the theme of Hitler's rise to power. To her, the graphical image underlined the emotional intensity of the subject matter in a manner not possible in the printed version: "The visual aspects contributed to the meaning on another level entirely. The paper leaves everything to the imagination but in the Web page the minute you open the page you get a hint about the content, or at least how I see the content." According to her own comments, Josie is aware that this is an additional mode of expression available to her in hypermedia composing, and she would like her use of them to affect her readers.

Although several students had originally intended to include sound files in their documents, most did not fulfill their plans because of logistical limitations—primarily the lack of technical assistance at the typically hectic end of the semester. In his Web page on the German reunification, Nathan incorporated sound files with the national anthems of the two divided Germanys in order to "add character" to his Web presentation as opposed to his print version: "Music touches me more than words sometimes, and specific musical pieces have even more symbolism, like national anthems. I couldn't convey that in my essay the same way, unless I put it on the Web, because the words relay something different than the tunes." Through the use of multimedia, Nathan felt he added a layer to the message not available to him on paper.

Adding graphical components such as pictures allowed students to generate intertextual references without naming them explicitly. In Victor's printed version of the fairytale *Cinderella*, he referred to generic characters (the prince, the stepmother, etc.), while in his hypertext version he added graphics bestowing the same characters with a real-life persona: Roman Herzog (then president of Germany) became Cinderella's father, and Ted Bundy, her prince. In a similar manner, Jim made references to his roommate in his fairytale but made these references explicit by linking to a page with graphics to show how the prince fit the description. Both Jim and Victor noted that the story itself changed with the addition of images, and Victor stated that "the story by itself is fine, but with the illustrations it's just more fun. It adds another level to the meaning. People will also want to read it more." To him, adding graphical elements was necessary to make the story worth reading, and his comment reveals that he cares who his audience is and whether or not they will want to read his story.

In spite of the reported benefits from composing with multimedia elements, students' incorporation of images was not always successful. In several examples, pictures were poorly juxtaposed with text or students neglected to identify picture contents or to explain the purpose of their inclusion when it was not apparent from context. Other pictures that related only remotely to the contents were given inappropriately prominent placement. In his Web page on the Reunification, Nathan quoted a guest lecturer from GW and included a large graphic linked to the university's homepage directly in the middle of his text on the lecturer's experience during the fall of the Berlin Wall. The placement of this graphic—one might argue even the inclusion of this particular graphic—can distract both the writer as he inserts the graphic and the reader who peruses the site. Such an application of graphics can detract from rather than expand the writer's message.

DISCUSSION

The examination of these advanced students' compositions and their self-reports on their own processes provides us with information about hypermedia composition and how it can be valuable in the L2 learning environment. First, we have seen that incorporating hypermedia as a context for L2 composition supports a learner-centered approach. Instead of having to adhere to a sequential and linear text organization as they did in their print documents, writers chose from a range of organizational patterns in composing their Web versions. Through both external and internal linking systems, they structured their presentations differently and in a manner that could better match their individual learning styles. Likewise, the multimedia (particularly graphical) components used in the Web pages revealed that students also chose nonverbal modes of expression, and their comments confirmed their sentiment that these combined features of hypertext reached their individual choices for expression and did not limit them as they felt the print mode did.

Second, composing with hypermedia fostered a communicative environment for L2 writing. The networked Web afforded writers an expanded audience to whom they could convey their meaningful message, thus encouraging a view of language as a means of communication rather than primarily as a system of grammatical structures to be learned. Even when the text of both versions was essentially the same, students felt the hyperdocument content was changed because it was part of the network which expanded both the context in which their communication took place as well as the audience to whom the writers communicated their message. Working in hypermedia where they could add graphical components and links to other sites, students felt that they were able to produce substantially different documents on the Web, and they reported that this was an advantage. In their own reports, students' awareness that knowing their Web version would be available to readers across the world influenced their choices in composing their Web pages. According to their comments, students made additions and changes based on their perceptions of the needs and interests of the public audience the Web afforded them, in contrast to the usual solitary recipient of the print version.

Finally, hypermedia afforded students a chance to contextualize their communication within the greater L2 discourse community by linking their own knowledge base (in the form of their text) with the knowledge base (in the form of others' texts) available to them on the Web. In making those connections (links), writers asserted their interaction with L2 texts intensified as they were virtually immersed in L2-rich context.

SUGGESTIONS FOR IMPLEMENTING HYPERMEDIA COMPOSITION IN THE L2 CLASSROOM

The successes and problems reported here can help formulate important and useful strategies to help teachers teach students to make the most of hypermedia's features. Although the suggestions that follow address specific issues raised by one group of advanced learners' attempts to employ hypermedia in L2 composition, they can apply to all levels of L2 writers planning to use the Web for writing. Further examinations of students' Web composition in other settings and on a range of L2 levels will augment and refine these strategies and advance our understanding of hypermedia's value as a tool for L2 writing.

Instruct writers to compose their text for the hypertext medium. Students participating in this pilot project primarily composed the text first and then transformed their text to fit the medium, restructuring, revising, and adding (links, graphics, etc.) as they worked. Yet as Warschauer (1999) notes, "If a goal is to teach students about particular ways of expressing meaning in this new medium, then designing documents specifically for the Web medium is necessary" (p. 160). Having students compose their entire composition in hypermedia would help students take the most advantage of the features and their contribution to the process of writing in the L2.

Place limits on links. While L2 learners benefited from engaging with the L2 input available on the Web, they were at times overwhelmed by the shear quantity of material to wade through; as Green (1997) has pointed out, "there is much that is not worth reading" (p. 259). By simply limiting the number of links required in an assignment, teachers relieve students of the burden of providing many links and simultaneously reduce the possibility of imprecise link-making. Teachers should provide assistance finding outside sources or connections expediently and efficiently while being careful not to squelch the writers' freedom to explore many avenues of meaning. Writers must learn to use search engines and limit their searches to pinpoint the most pertinent materials before they begin to read and select links.

Require link clarification. I noted earlier that several writers included links that at best did not correspond to their content or context of their essays and at worst undercut their message. Because there are no unified standards for link identification, some authors maintain that link "goals" should be as unambiguous as possible (Slatin, 1990). Even standardization would not resolve all the issues, since writers can make numerous different types of associations with links, and connections self-evident to one person may not be as obvious to another. If the link numbers are limited for an assignment (as suggested before), it is easier to require students to explain or justify all link choices within the context of their essay. They can do this by providing a separate explanation for the teacher; but a more effective way—and an approach that would also benefit readers—is to have students create a short tag line that appears in a dialogue box on screen when the mouse arrow is held over the link. In this box, writers explain as pithily as possible where the link leads, what type of information is available there, and why they included the link.

Scrutinize multimedia additions. While nonverbal (visual) expression is one of the most exciting and motivating aspects of Web composing, it may also be the least understood. Teachers should engage students in an ongoing discussion and critical evaluation of the use of multimedia resources to express meaning. An ideal way to involve students in such a discussion is to look at existing Web pages and analyze the authors' use of multimedia incorporation for the successful and less successful aspects. This same analysis can provide insight to develop strategies for text organization and link incorporation as well.

Provide technical training. Training in the technical aspects of Web composition is obviously a must. The more technological expertise Web writers possess, the more the constraints of the printed medium will be eradicated, and the more effectively they can express themselves via the new mode. Students in the current study experienced what Warschauer (1999) called "a profound sense of personal awakening to the power of technology" and likewise noticed a loss in power when they were unable to use the technology to accomplish what they wanted to do (p. 104). Even when training comes at the expense of language practice, students do not lose out: They gain other important skills, including technical skills useful across fields (Armstrong & Yetter-Vassot, 1994; Oliva & Pollastrini, 1995; Warschauer, 1999).

Keep communication the principal goal. As much as hypermedia appears to serve the L2 writer, researchers agree that the medium alone does not make the task or the message meaningful to the writer. Warschauer (1999) notes that L2 Web page creation is most successful when students perceive the task itself as relevant, as serving a real-world purpose. He observed that students' interest in the topic and not solely the fact that they were composing in hypermedia motivated students "to pay close attention to both the text and the overall design and layout of their pages, fostering an intensive and rewarding learning experience" (p. 161). The successful integration of hypermedia composition is at least partially dependent on the kinds of tasks and topics students undertook. In the project just discussed, students could choose their topic, and consequently their interest in their hypermedia productions was high. Even with this relative guarantee for success, writers were not always successful using the features of the medium in their composition. As more teachers incorporate Web composition in their L2 classrooms, more strategies addressing these new literacies will be developed for teaching writers to employ the features of the medium successfully to communicate a meaningful message and not merely to exploit the medium itself.

NOTES

1. Like others (Burbules & Callister, 1996; Landow, 1992; Warschauer, 1999), I use the terms "hypertext" and "hypermedia" interchangeably; however, I give precedence to "hypermedia" as the more inclusive term, precisely because it refers explicitly to other media types aside from text and in doing so draws more direct attention to learners' multiple means of expression (graphics, sound, etc.) in this medium. Additionally, although stand-alone

hypertext programs exist, I focus here only on documents composed for the Web. Hence in this chapter, the terms "hypertext," "hypermedia," and "Web documents" are synonymous.

2. For an in-depth comparison of hypertext and traditional print text, see Bolter (1991) or Snyder (1997). See also Warschauer, Shetzer, and Meloni (2000) for a similar comparison.

3. I have used pseudonyms for the students in the sections that follow.

4. As recently as five years ago, students had to learn the computer's language, HyperText Markup Language (HTML) in order to compose a Web page. Now, Composer and similar programs function much like a word-processing program such as Word for Windows, using a graphical user interface that in effect translates programming language into graphical features such as buttons and tool bars; thus, to create an effect (e.g., adding italics, tables, or graphics), authors simply press the corresponding button rather than having to write actual code.

REFERENCES

Armstrong, K., & Yetter-Vassot, C. (1994). Transforming teaching through technology. *Foreign Language Annals*, 27(4): 475–486.
Barnes, S. (1994). Hypertext literacy. *Interpersonal Computing and Technology: An Electronic Journal for the 21st Century*, 2: 24–36 (archived as BARNES IPCTV2N4 on LISTSERV@GUVM).
Bernhardt, S. A. (1993). The shape of text to come: The texture of print on screens. *College Composition and Communication*, 44(2): 151–175.
Blake, R. J. (1998). The role of technology in second language learning. In H. Byrnes (ed.), *Learning foreign and second languages: Perspectives in research and scholarship*, pp. 209–237. New York: Modern Language Association.
Bolter, J. D. (1991). *Writing space: The computer, hypertext, and the history of writing*. Hillsdale, NJ: L. Erlbaum Associates.
Burbules, N. C., & Callister, T. A., Jr. (1996). Knowledge at the crossroads: Some alternative futures of hypertext learning environments. *Educational Theory*, 46(1): 23–50.
Bush, M. D. (1997). Implementing technology for language learning. In M. D. Bush & R. M. Terry (eds.), *Technology-enhanced language learning,* pp. 287–349. ACTFL Foreign Language Education Series. Lincolnwood, IL: National Text-book Company.
Charney, D. (1994). The effect of hypertext on processes of reading and writing. In C. L. Selfe & S. Hilligoss (eds.), *Literacy and computers: The complications of teaching and learning with technology,* pp. 238–263. New York: Modern Language Association.
Chávez, C. L. (1997). Students take flight with Daedalus: Learning Spanish in a networked classroom. *Foreign Language Annals*, 30(1): 27–33.
Cononelos, T., & Oliva, M. (1993). Using computer networks to enhance foreign language/culture education. *Foreign Language Annals*, 26(4): 527–533.
Green, A. (1997). A beginner's guide to the Internet in the foreign language classroom with a focus on the World Wide Web. *Foreign Language Annals*, 30(2): 253–264.
Greenia, G. D. (1992). Computers and teaching composition in a foreign language. *Foreign Language Annals*, 25(1): 33–46.
Herron, C. A., & Moos, M. A. (1993). Electronic media in the foreign language and literature classroom: A fusion between science and the humanities. *Foreign Language Annals*, 26(4): 479–489.
Jor, G. (1995). Web Newsletter '95: A collaborative learning project for technical writing instruction. In M. Warschauer (ed.), *Virtual connections: Online activities*

and projects for networking language learners, pp. 368–374. Honolulu: University of Hawaii Press.

Kellner, D. (1998). Multiple literacies and critical pedagogy in a multicultural society. *Educational Theory,* 48(1): 103–122.

Kern, R. (1995). Découvrir Berkeley: Students' representation of their world on the World Wide Web. In M. Warschauer (ed.), *Virtual connections: Online activities and projects for networking language learners,* pp. 355–356. Honolulu: University of Hawaii Press.

Kost, C. (1997). Landeskunde im Internet: Eine computergestützte Unterrichtseinheit. (Geography and culture in the Internet: A computer-based instructional unit). *Die Unterrichtspraxis/Teaching German,* 2, 210–213.

Kramsch, C., & Andersen, R. W. (1999). Teaching text and context through multimedia. *Language Learning and Technology,* 2(2): 31–42.

Krashen, S. (1982). *Principles and practice in second language acquisition.* New York: Pergamon.

Lafford, P. A., & Lafford, B. A. (1997). Learning language and culture with Internet technologies. In M. D. Bush & R. M. Terry (eds.), *Technology-enhanced language learning,* pp. 215–262. ACTFL Foreign Language Education Series. Lincolnwood, IL: National Textbook Company.

Landow, G. P. (1992). *Hypertext: The convergence of contemporary critical theory and technology.* Baltimore: Johns Hopkins University Press.

Lee, L. (1997). Using Internet tools as an enhancement of C2 teaching and learning. *Foreign Language Annals,* 30(3): 410–427.

Lee, L. (1998). Going beyond classroom learning: Acquiring cultural knowledge via on-line newspapers and intercultural exchanges via on-line chatrooms. *CALICO Journal,* 16(2): 101–120.

LeLoup, J. W., & Ponterio, R. (1996). Choosing and using materials for a "net" gain in FL learning and instruction. In V. B. Levine (ed.), *Reaching out to the communities we serve,* pp. 23–32. NYSAFLT Annual Meeting Series 13. [Online]. Available: http://www.cortland.edu/www/flteach/articles/nysaflt96.html [1999, August 28].

Liu, M. (1994). Hypermedia assisted instruction and second language learning: A semantic network-based approach. *Computers in the Schools,* 10(3/4): 293–312.

Meloni, C. (1995). The cities project. In M. Warschauer (ed.), *Virtual connections: Online activities and projects for networking language learners,* pp. 211–215. Honolulu: University of Hawaii Press.

Nielson, J. (1995). *Multimedia and hypertext: The Internet and beyond.* Boston: AP Professional.

Oliva, M., & Pollastrini, Y. (1995). Internet resources and second language acquisition: An evaluation of virtual immersion. *Foreign Language Annals,* 28(4): 551–563.

Osuna, M. M., & Meskill, C. (1998). Using the World Wide Web to integrate Spanish language and culture: A pilot study. *Language Learning & Technology,* 1(2): 71–92.

Patrikis, P. C. (1995). Where is computer technology taking us? *ADFL Bulletin,* 26(2): 36–39.

Pennington, M. C. (1996). *The computer and the non-native writer: A natural partnership.* Creskill, NJ: Hampton Press.

Slatin, J. M. (1990). Reading hypertext: Order and coherence in a new medium. *College English,* 52(8): 870–883.

Snyder, I. (1997). *Hypertext: The electronic labyrinth.* New York: New York University Press.

Swain, M. (1985). Communicative competence: Some roles of comprehensible input and comprehensible output in its development. In S. M. Gass & C. G. Madden (eds.), *Input in second language acquisition,* pp. 235–253. Rowley, MA: Newbury House.

Vilmi, R. (1995). World Wide Web culture pages. In M. Warschauer (ed.), *Virtual connections: Online activities and projects for networking language learners,* pp. 360–362. Honolulu: University of Hawaii Press.

Walz, J. (1998). Meeting standards for foreign language learning with World Wide Web activities. *Foreign Language Annals,* 31(1): 103–114.

Warschauer, M. (1999). *Electronic literacies: Language, culture, and power in online education.* Mahwah, NJ: Lawrence Erlbaum Associates.

Warschauer, M. (ed.). (1995). *Virtual connections: Online activities and projects for networking language learners.* Honolulu: University of Hawaii Press.

Warschauer, M., Shetzer, H., & Meloni, C. (2000). *Internet for English teaching.* Alexandria, VA: TESOL Publications.

8

Online Readings and Discussions

Raising Intercultural Awareness and Exchange

Lina Lee

INTRODUCTION

Internet technology has become a powerful pedagogical tool for learning a foreign language in academic settings. Many foreign language educators have recognized the potential impact of the Internet on foreign language instruction. More important, research on the application of the Internet for foreign language teaching and learning has proven that online instruction has played an important role in foreign language acquisition (e.g., Bush, 1997; Lee, 1997; Warschauer, 1996). Previous studies show that online activities reinforced students' language skills, empowered their understanding of the target culture, and increased their motivation toward language learning beyond the classroom (e.g., Beauvois, 1998; Lee, 1997; Meunier, 1998; see also Gonglewski in this volume).

Internet resources provide different settings and levels of foreign language education. However, one of the major challenges for teachers is to learn how to create an instruction that balances the development of language skills and cultural competence. This chapter discusses a study using both Internet and Content-Based Instruction (CBI) to develop students' language and cultural competence. CBI focuses on reinforcing students' reading skills through the use of "authentic texts" from the World Wide Web. In addition, students "use" the target language to discuss the specific content of disciplinary areas via an electronic medium. Online interaction promotes students' thinking skills to allow them to focus on "communication" rather than "drill" language itself.

In this chapter, I first discuss CBI in foreign language instruction. I then describe the design of the study, including CBI and Internet tools, materials developments, and the procedures for planning activities and assessing learning outcomes. Finally, I report the results of the study and conclude with students' feedback and comments on the project and give suggestions for future improvement.

BRIEF REVIEW OF THE LITERATURE ON CONTENT-BASED INSTRUCTION IN FOREIGN LANGUAGES

It is not surprising to find that many of today's foreign language texts contain topic/theme-based materials and instruction in their chapters. The emphasis in foreign language learning has moved from a traditional approach—one that focuses on the study of the language itself—to a communicative approach in which learners acquire both linguistic and cultural competence. CBI fosters this goal of balancing the study of the subject matter and learning of the language itself (Stryker and Leaver, 1997). According to Stryker and Leaver (1997), CBI consists of three characteristics—subject-matter core, use of authentic materials, and appropriateness of the materials to the needs of specific learners. For instance, Kramsch and McConnell-Ginet (1992) have developed discipline-based approaches that emphasize an expansion of language study by making use of specific topics. Through the use of authentic readings, the learner receives the comprehensive input that is essential for foreign language acquisition (Krashen, 1985). In addition to the authentic readings, the process of acquiring communicative competence requires learners to use the target language to deal with specific topics such as science, art, business, and daily life.

Studies on using different content-based approaches such as topic-based or theme-based courses in the foreign languages have shown their effectiveness in developing students' communicative competence, cultural literacy, cognitive thinking skills, motivation, and self-confidence (e.g., Klahn, 1997; Sternfeld, 1997; Stryker, 1997). Among types of CBI are those methods developed for the specific needs of K-12 students and for adults in ESL and EFL programs and two U.S. government institutions—the Foreign Service

Institute and the Defense Language Institute (Adamson, 1993; Snow and Brinton, 1998; Stryker and Leaver, 1997). Many foreign language programs have adopted CBI. There are CBI courses in French at the University of Ottawa, political studies courses in Russian at George Washington University, and international business courses at Eastern Michigan University, Columbia University, SUNY-Binghamton, the University of Utah, the University of Minnesota, and Ohio University (Krueger and Ryan, 1993). These courses are taught entirely in the target language for Language for Special Purposes (LSP). Researchers have claimed that CBI can motivate, facilitate, and recontextualize the learning of foreign language (Krueger and Ryan, 1993).

Recently, CBI has become a part of regular university curricula identified as Foreign Language Across the Curriculum (FLAC) at the University of Minnesota since the mid-1980s (Klee and Metcalf, 1994). The purposes of the courses across various disciplines are to allow students to gain both language skills and cultural literacy as well as to develop students' analytic and critical thinking skills in the foreign language. Not only did these programs successfully integrate language and content, but all of them also significantly improved student foreign language proficiency. However, the results of the studies suggest that students' language proficiency levels should be determined before they participate in a CBI course (Klee and Metcalf, 1994). For instance, the Oral Proficiency Interview (OPI) from the American Council on the Teaching of Foreign Languages (ACTFL) is often used to determine students' proficiency level before CBI takes place.

In spite of the effectiveness of CBI in foreign language learning shown in the previous studies (e.g., Klahn, 1997; Sternfeld, 1997; Stryker, 1997), use of the combination of the content-based approach and Internet technologies to develop learners' language and cultural competence has not yet been explored. The core texts that the learners can obtain from the Internet are the authentic up-to-date information from different forms such as online newspapers, audio recordings, and video clips. The challenge is to devise strategies by which the instructor can make use of the materials found on the Internet efficiently and effectively.

In summary, previous research shows that CBI is an effective method to develop students' language competence so that they can interact with native speakers comfortably and successfully in real-life situations. This chapter describes a pilot project that used CBI as a methodology accessing the Internet to develop students' language skills as well as to enhance their intercultural awareness and understanding.

RATIONALE FOR THE INTEGRATION OF THE INTERNET INTO CBI

Many task-based online activities have been created to facilitate and enhance the process of foreign language acquisition. Previous studies have

shown the effectiveness of the Internet on students' foreign language acquisition. Not only have students' language skills improved but also their attitude
and motivation toward foreign language learning have changed (e.g.,
Paramskas, 1993; Lee, 1997, 1998; Warschauer, 1996). These studies also
illustrated different approaches for integrating Internet technology into foreign language teaching and learning. For instance, both receiving input and
producing output are essential for the development of a foreign language.
Students can receive input via online readings from newspapers, magazines,
and texts, as well as online communication that also allows them to produce
output in the target language.

Today it is not surprising to encounter students who pursue a double-major
degree for their undergraduate education, such as international affairs, political science, or Latin American studies combined with foreign language
education. The professional need of these students is to have both knowledge
of specific content areas in the target language and communicative skills. For
instance, students need to know vocabulary and intercultural understanding
and awareness related to business and nursing in order to do business in
Mexico or to deal with Hispanic patients in nursing homes or hospitals in the
United States. These special needs of the students encourage us to rethink the
way we structure language classes. The use of CBI as a framework, therefore,
is a potential way to help students achieve communicative competence as well
as gain the cultural knowledge of specific topics such as history, art, music,
and business.

Internet tools such as search engines or the existing foreign language
resources from personal, institutional, or commercial homepages provide
endless opportunities for learners to obtain the information on personal
interests and needs that is an essential aspect of CBI. Different sections
of online newspapers such as "politics," "economics," "arts," and "sports"
allow students to read about areas of interest in the target language. In
addition, the process of interpreting, analyzing, synthesizing, and evaluating
the cultural texts goes beyond the presentations of simple facts. Students'
reading skills and strategies in the target language, therefore, can be
improved. These resources can be used for CBI that covers specific content
areas of the target culture. In the following, I describe in detail the
Internet-based cultural project and the content-based approach constructed
for the students of an advanced Spanish course at a public state university
on a northern seacoast.

DESIGN

The goal of the application of CBI and Internet resources was to create a
learning environment wherein students practice their language skills and
acquire the target culture. The project, in particular, aimed to improve

students' reading and speaking skills through composing a content-based cultural project outside the classroom. The activities for the project were also integrated into the course syllabus. Thirty percent of the final grade was based on the project, making the project significant enough for students to be actively involved in the work.

When using the content-based approach with Internet resources, I take several issues into consideration. First, students' language proficiency and prior knowledge of the target culture need to be measured in order to identify their strengths and weaknesses. Second, authentic readings need to be selected based on students' proficiency level and interest. For example, the majority of the students in this class had either a major or a minor in Spanish. Some of them were double-majoring in Spanish and international affairs, political science, and communication. Students were encouraged to investigate areas related to their majors or the countries where they planned to study abroad. I also take measures to assure that appropriate reading texts from the Internet are provided to the students so that they know where to look for supportive materials. Third, students need to be informed clearly about the definition, purpose, content, procedure, and assessment criteria for the cultural project. Finally, when possible, samples of projects with different designs and topics should be available as models to them.

PROCEDURE

This project was divided into several stages that required collaboration among students, native speakers, and faculty from other disciplines. Structuring the project included assessing students' language skills before and after the project, selecting the Websites for reading materials, and planning the activities with pedagogical procedure both inside and outside the class. In the following, I describe each stage in detail.

Stage One: Assessing Students' Oral Skills and Cultural Knowledge

In order to identify the proficiency level of students' speaking skills before the project began, students in the advanced Spanish course took the Spanish Oral Proficiency Test (SOPT) designed by the researcher according to the ACTFL proficiency guidelines (1986). The researcher was interested in finding out what kind of oral skill students had acquired and how much help they might need to execute online activities. Students also took a test concerning the Hispanic world. The purpose of this test was to ascertain the students' cultural competence. Theme-based questions were used to identify specific areas of Hispanic culture with which students were familiar or unfamiliar. For instance, students answered questions such as "Briefly describe how

Mexicans celebrate the Day of the Dead" and "What is the political and economical situation in Chiapas, Mexico?"

The results of the SOPT showed that the majority of the students had an Intermediate-Mid proficiency and that a few had an Intermediate-High proficiency. None of the students had an Advanced level of proficiency. Surprisingly, the results of the Hispanic cultural test proved that this group of the students had very little knowledge of the Hispanic world. This further confirmed the strong need for work aimed toward enhancing students' knowledge of the target culture.

At the end of the evaluation, students were given a questionnaire to indicate what areas of Hispanic culture they would like to study. The following is a sample of the topics selected by the students:

- agriculture and rainforest in Costa Rica
- immigration and migration in the United States
- indigenous peoples of Mexico
- international business—North American Free Trade Agreement (NAFTA)
- Chilean poets—Pablo Neruda and Gabriela Mistral
- Fidel Castro and Cuba

The results of the cultural test thus confirmed the need for study of Hispanic culture using the content-based approach.

Stage Two: Selecting Topics and Building Resources

The topics for the cultural project selected were based on the students' needs and interests. An important principle for selecting topics was to study areas of which students had some prior knowledge through other disciplines. To avoid repetition, students who had selected very similar topics met with the instructor to discuss and select different aspects of the topic.

After the topics were defined, a list of resources from online newspapers or magazines, along with other materials located on a homepage for this course, was provided to the students so that they could begin their search. Faculty from the Spanish program and other disciplines, such as plant biology, anthropology, art, history, international business, and sociology, were invited to assist students in selecting reading materials. Approximately four to five readings, according to the length of the articles, were used for each topic. The selected readings were posted on the homepage so that other students could read them before the online discussion (see the website <http://www.unh.edu/spanish/lina/spanish631.html> for more information). After working with students for two semesters, a great amount of reading material was developed. In addition to the reading material, a collection of videos was available for students to use for their oral presentations in class. Students viewed the videos and selected segments they wanted to show in class. They also prepared a list of vocabulary words on the topic for the class so that other students learned words and idiomatic expressions along with the subject matter.

Stage Three: Executing Cultural Activities

At the beginning of the semester, students were informed about the cultural project using the content-based approach as part of their requirement for the course. They were also provided with a course syllabus in which the cultural project was described as a research project. Students were required to execute several activities during the semester to reinforce their language skills and increase their cultural knowledge. The activities were carried out both inside and outside the classroom. The procedure for the major activities is as follows.

Online readings and chats. The students were required to chat online once a week. Because it is extremely difficult to chat online with a group of fifteen students, the instructor divided the class into three groups. Each group consisted of four to five students. Each week students were assigned a theme-based topic for the online discussion. Most of the topics were related to the reading materials for the class, such as immigration and the law, the roles of men and women in Latin America, and the political situation in Latin America. After students read the online materials posted on the homepage, each group discussed the readings via a chatroom where they interacted with each other to express their opinions about and reactions to the texts. Each student worked collaboratively within the group by exchanging and debating ideas. Each group then shared its collective thoughts with peers in the class. Group collaboration among students was an important part of this activity. The collaboration promotes a supportive and nonthreatening environment that helps students build self-confidence in learning a foreign language.

Cultural presentations by native speakers. The focus of the activities was to provide students with more opportunities to use the target language in cross-cultural settings and to maintain balance between language and content. Native speakers from different countries on campus were invited to partici-pate and assist students in the project. The instructor met with six native speakers who were enrolled in different programs on campus. Two of them were biochemistry majors, one was in international affairs, one was in anthro-pology, and the remaining two were Spanish majors. These students gave talks about their countries, focusing on the aspects of the topics selected by the students for their cultural projects. The instructor scheduled each presentation into the course syllabus, and all talks were presented in the class. After the presentation, students interacted with native speakers. They asked questions and made comments. Students also wrote to native speakers for help with

Spanish language structure via e-mail. They also kept biweekly electronic journals sent to the instructor via e-mail.

Planning for cultural projects. The instructor met with each student to plan and discuss the final project. The instructor provided students with three hand-outs: (1) an outline of the project, (2) a brief summary of the project, and (3) a draft of the final project before their final interviews. Students were required to submit the work based on the three handouts. Students who investigated a similar topic worked together as a team to select different aspects of the same topic. For instance, three students worked on Aztec culture. One student wrote about the religion and gods of the Aztecs, another student focused on the wars between Spain and Mexico, and one student talked about the life of the Aztecs and their influences on the Mexican society of today.

As mentioned earlier, students were encouraged to contact professors from other disciplines to receive assistance in selecting readings for the topic. Some faculty on campus had done research in Latin America countries, especially in Mexico, Chile, and Guatemala. Students also received help from the Spanish faculty, who had traveled in Spain, Argentina, Honduras, and Mexico. The resources students gathered from different people enriched the course content and added a variety of aspects of the Hispanic world.

The different stages of writing necessary for carrying out this project not only reinforced students' writing skills but also helped them with their cognitive skills. They learned how to organize, classify, analyze, and summa-rize their writings under the guidance of the instructor. Based on the feedback received from the instructor, students revised the draft and produced the final copy of the project before the final oral interview. The writing process was very time-consuming for both students and the instructor. The instructor, therefore, requested a teaching assistant who was a graduate student to help students with their writing outside of the class.

Students' oral reports. Students also made fifteen-minute oral presentations to share the project with their peers and the instructor. The oral report counted for 5 percent of the 30 percent of their grade due to the cultural project. Pictures, charts, TV and video clips, and handouts were used to facilitate the presentations. Students were encouraged to rehearse the presentation at least once with their peers outside the class to ensure the quality of the oral report and to reduce the speaking anxiety in front of the class. A five-minute discussion among students after each presentation reinforced their listening and speaking skills, as well as promoting active learning.

Stage Four: Measuring Students' Learning Outcomes

Besides regular quizzes and tests, students wrote a five-page research paper concerning specific areas of Hispanic culture. A holistic assessment was used for this project. All the activities concerning this project were evaluated separately according to five categories: content, organization, language, style, and appropriateness. The scale of 5 = A, 4 = B, 3 = C, 2 = D, and 1 = F was used to keep track of students' work at each category. The instructor also conducted an oral interview with each student in the target language. All the interviews were recorded for the data analysis. The teacher-made evaluation form was used for the oral grade, which was 10 percent of the overall grade. The purpose of this interview was to find out students' perspectives and attitudes toward the cultural learning as well as the content knowledge gained from composing the cultural project. A self-evaluation form designed by the researcher was also used to further confirm students' reactions to the project and their perspective on the learning progress of their language skills, especially oral skills.

STUDENTS' FEEDBACK AND COMMENTS

At the end of the semester, students were given a questionnaire concerning their reactions to developing their language skills and cultural knowledge by the use of online resources and the content-based approach. Students were asked to indicate their level of satisfaction by ranking the following statements on a scale of 1 to 5.

1. I enjoyed working on the cultural project.
2. The theme-based instruction with online resources was an effective way to acquire a foreign language and culture.
3. Reading weekly online materials helped my reading skills and increased my knowledge of Spanish vocabulary.
4. Discussing online readings with my peers and native speakers via a chatroom was a meaningful way to improve my communication skills.
5. Native speakers and faculty from other disciplines on campus helped me with my cultural project.

The results showed that students responded very favorably to the cultural project. Most students agreed that using the content-based approach with Internet resources was an effective way to develop Hispanic cultural knowledge and improve their language skills.

During the final oral interview, the students were asked what they liked the best and the least about the project and also what needed to be improved for the future projects. Students provided many constructive comments concerning both the method and the content of instruction.

Content-Based Instruction

Based on the results of the questionnaires and the final interviews, students responded very positively to the content-based approach for the cultural project. Using CBI allowed the students to concentrate on studying specific content areas of Hispanic culture along with acquiring the language itself. Students viewed the theme-based instruction as a powerful way to gain cultural literacy and cross-cultural perspectives. Students understood that the activities fostered the development of communicative abilities through the examination of a content related to their interests. They were delighted that they could apply their knowledge acquired from other courses, such as economics, business, and art, to this project. Moreover, students felt a strong need to use the language for professional and personal needs, as many of them intended to live or study, travel, and work in the countries of the related subject areas. One student said,

> I had never taken a language course using the content-based approach to learn both language and culture at the same time. It was really a spectacular personal learning experience. It changed the way I think about learning a foreign language. Besides learning about specific topics of the target culture, it made me concentrate on how to use Spanish for communication rather than what I know about the language itself.

One of the main foci of content-based instruction was to foster awareness in the students themselves of their particular needs and motivations. The activities required the students to take charge of their own learning. For instance, students were responsible for reading all the assigned reading and their own reading for the project, although some of them complained about the reading load. They also were required to chat online and write biweekly electronic journals via e-mail. The majority of students agreed that a variety of activities helped them to learn the materials well enough that they could use the target language in an advanced way without thinking too much in English.

The study of subject matter was organized through collaboration among students, faculty, and native speakers. Participation in the project by native speakers and faculty on campus made a great impact on the students' progress in carrying out this project. The faculty members and native speakers spent time and made efforts to assist students in encountering readings and engaging them in online discussions. Some native speakers even spent extra time with students, helping them with their writings. Obviously, collaborative work was the key to making this project successful and meaningful for the students. Strategies for recruiting native speakers and faculty from other disciplines on campus and/or in the community need to be provided so that students can take advantage of resources from native speakers and the expertise of faculty. A small amount of compensation given to the participants for their contribution to the project can be useful.

Some of the students, however, preferred the more traditional approach, by which they learned the usage of grammar and other language skills with drills.

They were concerned about making errors in online chats and e-mail journals. Furthermore, students indicated that very little effort was made to help students to deal with linguistic errors in the process of composing the cultural project. Some students suggested that a certain portion of class time should be devoted to grammar review and error correction. It seemed that these students were not so convinced of the effectiveness of CBI. They wanted classroom activities to focus on language study rather than on learning cultural content. In addition, another student made the following comment: "There was just not enough time to do all the work required for this project, although pedagogically it sounded wonderful. I think this project should be worth more than thirty percent of the course grade."

Content and Reading Materials

In terms of the content, the majority of the students enjoyed reading a variety of cultural texts and found them interesting and stimulating. One student said that he had never thought how much he could learn from content-based instruction. Not only did he acquire better communicative skills through online discussions, but he also gained both vocabulary and cultural knowledge of a specific content area. A particularly important observation was that students experienced a different approach to learning Spanish, one that allowed them to explore both language and content at the same time. Most of the students no longer wanted to learn Spanish through the examination of grammar, structure, and drills. Instead, they appreciated the integration of the target culture into the language course.

However, some students were overwhelmed by the amount of material they had to read online. They commented that some of the materials were too hard to understand and that some articles were too long. They became frustrated by too much technical information in the texts. One student suggested that the instructor should give help with reading, such as a glossary or an explanation of complex structures along with reading strategies. A few students commented that because some topics were dry and boring, they had a difficult time becoming involved in the online discussions. These comments suggest that it is essential to provide learners with appropriate content and materials when using the theme-based approach for foreign language acquisition (Stryker, 1997).

Online Readings and Online Interaction

When asking students about the use of the Internet for this course, virtually every student favored online readings. Students especially appreciated information available on the homepage, which gave them easy access to the readings. In addition, students enjoyed chatting online with their peers and native speakers. For instance, one student commented, "Online discussions were very stimulating and the content was very informative. Chatting online was the best way I have ever learned to communicate with others in the target language." Moreover, students liked the interaction with native speakers via the chatroom. Students reported that online discussions reinforced their communication skills, and they felt less intimidated and more willing to get involved in the discussion than in front of the large class. Through the medium of the chatroom, students from varying levels of language background and different learning styles were able to engage in discourse based on their pace and needs. Students felt that they could take time to formulate sentences and could ask questions when needed. This confirmed the findings of my previous study concerning using the chatroom to develop students' speaking skills and thinking skills (Lee, 1998).

CONCLUSION AND IMPLICATIONS FOR FUTURE STUDY

Although some difficulties were noted by the students, the integration of the content-based approach and online resources for the development of students' language and cultural competence was a success. The main goal of this cultural project was to balance the study of language and content. CBI allowed students to learn specific areas of Hispanic culture while studying the language. The instructor's role was to become a facilitator of language acquisition. The instructor served as "language expert," while faculty from other disciplines served as "content experts." On the other hand, students were accountable for their own learning. Under the guidance of the instructor, they were in charge of selecting topics and readings for the project along with reading and chatting online with their peers and native speakers. In addition, students and participating faculty and native speakers on campus worked collaboratively to carry out the activities. Without a doubt, the collaboration had a great impact on the process and product of language learning.

New technologies make it possible to create a stimulating learning environment to benefit students by using online readings drawn from a variety of authentic materials, such as newspapers, magazines, and books and online discussions via a chatroom. Internet technologies provide students authentic, comprehensive "input" and "output" that are essential for them to become proficient in a foreign language. Not every student is a skilled reader or writer. Students have different learning styles. Online activities allow them to learn at their own pace without feeling the pressure they feel in front of the class. As a result, students' motivation and self-confidence about language learning are enhanced. More important, they gain specific cultural knowledge and understanding, which allows them to connect with other people around the Hispanic world.

In addition to outlining the advantages of the theme-based approach and online resources, this study emphasizes the importance of ascertaining the appropriate level of the readings. These authentic materials must meet the students' proficiency levels so that they are not overwhelmed. Students should be guided into acquiring strategies to cope with reading in the target language. A systematic assessment procedure needs to be established to ensure the quality of work based on theme-based instruction. In conclusion, the combined use of online technologies and the theme-based approach with an appropriate level of text proves to be an effective and vital tool in achieving the goal of empowering students to become autonomous learners and well-rounded individuals.

REFERENCES

Adamson, Hugh Douglas. (1993). *Academic competence: Theory and classroom practice: Preparing ESL students for content courses*. White Plains, NY: Longman.

American Council on the Teaching of Foreign Languages (1986). *ACTFL Proficiency Guidelines*. Hastings-on-Hudson, NY: American Council on the Teaching of Foreign Languages.

Beauvois, Margaret. (1998). Write to speak: The effects of electronic communication on the oral achievement of fourth semester French students. In Judith A. Muyskens (ed.), *New ways of learning and teaching: Focus on technology and foreign language education*, pp. 93–115. AAUSC Issues in Language Program Direction. Boston: Heinle & Heinle.

Bush, Michael D. (1997). Implementing technology for language teaching. In Michael D. Bush and Robert M. Terry (eds.), *Technology-enhanced language learning*, pp. 287–350. ACTFL Foreign Language Education Series. Lincolnwood, IL: National Textbook Company.

Klahn, Norma. (1997). Teaching for communicative and cultural competence: Spanish through contemporary Mexican topics. In Stephen B. Stryker and Betty Lou Leaver (eds.), *Content-based instruction in foreign language education: Models and methods*, pp. 203–221. Washington: Georgetown University Press.

Klee, Carol, and Metcalf, Michael F. (1994). Perspectives on foreign languages across the curriculum based on the University of Minnesota experience. In Stephen Straight (ed.), *Languages across the curriculum: Invited essays on the use of foreign languages throughout the postsecondary curriculum*. Binghamton: Center of Research in Translation, State University of New York at Binghamton.

Kramsch, Claire, and McConnell-Ginet, Sally (eds.). (1992). *Text and context: Cross-disciplinary perspectives on language study*. Lexington, MA: D. C. Heath.

Krashen, Stephen. (1985). *The input hypothesis*. New York, NY: Longman.

Krueger, Merle, and Ryan, Frank (eds.). (1993). *Language and content: Discipline- and content-based approaches to language study*. Lexington, MA: D. C. Heath.

Lee, Lina. (1997). Using Internet tools as an enhancement of L2 cultural teaching and learning. *Foreign Language Annals*, 30: 410–427.

Lee, Lina. (1998). Going beyond classroom learning: Acquiring cultural knowledge via online newspapers and intercultural exchanges. *CALICO*, 16(2): 101–120.

Meunier, Lydie E. (1998). Personality and motivational factors in computer-mediated foreign language communication (CMFLC). In Judith A. Muyskens (ed.), *New ways of learning and teaching: Focus on technology and foreign language education*, pp. 145–198. AAUSC Issues in Language Program Direction. Boston: Heinle & Heinle.

Paramskas, Donna. (1993). Computer-Assisted Language Learning (CALL): Increasingly into an ever more electronic world. *Canadian Modern Language Review,* 50: 124–143.

Snow, Marguerite Ann, and Brinton, Donna M. (1998). *The adjunct model of language instruction: Integrating language and content at the university.* Center for Language and Education Research. Technical Report #8. Los Angeles: University of California at Los Angeles.

Sternfeld, Steven R. (1997). Caterpillars into butterflies: Content-based instruction in a first-year Italian course. In Stephen B. Stryker and Betty Lou Leaver (eds.), *Content-based instruction in foreign language education: Models and methods,* pp. 56–77. Washington: Georgetown University Press.

Stryker, Stephen B. (1997). The Mexico experiment at the Foreign Service Institute. In Stephen B. Stryker and Betty Lou Leaver (eds.), *Content-based instruction in foreign language education: Models and methods,* pp. 177–202. Washington: Georgetown University Press.

Stryker Stephen B., and Betty Lou Leaver. 1997. "Content-Based Instruction: From Theory to Practice," In Stephen B. Stryker, and Betty Lou Leaver, *Content-based instruction in foreign language education: Models and methods,* pp. 1–28. Washington: Georgetown University Press.

Warschauer, Mark. (1996). Motivational aspects of using computers for writing and communication. In Mark Warschauer (ed.), *Telecollaboration in foreign language learning: Proceedings of the Hawaii Symposium,* pp. 64–81. Honolulu: University of Hawaii, Second Language Teaching and Curriculum Center.

APPENDIX A
Monthly Self-Evaluation

This worksheet is to help you evaluate your own progress in learning Spanish language and culture.

Checklist: Which of the following activities have you been participating in?

	Yes	No
1. Have you been reading online newspapers?	____	____
2. Have you been writing weekly journals?	____	____
3. Have you been working with native speakers?	____	____
4. Have you been chatting online?	____	____
5. Have you been participating in cultural presentations?	____	____

Reflective Questions:

6. What other things you have been doing to improve your Spanish?

_____

_____

7. What specific areas of Spanish do you think you need to improve? Why?

_____

_____

8. What have you learned from the online activities?

_____

_____

9. Which of the Internet activities have you enjoyed the most? Please briefly explain.

_____

_____

10. What have you learned about yourself as a learner by doing this cultural project?

_____

_____

APPENDIX B
End-of-Semester Oral Interview Questions

1. Briefly explain your experience in creating this project.
2. Describe your experience doing the online activities.
3. Share with me some of the cultural information in your portfolio.
4. Tell me what materials you used to support your cultural project, including where and how you found the materials.
5. Explain the most valuable and interesting part of this project and why.
6. Describe the most difficult or least important part of this project and why.
7. Tell me if this project met your original goals for culture learning and why.
8. Overall, tell me how the experience of this project improved your language skills.

9

Feature Films in Language Teaching

Possibilities and Practical Problems

Adam Knee

With the advent of video technology in the 1970s and, eventually, the development of a range of videotape productions designed specifically for language learning, many language teachers who would once have used feature films as a resource understandably shifted their efforts to the implementation of instructional videotapes instead. The new medium was and is more versatile and manipulable than its 16mm celluloid predecessor; and videos designed with language learning in mind can more directly target specific language structures than can commercial features designed for entertainment and/or artistic rather than pedagogical purposes (Altman, 1989; Berwald, 1985; D. Willis, 1983). This chapter makes the case, however, that despite the challenges they pose, feature films, in particular when presented through videotape or videodisc technology rather than film, can serve as a useful tool in the foreign language classroom.

I first offer here a brief outline of several justifications for using feature films as texts; I then make a general proposal about the specific ways features might be employed to help promote language learning; and last, I provide some practical suggestions for teachers trying to integrate film into their language classes. What prompts this discussion, in part, is the fact that widespread international interest in film—and in particular in commercial feature films—immediately suggests that viewing films might be a particularly fruitful means for promoting second language use among students. Yet, relatively few language textbooks offer any substantial focus on feature films, and such films are generally a very minor part of foreign language (and in particular EFL) curricula. While some of the reasons for the hesitancy to use films are indeed well-grounded (and I further address some of these concerns later), I hope I have made the case in this chapter that the substantial instructional potential in feature films can significantly outweigh their difficulties.[1]

WHY USE FEATURE FILMS?

Perhaps the most immediate answer to the question of why to use feature films is one to which I have already alluded: feature films—most significantly, Hollywood films—are texts in which students from most cultures have an almost unparalleled interest. Hence, nonnative speakers have a particularly high level of motivation as "readers" when encountering such texts in classroom instruction, all the more so because of their relative novelty. This motivational potential is, in fact, a key argument put forth in various forms for the more general use of video (e.g., Allan, 1985; Lonergan, 1984; Stempleski & Tomalin, 1990; see Part I of this volume about the importance of language learning motivation).

One might object that to choose an instructional text on the basis of its popularity represents a lowering of standards and—in the case of American feature films—effectively rewards Hollywood for (and institutionally reinforces) its global cultural hegemony. I think that indeed these are reasonable pedagogical and political objections but that a number of factors mitigate them. I do not presume to intervene here in the numerous ongoing high culture versus low culture and canonical text versus popular text debates, but I would assert that in the context of *language* instruction, concerns over matters of artistic or cultural value (themselves already suspect) could stand to be muted for pragmatic reasons. Moreover, the employment of "hegemonic" texts in the classroom does not mean that students are automatically indoctrinated with whatever ideologies such texts presumably propagate; ideally, the teacher will help establish a critical distance from said texts, to provide the student with the tools to "read against the grain," to cross-culturally interrogate both the films and the industry that produces them. Nor, of course, must a teacher work solely with Hollywood (or other mainstream) texts in order to reap some of their motivating benefits; one could, for example, start with a commercial blockbuster as a "hook" and move on to film texts that (debatably) have greater artistic value.

In addition to the benefit of motivating many students to pay more attention to class materials than they might otherwise, feature films also have the advantage that they are a cultural form in which most students are already highly literate, even if they are none too familiar with the spoken and written language employed within these texts. Films involve many layers of signification, some of which even beginning-level students are perfectly capable of understanding; one can comprehend a visual image, for example, or the syntactic relationship between images articulated through editing, even if one does not understand the words being spoken in a given scene. The vast majority of language students, moreover, already have a range of generic competencies related to film—a basic knowledge not only of the conventions of the very broad genre of feature film but also of those of such more delimited genres as the action film, the horror film, and so on. In the case of blockbusters and adaptations of widely known texts in particular, students often come to a film with a prior awareness of the plot from other sources, which further aids in their comprehension of the text as a whole; their prior knowledge of narrative structure helps them to fill in the gaps in their understanding of specific scenes or specific verbal exchanges.[2]

This kind of student comprehension is of course facilitated by the fact that the film's different layers of signification—verbal, visual, and narratological, for example—are often to some extent mutually supportive (Altman, 1989; Tomalin, 1986; J. Willis, 1983b); the overdetermined nature of the signifieds may allow students to apprehend them even if specific signifiers (in particular verbal ones) remain the source of some difficulty. Students are thus extended a degree of comfort and ease in understanding the text even though it involves some unfamiliar language, a comfort augmented in many cases by their aforementioned preexisting motivation in viewing the film text. This is, I would propose, a context in which students are able to begin to comprehend new language while relatively relaxed and not focusing directly on learning— a context that, many would argue, may help facilitate language acquisition. Put another way, when pleasurably immersed in the narrative, imagistic, and linguistic flow of the cinema, students' "affective filters" are arguably lowered, with greater language acquisition potential the result (Krashen, 1981; see also March in this volume on the aspect of *flow*).[3] This effect is amplified all the more for the reason that (even among the various moving image media and genres) feature films are a particularly affective, emotive form, one that by its very nature tends to "sweep away" its viewers.

Another reason for employing feature films in the foreign language classroom is that they provide many of the benefits sought in so-called authentic materials (Altman, 1989; Kerridge, 1982; Stempleski, 1992). Feature films tend to present language usage in extremely "high context" situations, even if these happen to be reconstructed, fictional situations; students get to watch the target language realistically employed (possibly even in a regional dialect) with a range of often culturally specific nonverbal cues as well as a range of true-to-life interferences: unclear speech, overlapping speech, external sounds, and so on. Foreign language films themselves are also "authentic," of course, in that they are in most cases texts actually circulated in countries where the given language is spoken, texts that might well be part of a native speaker's cultural background. In the special case of the Hollywood film used for EFL/ESL classes, the teaching text is indeed in a league with texts the students might encounter in many parts of the world, so broad is Hollywood's (and English's) reach. In this sense, cinematic English is a form of authentic English.

One further group of justifications for using feature films to teach foreign language takes its cue from certain arguments for employing literature in language teaching. In brief, these arguments posit that the separation of literature and language is a function of disciplinary and institutional politics, rather than rooted in any serious pedagogical reasoning; they suggest that literature is important as an authentic instantiation of language as it is actually used, and, most important, that literature can be employed to train students to examine multiple layers of meaning, ultimately allowing them to become more skilled, sophisticated readers (Collie & Slater, 1987; Kramsch, 1993; Sage, 1987). As noted, film likewise can be beneficial in exposing students to authentic language communication. And film involves multiple layers of meaning and thus can be employed to help students develop more advanced interpretation skills, applicable to functional texts and artistic texts alike. Language figures into this equation both through its use within the film text being read and in its use in processes of analysis and interpretation—for example, in class discussions of film and in critical writing assignments.

READING FILM AS FILM

My central suggestion regarding the use of feature films in language courses proceeds logically from some of the foregoing considerations. I would contend that if we are indeed using film to develop more advanced, sophisticated interpretation skills, to foster not just linguistic competence but also a broader communicative competence, we need to pay attention to the specificity of the medium being employed. Just as in teaching language through literature, when teaching language through film we need to pay some mind to formal technique. I emphasize this point in part because the very few textbooks and teaching guides in this area by and large do not pay much attention to the specifically cinematographic elements of film (Hennessey, 1995; Mejia & O'Connor, 1994; Williamson & Vincent, 1996).[4] Such texts instead tend to use films as a springboard for discussions of theme, plot, and sometimes genre, also offering exercises based upon film dialogue to a lesser degree. This tendency is completely understandable if one takes into account the particular instructional context, the utilization of film as a vehicle for teaching language rather than for teaching the basics of cinema studies. However, while thematic debates, plot analyses, and dialogue exercises are all helpful activities, they are also only part of a broader range of possible tasks, some of which should involve reading film as film. Only in this way will students be encouraged to become critically active readers of foreign-language texts of various sorts, rather than merely conditioned to derive an understanding of the target language.

Interestingly, Anthony Jennings (1996) has posed an argument explicitly counter to this position, claiming that when film is brought into the language and literature classroom, the focus should be on theme rather than technique. His reasoning is that his approach will produce the more perceptive reader in part because it is theme, rather than technique, that holds the students' interest. A focus on formal technique, he claims, will usurp too much class time and drain the excitement from the text, thus negating one of the reasons for using film. In order to make this argument, Jennings is forced to summon the specter of a mythical, monolithic formalist, to attack a straw man who completely disregards meaning in the quest for an analysis of technique. In actual practice, of course, paying some heed to cinematic technique does not automatically require that one neglect other aspects of the text. Any approach can go awry if it is pushed to an all-encompassing extreme. What I am advocating here, however, is an integration of these "formal" considerations into the broader fabric of the curriculum. Increasing the range of textual elements a student examines is hardly a cause for alarm about lessened student perceptiveness.

Another, more pragmatic objection to a focus on film form in the language class is simply that the vast majority of language teachers have not received any formal training in film analysis. Certainly, an instructor leading a class that involves issues of film technique should have some prior awareness of said technique. But, at the risk of devaluing my own primary discipline of cinema studies, let me also assert that some degree of technical awareness can be achieved by an instructor new to the critical study of film with just a few hours' perusal of a college film-studies textbook; a basic knowledge of some of the descriptive vocabulary employed in film studies, along with the instructor's preexisting skills in textual analysis, should, I think, suffice for a foreign language (rather than a cinema studies) course. It is not necessary for one to be an expert in cinema, but merely for one to be capable of guiding students to focus more broadly on the various levels of film texts.

PRACTICAL OBSERVATIONS AND SUGGESTIONS

Indeed, my own recent initial efforts to put some of these thoughts into practice involved the organization of an advanced-level EFL/film course at Assumption University in Thailand with a fellow lecturer who held a doctorate in TESL but had no formal background in film studies. The novelty of the material did require him to do a bit of extra background reading but did not pose the least hindrance in his teaching of the class. Each of us taught our own section of the course, which was offered as a six-week, 60-hour module of a semester-long program rather ominously entitled "Terminals." The Terminals program is designed for Assumption students (mostly Thais, along with some other nonnative speakers of English) who are having particular difficulty passing regular-track English courses. Film was therefore tried out, in this particular case, as a new means of motivating the students in their language studies.

Subject Organization

The module was organized in large part around various film genres—both to highlight conventions with which students were already aware and to develop new schema to be engaged in later screenings (an emphasis endorsed in both Swaffar & Vlatten, 1997, and Williamson & Vincent, 1996). We began with an introductory overview of the contemporary status of Hollywood filmmaking, placing particular emphasis on the industry's dominance in global markets, and then moved on, week by week, to such genres as the science fiction film, the spy film, and the documentary, including where possible films with English spoken in accents other than American. Through class discussion and analysis, students were able to become more cognizant of their own already-existing generic competencies, their own accrued awareness of the conventions of various popular textual forms. When such analysis began to cross over into questions of film technique, the occasion was taken to introduce some basic technical vocabulary, such as terms to describe differing camera positions (low angle, high angle, oblique, bird's eye) and movements (tracking, panning, craning, zooming); students thus received their new critical vocabulary in a practical, contextualized manner.

Student Assignments and Assessment

The module built upon newly developed generic and technical vocabularies by bringing these to bear in the writing of various kinds of film reviews as homework assignments; some of the students particularly enjoyed writing about Hollywood films then playing in Bangkok's theaters, which also led to some involved (and opinionated) in-class discussions. Readings included excerpts from introductory English-language college film texts and film reviews and feature articles from local and overseas newspapers and magazines.[5] Regular quizzes and exams verified knowledge of some of the factual material covered in class and in readings (by way of short-answer questions and identifications), but also asked, more substantially, for impromptu reviews of films screened or short essays on topics related to class discussion (e.g., an essay on what *Robocop* [1987] appears to say about the role of technology in modern life). The final exam also required students to write a description of the shots in a video sequence they were shown (the film clip was repeated a number of times at intervals, to allow students time to revise their descriptions) and to transcribe the dialogue in another sequence. Such transcription exercises can be quite time-consuming for an exam format (not to mention most challenging for the students!), but they may be of use, on occasion, for an instructor wanting to focus intensively on listening skills.

While this module proceeded without any major mishaps, it also became clear to us that using film to teach a foreign language presents quite a few practical problems and challenges present in neither the traditional language class nor the traditional cinema studies class. Some of these potential problems—and possible solutions to them—are outlined next.

Choice of Materials

First, while students are indeed motivated to watch popular films, getting them to remain attentive and engaged for the entire duration of a film not in their native language can pose a considerable problem—particularly if the language level of the film is too difficult. This means that the instructor must carefully preview any film being used for a language class not only for language difficulty (in areas of vocabulary, regional dialect, speed of delivery, and clarity of sound recording), but also for cultural appropriateness (Arcario, 1992; Joiner, 1990).[6] A comedy, for example, may be widely popular in its country of origin, but feature a comedian whose quick speech and "in" (that is to say, very culturally specific) jokes are far beyond the reach of students. A documentary or action film might present its dialogue with such a high level of literal and figurative contextual "noise" as to make it unintelligible. The teacher must therefore keep the students' language level in mind when previewing a film and also consider how important listening comprehension is to a given class's goals.

Viewing Procedures

Once an appropriate text is chosen, the instructor must also be ready to present it in a manner that will keep students actively and critically engaged and paying at least some mind to language; the dangers of slipping into a passive viewing mode are emphasized by many who have discussed using video or film to teach language (e.g., Cooper, Lavery, & Rinvolucri, 1991; Hill, 1989; J. Willis, 1983a). Pre-viewing activities, it has not surprisingly been demonstrated, can help ensure that video viewing is productive for students (Herron, 1994); pre-film readings and discussion could, for example, introduce pertinent vocabulary items, highlight a film's generic traits and thematic emphases, and anticipate potentially confusing plot elements. Once the screening has begun, the instructor should also be ready to stop the film at appropriate points for class discussion, as well as to ensure that no students are too lost to follow the plot (Donchin, 1985). If a particular bit of dialogue has confused students, the sequence can be replayed one or more times before viewing the film continues. Similarly, if a significant formal technique has been employed or an important narrative pattern has begun to emerge, appropriate illustrative sequences can be replayed before the viewing continues. One might object that this stop-and-go approach detracts from the immersive, affective effects of film viewing I outlined earlier, and indeed, to a degree I would agree that this is so. Nevertheless, I would contend that the technique is crucial for keeping students critically engaged with a foreign-language film text. Viewing a feature film straight through from start to finish might be suitable on occasion if the language is accessible enough, in order to give students a more authentic viewing experience, but in general this should be avoided— especially in the case of beginning- or intermediate-level students.

Technical Considerations

Next, the teacher also needs to ensure that the viewing environment and facilities are adequate for class needs. In general, I would recommend leaving classroom lights on during film viewing, for the same reasons I would recommend stopping the film on a regular basis—to keep the students from getting too relaxed to pay adequate attention to elements of the text. It is also crucial that your video monitor have adequate sound reproduction; the sound is often garbled enough to begin with in film texts designed for native listeners, and unintelligible dialogue can quickly become frustrating for students. Indeed, for this reason, it is also best to examine the specific videocassette being used in a class in advance; even if you have already previewed the film from another source, you might be unpleasantly surprised to find that the tape you have acquired happens to have poor-quality sound. You need be particularly wary in countries where video piracy is prevalent, as your software may turn out to be not only of unusable quality, but illegal as well. If you are teaching your students in their native country, you likely must also deal with the problem that the most readily available foreign language videos are subtitled in the national language, and it is, of course, generally best to avoid such tapes, as students will tend to rely primarily on the subtitles. The ideal solution to this problem might be for your institution to get non-subtitled videos from a mail-order firm in advance. The practical reality, however, is that you may well have to work with a subtitled video, in which case it is best to design a mask for the bottom of the television screen so that the titles will not be visible—though you might opt to reveal them in certain less intelligible sequences.

PRELIMINARY CONCLUSIONS

Admittedly, from our brief, preliminary effort at using film in an EFL context, one could hardly draw any basic conclusions about the effectiveness of film for facilitating language acquisition. I cannot definitively "prove" that language acquisition occurred any faster, or even at the same rate, as with other methods of instruction. But I can say that the method did appear to meet our most immediate goals of getting students involved with the classroom work and encouraging them to use the target language. Students did by and large appear to find the film texts (primarily from Hollywood) quite engaging, and most of the students were, with a bit of assistance, able to follow the narratives and take some note of technique. I was quite happy to see that the students were not at all put off by learning new technical vocabulary for describing film. To the contrary, they seemed much interested in it, and some were already familiar with a few of the terms. More important, the students were able to use their oral and written language skills not only to recount plot elements and describe images but also, gradually, to contribute to discussions of the films' genre conventions and prevalent themes.

I recall one class discussion late in the term on the James Bond film *Thunderball* (1965), in which we had touched on the film's similarity to other Bond films and spy movies. I asked whether anyone could pick out a deeper theme to the film, which was plainly an unabashed entertainment vehicle. In short order, a student raised her hand and quietly informed us, "The theme is the conflict between emotion and duty." While this response—which in fact hit the nail on the head—might not seem earth-shattering from a native English speaker in a Western classroom setting, for it to come so succinctly and with such minimal prompting from a Thai undergraduate in a native classroom setting marked, I think, a moment of triumph: It required that her English listening skills and critical analysis skills be developed enough that she could consistently follow key plot events and look beyond their entertainment qualities to their thematic implications, later note a pattern in these thematics, and then concisely formulate the pattern in plain English, feeling confident enough to voice her opinion in the presence of a close-knit group of peers much more used to learning by emulation than by independent analysis.[7]

Certainly not all of the students became comfortable with independently describing and analyzing films—and I would not want to claim that any quantum increase in skills was observable after such a short teaching unit. Moreover, our approach to the material did not allow for much concentrated focus on targeted language structures, though we were able to take the time to work on rhetorical strategies for describing images and reviewing films. But what we may have sacrificed during the few weeks in terms of technical language mastery I suspect we more than gained back in other less "surface" language skills, in exposing students to new kinds of interpretive strategies and starting to develop a critical, intercultural awareness of both non-Thai texts and non-Thai approaches to understanding texts.

What much of the foregoing undoubtedly suggests is that effectively using feature films in the language classroom can be quite labor-intensive for the instructor. At the same time, however, such films may provide a useful, enriching, and entertaining supplement to more traditional texts in the foreign language or ESL/EFL curriculum.

NOTES

1. I gratefully acknowledge the contributions to this work of Dr. Elango Kandan (now at Loyola College of the University of Chennai, India), the coordinator of the Terminals subject described herein and my co-teacher in the film module, and Dr. Stephen Conlon, Director of Research at Assumption University's Institute for English Language Education.

2. Interestingly, one of the ways the earliest filmmakers ensured that audiences not yet "fluent" in the language of the new medium would understand their film narratives was by resorting to story materials with which viewers would already have been familiar—contemporary events and political cartoons, for example (Musser, 1984/1990).

3. Stephen Krashen puts particular stock in the worth of voluntary pleasure reading (even of comic books) for language acquisition, and it is significant that many of the characteristics he values in such reading contexts are also present in the filmgoing context: The texts offer a high level of comprehensible input (ensured in films through visual cues) and are received with high motivation and little anxiety (1985, 1985/1989, 1993).

4. The cited textbook by Williamson and Vincent (1996) does in fact offer a perfunctory review of some technical film terms (and a derivative account of several approaches to film criticism) in an opening section, but these do not figure importantly in the remainder of the book. On the other hand, a recent essay by Swaffar and Vlatten (1997) is a rare exception to the tendency described here, as it takes substantial note of the significance of cinematically specific codes for the interpretive activities of language students—although many film scholars would want to qualify the broad generalizations about film language offered in the appendix on "How Visual Images Construct Viewer Consciousness" (p. 185).

5. Recent college film textbooks at a level appropriate for many advanced EFL students include Prince (1996) and Phillips (1999); also available in British and Australian markets are several film textbooks designed for secondary education, which may be adaptable for EFL use as well.

6. For example, is the material too sexually oriented, or do culturally specific references come so frequently that students will not be able to comprehend much of the film?

7. For discussion of Thai learning styles see Knee, 1999; Mulder, 1996, pp. 106–112, 139–144.

REFERENCES

Allan, M. (1985). *Teaching English with video.* Essex, England: Longman.
Altman, R. (1989). *The video connection: Integrating video into language teaching.* Boston: Houghton Mifflin.

Arcario, P. (1992). Criteria for selecting video materials. In S. Stempleski & P. Arcario (eds.), *Video in second language teaching: Using, selecting, and producing video for the classroom,* pp. 109–121. Arlington, VA: Teachers of English to Speakers of Other Languages, Inc.

Berwald, J.-P. (1985). Video and second language learning. *Studies in Language Learning,* 5(1): 3–16.

Collie, J., & Slater, S. (1987). *Literature in the language classroom: A resource book of ideas and activities.* Cambridge, England: Cambridge University Press.

Cooper, R., Lavery, M., & Rinvolucri, M. (1991). *Video.* Oxford, England: Oxford University Press.

Donchin, R. (1985). Video in language learning. *Studies in Language Learning,* 5(1) 61–66.

Hennessey, J. (1995). Using foreign films to develop proficiency and to motivate the foreign language student. *Foreign Language Annals,* 28: 116–120.

Herron, C. (1994). An investigation of the effectiveness of using an advance organizer to introduce video in the foreign language classroom. *Modern Language Journal,* 78: 190–198.

Hill, B. (1989). *Making the most of video.* London: Centre for Information on Language Teaching and Research.

Jennings, A. (1996). "Viewer, I married him": Literature on video. In R. Carter & J. McRae (eds.), *Language, literature & the learner: Creative classroom practice,* pp. 185–203. New York: Longman.

Joiner, E. (1990). Choosing and using videotexts. *Foreign Language Annals,* 23: 53–64.

Kerridge, D. (1982). The use of video films. In M. Geddes & G. Sturtridge (eds.), *Video in the language classroom,* pp. 107–121. London: Heinemann Educational Books.

Knee, A. (1999). An American in Bangkok: Reconsidering pedagogical values. Association of Departments of English: *ADE Bulletin,* 123, 31–35.

Kramsch, C. (1993). *Context and culture in language teaching.* Oxford, England: Oxford University Press.

Krashen, S. (1981). *Second language acquisition and second language learning.* Oxford, England: Pergamon Press.

Krashen, S. (1985). *The input hypothesis: Issues and implications.* London: Longman.

Krashen, S. (1989). *Language acquisition and language education: Extensions and applications.* New York: Prentice-Hall International. (Originally published 1985.)

Krashen, S. (1993). *The power of reading: Insights from the research.* Englewood, CO: Libraries Unlimited.

Lonergan, J. (1984). *Video in language teaching.* Cambridge, England: Cambridge University Press.

Mejia, E. A., & O'Connor, F. H. (1994). *Five star films: An intermediate listening/speaking text.* Englewood Cliffs, NJ: Prentice-Hall Regents.

Mulder, N. (1996). *Inside Thai society: Interpretations of everyday life,* 5th edition. Amsterdam: Pepin Press.

Musser, C. (1990). The nickelodeon era begins: Establishing the framework for Hollywood's mode of representation. In T. Elsaesser (ed.), *Early cinema: Space-frame-narrative,* pp. 256–273. London: BFI Publishing. (Reprinted from *Framework,* Autumn 1984.)

Phillips, W. (1999). *Film: An introduction.* Boston: Bedford/St. Martin's.

Prince, S. (1996). *Movies and meaning: An introduction to film.* New York: Prentice-Hall.

Sage, H. (1987). *Incorporating literature in ESL instruction.* Englewood Cliffs, NJ: Prentice-Hall.

Stempleski, S. (1992). Teaching communication skills with authentic video. In S. Stempleski & P. Arcario (eds.), *Video in second language teaching: Using, selecting, and producing video for the classroom,* pp. 7–24. Arlington, VA: Teachers of English to Speakers of Other Languages, Inc.

Stempleski, S., & Tomalin, B. (1990). *Video in action: Recipes for using video in language teaching.* New York: Prentice-Hall.

Swaffar, J., & Vlatten, A. (1997). A sequential model for video viewing in the foreign language curriculum. *Modern Language Journal,* 81: 175–188.

Tomalin, B. (1986*). Video, TV & radio in the English class: An introductory guide.* London: Macmillan.

Williamson, J. A., & Vincent, J. C. (1996). *Film is content: A study guide for the advanced ESL classroom.* Ann Arbor: University of Michigan Press.

Willis, D. (1983). The potential and limitations of video. In J. McGovern (ed.), *Video applications in English language teaching,* pp. 17–27. Oxford, England: Pergamon Press.

Willis, J. (1983a). 101 ways to use video. In J. McGovern (ed.), *Video applications in English language teaching,* pp. 43–55. Oxford, England: Pergamon Press.

Willis, J. (1983b). The role of the visual element in spoken discourse: Implications for the exploitation of video in the EFL classroom. In J. McGovern (ed.), *Video applications in English language teaching,* pp. 29–42. Oxford, England: Pergamon Press.

Part III

Relationships for Learning

10

Talking to Learn

Socializing the Language Classroom

Robert Weissberg

More than twenty-five years since the advent of communicative language teaching, many foreign language (FL) and second language (L2) classrooms are still characterized by lockstep, teacher-fronted, whole-class instruction (Thornbury, 1998). Why the traditional transmission model of instruction should persist despite a wealth of evidence for the effectiveness of less teacher-centered instructional models (see Jacob et al., 1996, for an excellent review of this research) is puzzling. Perhaps it is the belief on the part of some teachers that group work exposes language students to too many verbal errors in the speech of their classmates. Perhaps for some teachers it is a reaction to classroom experiences where certain groups didn't work well together. In other cases it may be that instructors have felt uncomfortable with the hubbub that often accompanies social activities in class.

Certainly, the student-centered classroom is neither a quiet nor always an orderly one. But the absence of group work deprives students of a natural and motivating environment in which to develop their language skills: the conversational give-and-take of people using language to accomplish something.

Thus, eliminating social interaction from the FL and L2 classroom is justified on neither linguistic nor classroom management grounds; a better understanding of how classroom talk shapes the learning environment is essential in order to realize the necessity of providing for social interaction in the language classroom.

SOCIAL ORGANIZATION AND CLASSROOM DISCOURSE

Strict adherence by the instructor to teacher-centered, transmission-style teaching can increase the boredom factor in any classroom regardless of subject matter; however, its impact is even more serious in FL and L2 classrooms, where listening comprehension and linguistic accuracy are only two of the many skills that need to be mastered. As Ernst (1994) remarks, "There is more to learning a language than the structural aspects. Students need to learn when it is appropriate to speak, how to gain the right to speak, how to gain the floor, how to change the topic, and how to invite others to speak" (294).

In other words, a whole constellation of sociolinguistic skills must be practiced if one is to become an effective FL or L2 user. The most effective way in which they can be acquired is through something approximating normal conversational give-and-take. In order to expose students to a full range of conversation functions and to provide them with opportunities for authentic language use, the instructor must organize learning activities in such a way that they result in language use that approaches authentic social interaction. This is in fact the central, guiding principle of Communicative Language Teaching (Celce-Murcia et al., 1997).

Studies of classroom discourse indicate that this is unlikely to occur in conventionally structured lessons, where teachers tend to do most of the talking and where student discourse is limited and highly stylized. In many classrooms this is evidenced in the repeated occurrences of the Teacher Initiates–Student Responds–Teacher Evaluates discourse pattern. The first step in the pattern often consists of a "display question," that is, a question to which the teacher already knows the answer (Ernst, 1994). Mehan's (1979) classic example of the I-R-E discourse cycle is: (I) "What time is it, Denise?" (R) "It's two o'clock." (E) "That's good, Denise!" Extended I-R-E chains result in a style of classroom discourse that is impoverished in terms of both quality and quantity (Long & Porter, 1985).

To realize the full potential for socialization inherent in any language classroom, it is helpful to envision the ideal lesson as fluid organism, capable of shifting back and forth from whole-class to large-group to small-group to dyadic participation patterns. While constantly managing the flow and monitoring the participant structures in her class, the teacher is only at times the center of attention in the lesson. By deliberately removing herself from the center at crucial junctures in the lesson, she creates a dynamic and participatory social climate. By learning to maximize the social potential of the classroom on a daily basis, she makes it possible for the target language to be not just an object of study but also a genuine medium of communication for students as well.

In this chapter we review various ways in which socialization of the classroom through the principled use of small-group and dyadic activities breaks down the rigid discourse structure of conventional lessons and promotes FL and L2 acquisition. In the next section we review the theoretical arguments supported by classroom research that led to the development of student-centered language teaching in the 1970s and 1980s. Following that, a framework is offered for evaluating a variety of group and paired tasks, as well as a discussion of how each task type employs social activity in order to promote the acquisition of oral language skills. Finally, we consider how social tasks can also promote the acquisition of FL and L2 literacy.

TALKING TO LEARN: SOCIAL APPROACHES TO LANGUAGE LEARNING

In a lockstep, teacher-fronted classroom, conversation among students is often viewed as off-task and disruptive. In the fully socialized language classroom, on the other hand, informal talk is the key to learning. This view of speech as a vehicle of learning goes back at least as far as Vygotsky (1962), who saw the social function of children's language as a necessary precursor to the internalization of speech as the vehicle for thought and cognitive growth. Social interactionist views of foreign and second language learning have developed from this notion of talking to learn. Thornbury (1998), for example, states that the more truly conversational classroom talk becomes, the more effectively it serves as the vehicle of language learning:

> [Communicative language teaching] require[s] of teachers not so much the learning of new pedagogical skills but the accessing of the interpersonal communication skills that characterize real talk. These are skills that, curiously, teachers with no prior training often resort to, especially in small-group settings. (113)

Swain (1985) viewed self-generated learner talk (or "comprehensible output") as the necessary complement to Krashen's (1982) notion of "comprehensible input." That is, she saw that the mental formulation of the message on the part of the speaker, and the resulting act of speech itself, is as important to the development of proficiency as is comprehension. This is not simply an argument for quantity of student talk (obviously, the less teacher-fronted instruction there is, the more time there is for students to converse), but for quality as well. Long and Porter (1985) and more recently Jacob and associates (1996) have summarized research showing that task-oriented group work allows for a greater variety of speech acts (e.g., suggesting, inferring, qualifying, hypothesizing, generalizing, disagreeing) and negotiation of meaning (i.e., clarification requests, confirmation checks, comprehension checks, requests for repetition, etc.) than does teacher-fronted instruction. By engaging in a wide variety of speech acts, students are practicing a more representative sample of language behavior than is possible within the I-R-E discourse paradigm.

In summary, natural conversation carried on in a well-managed learning environment can be a powerful learning tool for language acquisition. The realization of this fact has given rise to powerful new approaches to L1 and L2 teaching and learning, including communicative language teaching (Celce-Murcia et al., 1997) and its offspring Whole Language (Heald-Taylor, 1991), cooperative learning (Brechtel, 1992; Jacob et al., 1996), and proficiency-based foreign language teaching. With their emphasis on natural language use, these pedagogies are able to unleash the social potential of the classroom by removing the teacher from stage center and allowing interdependent groups and pairs of students to work together to accomplish interesting tasks (see also Bräuer in this volume).

During the time that students are engaged in such projects, conscious attention to the linguistic features of target language may take a backseat to accomplishing the task itself. Although there are some who are concerned about the eventual outcome of this emphasis on language fluency at the expense of accuracy (Hammerly, 1991), the social interactionist school of language acquisition posits that it is at precisely these moments that students experience something approximating the natural conditions in which they learned their first language.

How can social learning be best supported in the classroom through group and paired tasks? Perhaps most important for FL and L2 teachers, what can we expect to achieve in terms of students' oral and written language proficiency through the use of social tasks? These are the questions we consider in the next two sections.

TASKS AND TALK

To address the first question, we examine here several features that are useful in understanding and categorizing tasks. Nunan (1989) defines a task as "a piece of classroom work which involves learners in comprehending, manipulating, producing or interacting in the target language, while their attention is principally focused on meaning rather than form" (10). He identifies three elements of task design: (1) the pragmatic *goal* (what students must accomplish during the task, e.g., exchanging personal information); (2)

input (i.e., the materials—handouts, pictures, etc.—used to facilitate the task); and (3) *activity* (i.e., what students are actually expected to do during the task—interview each other, for example). (For a full discussion of these elements, the reader is referred to Nunan.)

Also to be taken into consideration are *language modality* (i.e., whether the activity promotes oral or written language practice, or a combination of the two); *group configuration* (the number of students involved and their relative proficiency levels in the target language); *linguistic focus* (what formal language features the task is intended to reinforce, or whether the task is designed simply to enhance students' overall fluency); and *cognitive demand* (whether the task promotes convergent or divergent thinking, and how the input information necessary to complete the task input is apportioned among students). We will focus here on the latter three elements (see Figure 10.1)

Group configuration. Whether students are working in pairs or in small groups, the issue of their relative proficiencies in the target language must be considered. Some authors have recommended the use of heterogeneous groups (Bell, 1991; Scane, Guy, & Wenstrom, 1994). This arrangement has the advantage of bringing the class together as a diverse community of learners, rather than becoming permanently split along ability lines and the patterns of individual dominance and leadership that result. In some cases, a given task may require heterogeneous grouping, as in peer tutoring.

On the other hand, lower-proficiency students who are constantly grouped with stronger speakers may have difficulty developing the self-confidence they need to create practice opportunities for themselves. A good example of the conflicting interests encountered with mixed proficiency grouping is that of the "Talking Circle" task (Ernst, 1994). In this warm-up activity, all members of the class sit together in a circle and discuss any topic that comes to mind (e.g., sports events, movies, personal experiences, anecdotes, feelings about the course). The discussion is moderated by the instructor, who intervenes only when necessary. While the lower-level students have the advantage of being exposed to higher levels of the target language from their more proficient classmates, they may feel intimidated by a level of language they themselves cannot produce and choose to listen a lot and participate very

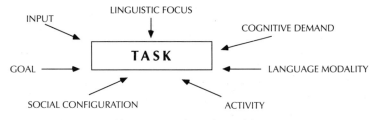

Figure 10.1. Elements of language tasks (adapted from Nunan, 1989)

little, if at all. In the end, the issue of heterogeneous versus homogeneous grouping must be considered within the context of each individual task and the linguistic benefits it is expected to produce for students.

Linguistic focus. In the task-based activities described by Nunan (1989), there is no overt focus on grammatical form. Students engage in an activity with the sole intent of completing the task. An example is the "Simulation," in which a group of students work through a problem together to reach a consensus decision. (A good example is the "Scholarship Committee," where students take the roles of the members of a scholarship granting board and must choose two winners from a pool of candidates by examining and discussing the applicants' resumes. Other similar simulations are presented in Rooks, 1994, and Shoemaker & Shoemaker, 1991). In this type of task the material is complex, and the decision-making process can be a difficult, even an emotional one. For students (especially less-proficient ones), it is extremely difficult, if not counterproductive, to try to attend simultaneously to the task at hand and, say, the correct construction of adjective clauses.

A focus on form is not out of place, however, in other tasks. If the focus is restricted to a single grammatical element, or subset of elements, and if the task is cognitively simple enough, both can be managed. The advantage in this case is that students can increase their automatic control over the grammar feature as they accomplish the task. A social activity designed to accommodate focus on a linguistic feature thus accomplishes two objectives at once: practice in both fluency and accuracy. For example, the "Talking Circle" described earlier can be adapted for use as a grammar re-enforcement task. We may refer to this activity as the "Speed-Talk Circle,"[1] a good example of a social activity designed to practice a specific linguistic element. Students are seated in two concentric circles, the inner circle facing the outer one (Figure 10.2). The inner-circle students are instructed to discuss a carefully selected topic (e.g., their activities during the previous weekend) with their

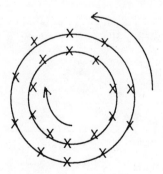

Figure 10.2. The Speed-Talk circle

partner in the outer circle, and to concentrate on a specific language form as they do so (in this case, regular and irregular past-tense verbs). In the first go-round, the inner-circle students have three minutes to relate their narrative to their opposite numbers. At that point, the inner circle students rotate one seat clockwise and repeat the same spiel with a new partner (the outer-circle students remain stationary), but this time taking only two minutes. Again, students are asked to concentrate on using the correct past-tense verbs, and examples from some of the student narratives are elicited. In the final stage, the inner-circle students move once again to their right and repeat the same information with a new partner, this time condensing the narrative into one minute. The entire procedure is then repeated with students in the outer circle, rotating in the opposite direction. (The communicative nature of the task can be further enhanced by including time for the listener in each phase to ask questions of the narrator.)

Cognitive demand. When considering whether or not to focus on linguistic items during a task, it is important for the instructor to take into account not only the difficulty of the task but also the style of thinking that it demands of the participants—that is, whether it prompts convergent or divergent thinking in the participants. Students will likely find it more taxing to keep their attention focused on grammatical items while engaging in divergent thinking activities. The "Scholarship Committee" is an example of a semidivergent task; there is no predetermined outcome, although there are a limited number of options. Students must negotiate, argue, and eventually come to a consensus. This is not an appropriate task in which to ask students to attend to discrete grammatical items, say, the use of articles with mass and count nouns.

Another divergent task, well suited to lower-level learners, involves "Designing the Bulletin Board." Groups of students work together to create a design for a classroom bulletin board, using materials provided for the task. When they have reached consensus on the overall plan, the groups gives directions to other students to set up bulletin board following their oral directions. This activity calls for extensive intragroup as well as intergroup negotiation. The task includes two different levels of cognitive complexity; the first (planning) phase is completely divergent—students can come up with any design that the materials provided allow; the second (giving directions) phase is convergent—there is only one acceptable outcome. Thus students may find it easier to attend to a specific linguistic focus during the latter task than during the former.

In fully convergent tasks, that is, those in which there is not only one predetermined outcome but also only one way to get there, it is more reasonable to ask students to focus on formal aspects of language throughout the activity. An example is Olsen's (1977) dyadic "Direction-Giving Exercise." Each student in the pair is given a street map of the same downtown area, with streets clearly named. The only difference is that different, but complementary locations (e.g., bakery, high school, hardware store) are identified on each partner's map. Students learn the location of the unknown destinations on their own maps by following street directions given by their partners. Since the task is convergent (there is only one correct location for each destination) and repetitive, it is relatively easy for students to practice a set of fixed expressions ("turn left," "go straight ahead," "it's on your right," etc.).

There is some evidence that divergent tasks are more prone to communication breakdowns within the group, but that they also yield greater learning than simpler tasks (Jacob et al., 1996). This may be due to the fact that miscommunication opens the door for students to engage in conversational repair, in which their attention is turned from grammatical accuracy to larger discourse strategies. A task for beginning-level students that takes advantage of the ambiguities of divergence is the "Family Album," in which one student presents a short, extemporaneous presentation about a family member, showing a photo of the person, if possible. The class listens, asks questions, and then breaks into small groups to review all the information collected about the person in question. During the group discussions, misinterpretations are corrected and accurate information concerning the family member in question is confirmed. If disputes within the group cannot be resolved, the group may appeal to the original student speaker. A final set of notes can form the basis of a group paragraph-writing exercise.

A similar activity involving academically sophisticated material is accomplished in the "Seminar" (Lynch, 1995), in which individual students present short talks on topics from their major fields of study, followed by a general question-and-answer session. The informational content of both these tasks is totally unpredictable, and thus the chances for misunderstanding are legion. Consequently, there is much to be gained in the discourse arena through the use of repair strategies. Students practice making requests for clarification, repetition, and confirmation as well as making speculative or hypothetical comments. In addition, they learn strategies for holding the floor and yielding it and for interrupting politely.

Another factor affecting cognitive demand in a task is how the information needed to complete the task is distributed among participants. In a *one-way task* (usually carried out in dyads), the flow of information is one-directional. One student provides all the information needed by the other to complete the task, for example, filling out an interview form on personal information. Another example of a one-way task is the "Picture Dictation" (Christison & Bossano, 1987), in which one student prepares a grid with pictures of different objects in each cell; she then communicates the items and their locations to the other student, who fills in a blank grid according to the directions. (Neither partner is allowed to see the other's grid during the task.)

In a *two-way task*, on the other hand, each member of the pair possesses different pieces of the information needed to complete a task. Partners must share and coordinate the pieces of information they have been provided in order to complete the task. An example is a variation on the picture dictation described earlier, in which each student's grid has different cells already filled in; the students' task becomes one of requesting and confirming information from each other to fill in the empty cells so that the end result is two identical grids. Again, this is all done orally; there is no visual access to each other's grid. (The familiar board game "Battleship" is an extension of the two-way task.)

In a *jigsaw activity,* pertinent information is shared among groups of students. First, all students are assigned to "expert groups" to prepare and consolidate different pieces of the information needed to complete the task. Then the experts are dispersed into mixed groups, where each member's expert information is fit together to complete the task. Jigsaws can be applied to simulations, such as the "Factory Accident" (Coelho et al., 1989), in which each group prepares the testimony of one interested party in a fatal accident on the job site (e.g., a union leader, a safety engineer working for the company, a local emergency officer, a friend of the dead worker, etc.). In the jigsaw group, representatives from each expert group meet together to determine responsibility for the accident. (The famous Japanese film "Roshamon" is a literary precursor of the classroom jigsaw.)

Each form of information distribution just described produces a different pattern of classroom discourse and a different level of cognitive difficulty. One-way tasks are simplest for students to execute but linguistically impoverished, since only one member of the pair has the opportunity to use negotiation strategies (comprehension checks, clarification requests, etc.). Two-way tasks multiply the potential for verbal negotiation. Divergent jigsaw tasks provide the most opportunities for negotiation and creative language use; they are also the most cognitively demanding for students, since there is no fixed outcome and negotiation is carried out in a group setting. Of the three distribution patterns, the jigsaw is likely to result in the most natural classroom discourse, while at the same time producing the greatest cognitive load on students.

If the instructor wishes students to practice a particular language item during the activity, convergent one- and two-way tasks may best serve the purpose. Since they are by nature repetitive and do not create a heavy cognitive demand, students are better able to monitor their target language output while at the same time completing the task. For example, in the direction-giving exercise described earlier, pairs of students have multiple opportunities to practice and refine embedded questions like "Do you know where the supermarket is?" or "Can you tell me how to get to the bakery?" Again, the language goals of the lesson should determine the type of task selected for use.

SOCIALIZING L2 LITERACY LEARNING

The preceding discussion examined social learning tasks designed primarily to develop L2/FL students' oral language proficiency. The socialization of the language classroom can also be harnessed for the benefit of students' literacy development. Language educators and researchers have long known that native speakers' reading and writing skills develop naturally from their oral knowledge of the language (see Weissberg, 2000, for a review of the social interaction school of literacy education). We place a tremendous burden on FL/L2 learners when we expect them to develop fluent reading and writing skills without giving them recourse to the linguistic support of social activity. In this section we review some of the social tasks that have been designed for use in FL/L2 reading and writing lessons.

A multitude of social opportunities are available in writing lessons. Natalie Hess (1999) has used a "Picture Discussion" technique to inject socialization into a writing lesson for ESL students. A set of provocative pictures is laid out on the floor; each student chooses one and tapes it to the wall of the classroom to form a gallery. Then students visit with each other informally about the pictures they have chosen; they are instructed to tell each other why they chose a particular picture and what it reminds them of. Finally, students write about their pictures, again focusing on how the images remind them of something in their own lives. The gallery chat serves as a kind of pre-writing stimulus for topic development and exploration.

The author has used "Group Composing" in college ESL writing courses for a similar purpose. Preparatory to writing, the class as a whole brainstorms a given topic, while the instructor acts as scribe, jotting ideas on the board as class members volunteer them. In a variation on this technique, the group as a whole composes a paragraph, which the teacher transcribes on the board. During this task, not only are students composing aloud, they are also negotiating with each other over precisely what will go up on the board next (the teacher makes minimal comments throughout this process, just sufficient to keep the group on task and to adjudicate among competing suggestions from various students). This activity is especially effective, since it allows students to interact socially for the specific purpose of producing a text in the target language.

Other group writing/reading projects are more elaborate. Hirvela (1999) has described a "Group Writing Project," in which groups of students read a text together and then plan and compose a single group response. The class as a whole responds to each group's written product, after which the small groups have an opportunity to revise their papers. Weissberg and Büker (1990) suggest an even more elaborate social activity for advanced L2 students in which teams of students jointly formulate a research question, gather background material from the library, conduct a research project, analyze the results, and finally write up the results in a joint report.

Probably the most common group task in the L2 writing classroom is the use of "Peer Response" groups, in which students read and critique each other's written products. Although there is some controversy in the L2 writing pedagogy literature as to the positive effects of peer revision on student writing (Silva, 1998), this technique does give students exposure to their classmates' writing, and individual writers receive feedback from readers other than the teacher. If nothing else, exposing student writers to peer response groups gives them an authentic audience to write for.

Even traditional grammar instruction can be given a social twist. Students can work in study groups to check answers to homework exercises or to prepare group presentations to the rest of the class on grammatical points. In a variation on a group writing technique called "Noticing" (described by Martone, 1998), students work in groups on a text provided by the instructor. Their task is to identify grammatical structures in the text that they would like the rest of the class to note. Group analysis and preparation is followed by short presentations to the class as a whole.

MAKING GROUPS WORK

Social tasks in the language classroom are not without their pitfalls. Some groups of students simply don't work well together. Bell (1991) notes that for this reason it is best not to maintain fixed group membership throughout the duration of a course. Additionally, some students are unaccustomed to group work and may view the whole enterprise as a waste of time. Such students may opt to drop out of active participation. Jacob and associates (1996) observed many "missed opportunities" for language development in the ESL groups they studied. Groups sometimes misunderstood or lost focus on the assigned task or deliberately changed a task that didn't suit them (271). They found that successful group work requires constant teacher supervision and, if necessary, intervention. As these authors note, "Cooperative learning is not a silver bullet; neither does it deserve to be one more innovation that is tossed out when it does not work" (274).

To overcome some of these difficulties, a number of practical suggestions have been made for maximizing the effectiveness of group work in language classrooms (Bell, 1991; Scane, Guy, & Wenstrom, 1994; Brechtel, 1992). Among those most commonly mentioned are:

1. Keep group membership heterogeneous in terms of target language proficiency.
2. Keep group size small, between three and seven participants.
3. Avoid fixed group membership.
4. Give group work a second chance; it may not go well the first time.
5. Give each group member a specific role in completing the task.

6. Make individual students as well as the group as a whole accountable for its outcomes.
7. Monitor groups continually to answer questions, ease them over hard spots, keep them on task, and provide native-speaker feedback on the linguistic focus of the exercise.
8. Alternate group work with pair work and whole-class instruction.

Students need training in order to get the most out of social learning activities. For this reason the first group activity to be introduced in a class should be an easy one with a quick payoff. As students become more accustomed to group tasks, more divergent, open-ended tasks can be attempted. In setting up a class's first small-group experience, it is important for the instructor to give extremely precise directions so that each group knows exactly what it must accomplish; it is also helpful to set an explicit time limit within which the task is to be completed. After several experiences, students will need few if any preliminary directions.

In the case of a highly complex task, such as peer revision in a writing class, it may be necessary to model the group process for the class before it is attempted. For example, highly practiced writing response groups can be videotaped, and the resulting tape can be used later to model the process for neophyte groups.

Just as FL and L2 students need preparation and training for group work, so often do their instructors. As noted earlier, for a variety of reasons some language teachers resist using group and pair work in their classes. Clair (1998) proposes an interesting solution to this problem: groupwork and teamwork should be a regular part of teacher training programs. The best way to train future teachers in alternative methodologies is for their own education professors to model the desired techniques in their courses, in this case by including plentiful opportunities for participation in group tasks. When FL and L2 teachers-in-training become accustomed to cooperative learning as part of their own education (and assuming they experience success with it), they are more likely to carry it over into their own classrooms.

The group-work ethic can be extended beyond teacher education programs to in-service training programs as well. Clair (1998) encourages language teachers to form cooperative study groups to deal with problems of multicultural language education in their own schools, rather than bring in outside experts to do one-shot workshops. In the results of her study she found that group participation helped build teachers' self-confidence, independence, and trust in each other's professional expertise.

Clair's findings for language teachers reflect the kind of outcomes we can expect for their learners as well. Students who participate in well-managed social tasks discover over time that they are not dependent on their instructors for the development of their FL or L2 skills. Working interdependently with their classmates, they come to rely increasingly on their own resources to solve learning problems. Thus, the socialized classroom allows them to grow into autonomous language learners and users.

NOTE

1. This activity, as well as most of those described in this chapter, is not original with me. I acknowledge the long-ago ESL instructor who first told me about it.

REFERENCES

Bell, J. (1991). *Teaching multilevel classes in ESL.* Carlsbad, CA: Dominie Press.

Brechtel, M. (1992). *Bringing the whole together: An integrated whole language approach for the multilingual classroom.* Carlsbad, CA: Dominie Press.

Celce-Murcia, M., Dornyei, Z., & Thurrell, S. (1997). Direct approaches in L2 instruction: A turning point in communicative language teaching? *TESOL Quarterly,* 31: 141–152.

Christison, M., & Bossano, S. (1987). *Look who's talking: Activities for group interaction.* Hayward, CA: Alemany Press.

Clair, N. (1998). Teacher study groups: Persistent questions in a promising approach. *TESOL Quarterly,* 32: 465–492.

Coelho, E., Winer, L., & Olsen, J. (1989). *All sides of the issue: Activities for cooperative jigsaw groups.* Hayward, CA: Alemany Press.

Ernst, G. (1994). "Talking circle": Conversation and negotiation in the ESL classroom. *TESOL Quarterly,* 28: 293–322.

Hammerly, H. (1991). *Fluency and accuracy: Toward balance in language teaching and learning.* Clevedon, U.K.: Multilingual Matters.

Heald-Taylor, G. (1991). *Whole language strategies for ESL students.* Carlsbad, CA: Dominie Press.

Hess, N. (1999). Poetry for language skills. Paper presented at 16th Rocky Mountain Region TESOL Conference, Las Cruces, NM, October 15.

Hirvela, A. (1999). Collaborative writing instruction and communities of readers and writers. *TESOL Journal,* 8: 7–12.

Jacob, E., Rottenberg, L., Patrick, S., & Wheeler, E. (1996). Cooperative learning: Context and opportunities for acquiring academic English. *TESOL Quarterly,* 30: 253–280.

Krashen, S. (1982). *Principles and practice in second language acquisition.* Oxford: Pergamon Press.

Long, M., & Porter, P. (1985). Group work, interlanguage talk, and second language acquisition. *TESOL Quarterly* 19: 207–228.

Lynch, T. (1995). The development of interactive listening strategies in second language academic setting. In D. Mendelsohn & J. Rubin (eds.), *A guide for the teaching of second language listening.* Carlsbad, CA: Dominie Press.

Martone, D. (1998). Second language students in the writing classroom: How can the writing teacher help them effectively? Workshop presentation, Conference on College Composition and Communication, Chicago, April.

Mehan, H. (1979). *Learning lessons.* Cambridge, MA: Harvard University Press.

Nunan, D. (1989). *Designing tasks for the communicative classroom.* Cambridge: Cambridge University Press.

Olsen, J. (1977). *Communication starters and other activities for the ESL classroom.* Hayward, CA: Alemany Press.

Rooks, G. (1994). *Let's start talking.* Boston: Heinle & Heinle.

Scane, J., Guy, A., & Wenstrom, L. (1994). *Think, write, share: Process writing for adult ESL and basic education students.* Carlsbad, CA: Dominie Press.

Shoemaker, C., & Shoemaker, F. (1991). *Interactive techniques for the ESL classroom.* Boston: Heinle & Heinle.

Silva, T. (1998). Second language students in the writing classroom: How can the writing teacher help them effectively? Workshop presentation, Conference on College Composition and Communication, Chicago, April.

Swain, M. (1985). Communicative competence: Some roles of comprehensible input and comprehensible output in its development. In S. Gass & C. Madden (eds.), *Input in second language acquisition.* Rowley, MA: Newbury House.

Thornbury, S. (1998). Comments on Marianne Celce-Murcia, Sotan Dornyei, and Sarah Thurrell's "Direct Approaches in L2 Instruction: A Turning Point in Communicative Language Teaching?" *TESOL Quarterly,* 32: 109–116.

Vygotsky, L. S. (1962). *Thought and language,* E. Haufmann & G. Vakar (eds. and trans.). Cambridge, MA: MIT Press.

Weissberg, R. (2000). On the interface of speech and writing: Dialog journal writing and the acquisition of syntax by adult ESL learners. In G. Bräuer (ed.), *Writing Across Languages.* Greenwich, CT: Ablex, 71–88.

Weissberg, R., & Büker, S. (1990). *Writing up research: Experimental research report writing for students of English.* Englewood Cliffs, NJ: Prentice Hall.

11

Writing Consultation for Foreign Students

Stella Büker

Since 1998 the University of Bielefeld has been working on a project entitled "PunktUm—Discipline-specific Language Training & Writing and Speech Consultation for Foreign Students."[1] As the name states, the project's two main objectives consist of oral and writing training in order to improve the discipline-specific oral and written competence of foreign students. This chapter presents the concept and experiences of a project, which in its design is unique in Germany.[2] In order to do so we pose the following question: What were the reasons that led to the establishment of this kind of support offered to foreign students? This requires a look at the specific difficulties learners from foreign countries face during their studies in any subject area. Additionally, the writing consultation is described in its inner structure and by its concrete results, but always as an integrated part of the entire project. A few examples illustrate advising strategies that point out the potential advantages of this kind of assistance. To start with, we explain the theoretical framework.

THE SITUATION OF FOREIGN STUDENTS AT THE UNIVERSITY OF BIELEFELD

Each term about 200 foreign students[3] register at the University of Bielefeld after having passed a language proficiency test. To prepare the students for this test the university offers different language courses free of charge. Depending on their level of German language knowledge, the students may take a three-, six-, or twelve-month course. In the past, this was the only help available at the university; once the students had taken up their study of a certain discipline, they would not receive any further language assistance.

The area of general information, study organization, and social integration has been covered for more than a year by a program called "Brother and Sister," which arranges tandems between foreign students who have recently registered at the university and a German peer. The International Office and the Society for the Promotion of Foreign Students schedule special consulting hours. In addition, every term there are general orientation events and cultural activities in which foreign students may participate. Within the scope of universities in Germany, the service provided for foreign students at the University of Bielefeld is about average. Only very few German universities (e.g., Hanover and Leipzig) have set up discipline-specific assistance for foreign students[4] and offer language courses on discipline-specific terminology, and, less frequently, sessions on how to improve academic working and writing techniques.

Despite the fact that students and teaching staff occasionally report severe learning problems among foreign students, it can be stated that the majority of them receive hardly any help when facing difficulties in their discipline-specific studies. Also, it is quite difficult for the individual student to organize qualified help on a private basis, since this often requires financial means most students do not possess.

The project "PunktUm—Discipline-specific Language Training & Writing and Speech For Foreign Students," established in June 1998 at the University of Bielefeld, was an answer to that situation. The project benefited from the political discussion about the inadequate internationalization of German universities. This debate helped to draw official attention to the needs of foreign students and to create an environment that may attract more learners from other countries.

DEVELOPING A CONCEPT FOR THE PROJECT

Because of the lack of established and successfully working projects of such a kind in Germany, it was quite a challenge for us to develop a concept to support foreign students during their discipline-specific studies. We had to do pioneering work and be always willing to experiment. We used a kind of trial-and-error method, in which we alternately recorded in detail the problems of our clients and then tried to apply fragments of already existing concepts as well as some of our own approaches. These early experiences provided new insights regarding the needs of our clients, which, in turn, led to the modification of our concept.

Problem Analysis

Earlier studies that investigate the problems of foreign learners in higher education largely focus on the psychosocial dimension, showing problems in social integration (especially in the academic environment), the psychological state of the individual learner, or his/her financial situation. Those studies also reveal difficulties in dealing with German authorities, with formal requirements of registration at the university and the procedures of recognition of the credit received in the respective country of origin (see Grieswelle, 1978; Skillen, 1985; Projektgruppe Ausländerstudium, 1987; Buchrucker & Meinhardt, 1991; Chen, 1996; Rosen, 1997). A majority of the studies identify a deficiency in knowledge of German as the main cause of the problems mentioned earlier. Some recent studies focus on the difficulties foreign learners face in using discipline-specific language (Ehlich, 1999). Others highlight the students' problems in academic writing and analyze, for example, whether those problems may be attributed to culturally different learning systems or culturally based text norms (Eβer, 1997).

Büker, in an empirical study (1998), investigates the complex process of writing a final thesis as a vital source of insight into a variety of problems, which many of the interviewed students perceived to be very stressful. Figure 11.1 is based on this empirical study, which has been crucial to the development of our project concept. Contrary to other studies, which reduce the problems of foreign students to either lack of linguistic knowledge or insuf-

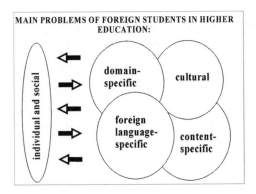

MAIN PROBLEMS OF FOREIGN STUDENTS IN HIGHER EDUCATION:

individual and social

domain-specific

cultural

foreign language-specific

content-specific

Figure 11.1.

ficient adjustment to the learning system in Germany, the concept of our project applies five interdependent levels.

The problems foreigners confront when working academically may be analyzed at five different levels: the cultural level, the domain-specific level, the level of foreign language proficiency, the content-specific level of the discipline, and the social and individual level. Problems concerning the social and personal realm differ from those of the other levels in that they may influence and add stress to the situation but do not directly affect the work process. Nevertheless, students' social and individual situations may have a positive or negative effect on their academic performance and vice versa. Problems belonging to the other four levels refer to deficiencies that may be classified as problems in study technique. The different levels may be characterized as follows.

The *content-specific level* refers to problems of content knowledge of the discipline, such as the correct understanding of a theory or an argument, the kind of methods applied in the discipline, its key literature, and so on.

Domain-specific problems occur with regard to the formal conventions of an academic field that any student, native speaker or not, has to observe in presentations, term papers, contributions to a discussion, assessment of scientific literature, and the like.

Cultural problems take into account actual or assumed differences in the concepts of academic work done in Germany and the country of origin, such as how to write a term paper, how to compose an essay, or how to deal with academic/scientific literature.

Problems caused by improper use of discipline-specific foreign language belong to the level of *foreign language* deficiency. Difficulties may range from specific (e.g., use of tenses, sentence structure, word formation) to general questions and individual insecurities (e.g., "I have difficulties understanding a text in the foreign language." "Does my German really express what I mean?" "I have problems distinguishing colloquial from academic language."). Problems on this level often coincide with problems on the domain-specific level, as evident in questions like how to give a presentation when the student does not have adequate foreign language skills or how to deal with foreign language literature one does not understand sufficiently.

Social and personal/individual difficulties like loneliness, illness, or financial pressure may be additional obstacles to successful academic work and should not be neglected when diagnosing a student's situation.

Foreign students face a variety of difficulties, on different levels. According to Büker (1998), the complexity of the problems is usually hidden to the foreign student. The person is often aware of a linguistic difficulty, but not that the problem may also be present on a social, domain-specific, cultural, or content-specific level. The levels mark different areas that have to be dealt with separately in the beginning to provide assistance successfully.

The Concept

Our project focused on issues that belong to the domain-specific, cultural, and foreign language competence levels. The content-specific level was omitted, for two reasons: First, its inclusion would require the advisors to be expert in the respective disciplines of the students seeking help. Second, academic performance is assessed in regard to content according to the instructors' discipline-specific criteria. Problems on this level have to be identified accordingly and solved with the help of the respective faculty. This way, dialogue between teachers and students is not replaced by our service, but enhanced.

Our project, based on fundamental criteria of academic work valid for all departments, aims to provide general assistance. Specifics of the various disciplines are integrated to the extent necessary to solve problems on a general level. Moreover, if social and personal problems are diagnosed that constrain the academic performance of a student, he or she is referred to psychological counseling. Figure 11.2 shows the different components and structures of the project.

The general orientation of the project did not require an affiliation with a specific discipline. Nevertheless, there were two good reasons to connect the project to the Department of German as a Foreign/Second Language: The content of the work closely corresponds to the department's effort, and most of the advisors are part of the department. Furthermore, it was important to provide a protective setting to our clients. If foreign students decide to talk about their difficulties, one has to ensure that there is no control or even influence from the student's own department.

The content of the project covers the whole range of academic writing (term papers, final theses, written tests and exams, protocols), oral performance

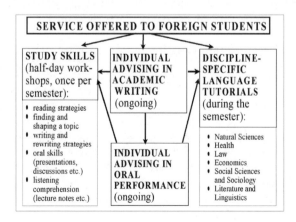

Figure 11.2.

(presentation, oral tests, discussion skills), and the improvement of discipline-specific language competence. Assistance for the latter explicitly meets the needs of the respective departments, that is, natural sciences, health, law, economics, social sciences and sociology, and literature and linguistics.

The cross-disciplinary assistance in academic writing and oral performance is frequently confronted with domain-specific and cultural problems. Advising starts with the process of academic work and helps with the conventions that have to be observed when further developing an academic product, as well as teaching the working techniques that enable the students to fulfill their assignments efficiently. Advising a student *during* the process of her or his academic work ensures proper timing: Problems are detected and solved in the order and at the moment they surface and not at a time when work has been concluded.

Assistance is given in the form of individual advising. In developing the consultation for foreign students, we were able to draw on the concept of the Writing Lab, which has been in place at the University of Bielefeld since 1993. The Writing Lab is open to all students and faculty regardless of the department they study or teach in. The lab advises all who want to learn about or teach academic writing. However, the Writing Lab will not assist foreign students, whose problems due to discipline-specific foreign language deficiencies are often too complex. The success of the service offered by the Writing Lab to native speakers inspired us to create a similar assistance to foreign students. In order to achieve a concept that would also work on the language and the cultural level, we extended and modified the existing Writing Lab concept. In addition to individual advising, we offer half-day workshop modules on academic writing and speech for students who wish to know more about specific problem areas. Workshop participants can exchange experiences and improve their problem awareness.

In general, discipline-specific language is taught in tutorials during the semester, but problems due to individual language deficiencies can also become part of personalized advising. Students who feel further need or desire to improve their discipline-specific language competence may also participate in one of the tutorials offered by their respective departments.

Theoretical Framework

As mentioned earlier, there was no existing practical and theoretical concept that we could apply directly to our project. Therefore, we had to take bits and pieces from other concepts and modify and rearrange them to something new. The theoretical framework reflects this inasmuch as the design of the special project services varies depending on the consultation needs, offering writing consultation, oral performance advising, and tutorials in the language of a discipline. The framework we used for the writing consultation has been drawn from writing process research, writing pedagogy, and contrastive linguistics.

The writing process research important to us includes various cognitive writing process models (see Hayes & Flower, 1980; Bereiter & Scardamalia, 1987; for foreign language writing, see Krings, 1989; Börner, 1987) with the common notion that academic writing is an extremely complex task. This complexity becomes particularly clear when the process is broken down into its various stages, in order to illustrate the different cognitive demands placed on the writer. This knowledge has been put into practice in writing pedagogy (see Kruse, 1993; Ruhmann, 1995, 1996), which makes it possible and necessary to advise *during* the actual writing process, that is, to break down the complexity of the process in order to make occurring problems more visible and manageable. Tasks like gener- ating ideas, planning a text, and structuring a text should not be dealt with simultaneously, but rather in succession. This approach introduces the writing process as the main aspect influencing the outcome of any product, thus adding another perspective to the writing consultation, besides ana- lyzing text criteria and the teaching of the same. Studies in contrastive linguistics regarding the conventions of academic texts within specific academic cultures contribute to the analysis of our clients' difficulties in a more comprehensive way (see, e.g., Clyne, 1987; Anderson, 1990; Eβer, 1997). So far, the teaching of academic writing in German as a foreign language has developed very few didactic approaches worth mentioning, which are process-oriented.

METHODS AND APPLICATIONS

The Writing Consultation offers office hours for foreign students three times per week. The students explain their problems; advisors get a first impression of the situation, inform the client about the project services (workshops on learning techniques, tutorials in the language of the discipline, individual advising sessions); and finally, client and advisor decide together on an action plan. If there is a need for individual advising, a separate appointment will be arranged.

The individual advising session usually takes one hour. While the client describes his or her problems, the advisor will ask further questions for the purpose of locating the levels at which problems appear during the process of academic work. The next step is to identify what exactly causes the problems. The advisor has to look at two levels: First, is the problem one that has to be solved elsewhere (psychological counseling, faculty of specific discipline). Second, when and in what sequence do the problems occur? If there is a problem at the beginning of the process (such as literature that has not been understood, putting constraints on the writing process), all remaining tasks will be affected by the initial problem. In this case, it is not the writing process itself but the assessment of literature that should be addressed first. Persistent constraints in the writing process after the initial problem is solved may be diagnosed in further consulting sessions.

Often the initial reason that foreign students contact the Writing Consultation is a language problem that hinders the process of academic work as a whole. Not having understood their readings, students either do not write at all or are in desperate need of feedback about the quality of their text. In a few cases, the opposite holds true: There are no language deficiencies, but content-specific problems instead. Furthermore, a majority of students mention social and individual/personal problems, communication and social contact being the most common of these. They complain about feelings of isolation and loneliness at the university and feelings of insecurity and anxiety when interacting with faculty.

Usually, the first session reveals that the problem initially described by the student is not the only one and not even the most urgent, as the following example shows. This example also gives an idea of the inner dynamics between student and advisor in the process of shaping the diagnosis of the problem.

A Korean student visits the Writing Consultation during her second term because she has experienced problems writing her term paper in German Literature. She explains that this is her first term paper and that she does not know how to work with quotations. First, the assignment specifics (deadlines, stage of the work, name of the professor) were taken down. Nothing unusual was noted, and therefore the advisor proceeded to diagnose the student's problem.

A variety of causes may have led to the student's problem of not being able to write the paper:

- She did not understand the texts (content-specific and/or foreign language deficiencies).
- Her chapter lacks a clear structure.
- She does not know the formal conventions of academic writing, such as how to work with quotations (cultural context).
- She is not sure about the relevant information (did she gather the information necessary to solve the task?).
- She did not systematically evaluate the literature she read and therefore is not able to write about it.
- She has a writing block—the problem might be located on the psychological level.
- She has not worked out a clear research question for her paper.

The following conversation revealed that the student had simply taken the course title for her paper without actually designing her own project. She did not know that she had to choose her own research topic and to work out a research question, based on which she then would develop a work strategy. During her studies back home she mostly wrote tests and summaries. In the light of this experience she had tried to apply familiar working techniques and conventions of her native culture to academic performance in Germany. Even though she wanted to write up a summary of the texts she had read, she could not find a structure that allowed her to connect the different readings.

During the advising session the student was told why the elaboration of a research question was the first step toward a solution of her problem. The student was quite astonished to learn about the German way of academic work. Now she realized the meaning of her teacher's remarks when she consulted him earlier. She explained that during their meeting she was ashamed to ask about what she hadn't understood. At the end of this first consultation, the advisor told the student to select a research topic, work out a research question, and decide what literature she wants to use.

During the next three sessions the student further developed her research question, which then was reconfirmed with her professor. This unusually long period of consultation was due to the highly demanding topic the student had chosen. The advisor pointed out that the overall degree of difficulty of her paper was creating another problem, a fact the student had not been aware of before. She had assumed that the chosen level was the expected standard. Both advisor and student came to the conclusion that she would have to work extremely hard to reach her own expectation and that it could become difficult to meet the assignment deadline. Despite hard work, the result would probably still be only average. Taking this into account, advisor and student came to the mutual conclusion that it might be more rewarding to write her first term paper in a different course, one closer to her current level of linguistic ability. Nevertheless, the student preferred to go ahead with the original topic and course. However, she now realized that her problems resulted from the degree of difficulty of the research topic and had nothing to do with her intellectual ability. Furthermore, she was able to understand that an average grade received for her work would mean, in her situation as a nonnative speaker, that she had done very well.

The next problem analyzed during consultation was that the student did not understand the texts, because of the extreme difficulty of the research topic and a discipline-specific language deficiency. She also did not have any strategies for reading comprehension and assessment of the text. The advisor introduced different working techniques and respective exercises. Further difficulties included the development of the main argument (structuring exercises were done) and the conventions used in her discipline for citing sources.

Finally, when the first draft was completed, the student received feedback from her advisor. While she had done well with regard to the structure of the chapter, there were deficiencies in her attempt to improve the draft that originated from our advising session. Furthermore, it became evident that the student had quoted extensively from texts without marking those passages. When asked, she explained that she simply had not been able to understand the text and therefore had tried to stick as closely to the original as possible. There were also problems with syntax, morphology, and semantics. With the deadline approaching, there was little time for a final review of the paper. When the paper was turned in, a total of twelve individual advising sessions had taken place. Later the student informed the advisor that the paper had been graded with a C.

This is an example of how the Writing Consultation works: diagnosing the problems, separating them into consecutive stages, and working on them one after the other. Furthermore, it gives an idea of the kind of problems that actually complicate the process of academic writing in a foreign language. They are typical not only of nonnative speakers but also of the majority of mother-tongue students. The example also shows the efficacy of the writing counseling. Without this kind of assistance the student most likely would not have been able to finish her term paper.

The conceptual work on the improvement of the Writing Consultation consists of the following aspects: There is a great need for new exercises that can be used during the advising sessions. Since there is a general lack of satisfactory sources, we have to develop most of the exercises ourselves.

Nevertheless, the major problems we face are those involving discipline-specific foreign language competence and textual feedback. The Writing Consultation works on both cross-disciplinary and general academic levels. If students are confronted with second language problems, the advising has to take as a starting point the area of general academic language. Discipline-specific language skills have to be acquired somewhere else, which may prove difficult for students.

We are trying to work out solutions for the latter problem as well as for those in the area of effective writing feedback. These activities take up almost 50 percent of the time of the Writing Consultation. The insights gained from exemplary feedback usually enable native speakers to independently review future writings. The situation of nonnative speakers is different: Foreign language problems often do not allow for independent reviewing. We are also trying to solve problems in this area.

"WRITING CONSULTATION"
INTERVENTION FORM

I conclude with a summary of the successes and difficulties we experienced in working with the intervention form "Writing Consultation," which has the objective of improving the discipline-specific language and writing competence of foreign students.

The preceding example shows that individual advising is an effective way to diagnose the complex problems of foreign students in the process of their academic writing. I doubt that most students are able to gain this kind of insight into the multilayered difficulties without individual advising. These insights, however, are necessary in order to solve the problems step by step.

Moreover, individual advising provides a protected setting: There is no control as to discipline-specific performance. This favors a special student-advisor relationship based on confidence, which has to be considered highly important for two reasons: First of all, students will talk openly about their difficulties, which has to be understood as a great relief for them. Students are generally happy to hear that many of their peers face similar problems. Second, because of the insight gained during the individual advising session, assistance is designed to meet the specific needs of the client.

Individual advising sessions always start with the most urgent problem, that is, the students are always "met where they are," whereas workshops often deal with issues that do not address the most pressing needs of individual participants. Compared to the workshop, the student in a consultation is actively involved in gaining the insight necessary to solve his or her problems. An intervention in the form of individual advising sessions also saves time and increases efficiency by avoiding misunderstandings and inadequate challenge. All this is confirmed through our experience, which has shown that individual advising encourages students to use this service and to actively confront their problems. The fact that only a few students missed appointed sessions (in contrast to the high average of cancelled workshop participation) speaks in favor of the program. The bigger commitment resulting from the intensity of the student-advisor relationship may account for that. The high degree of organizational flexibility also has a positive effect: A session may take place when needed, in situations of acute crises, and at short intervals. The students will be accompanied during the process of academic work according to their needs.

Only a few negative experiences, compared to the long list of positive effects, resulted from the individual advising provided by the Writing Consultation. They are not fundamental criticisms of the Writing Consultation itself, but indicate weak aspects that have to be resolved or at least limited in the near future. Individual advising of foreign students implies a high work input on the part of the advisors; therefore, the costs are higher compared to workshop-based assistance. Another drawback is that the one-on-one consultation does not foster contact between students. We try to meet these disadvantages by offering additional events that allow students to communicate and share, which at the same time helps to reduce the costs of the project. When it becomes clear that certain problems can be solved in workshops, we urge the student to continue there. This means that individual advising sessions will be held only when considered absolutely necessary.

NOTES

1. In this chapter the term "foreign students" includes all students of foreign descent, not only those with a foreign passport and/or German as their second language.

2. It was not until the winter term of 1999/2000 that Sprechberatung/Speech Tutoring was introduced as a modified offering of the project. Because of its short time of operation and the few experiences gathered, the area of speech tutoring has not been included in this chapter.

3. Approximately 1,500 of the ca. 20,000 students at the University of Bielefeld are students from other countries.

4. The results refer to Internet research dated July 1999.

REFERENCES

Anderson, L. (1990). Learning to write in L2 in institutional contexts. In R. Duda & P. Riley (ed.), *Learning Styles,* pp.135–154. European Cultural Foundation. Proceedings of the First European Seminar. Nancy, 26–29 April, 1987. Nancy: Presses Universitaires de Nancy.

Bereiter, C., & Scardamalia, M. (1987). *The psychology of written composition.* Hillsdale, NJ: Erlbaum.

Börner, W. (1987). Schreiben im Fremdsprachenunterricht: Überlegungen zu einem Modell. In W. Lörscher & R. Schulze (eds.), *Perspectives in Language in Performance,* pp. 1336–1349. Tübingen: Narr Verlag.

Buchrucker, J., & Meinhardt, R. (eds.). (1991). *Studium und Rückkehr: Probleme und Erfahrungen ausländischer Studierender in der Bundesrepublik.* Frankfurt a.M.: Verlag für Interkulturelle Kommunikation.

Büker, S. (1998). *Wissenschaftliches Arbeiten und Schreiben in der Fremdsprache Deutsch. Eine empirische Studie zu den Problem-Lösungsstrategien ausländischer Studierender.* Baltmannsweiler: Schneider Verlag Hohengehren.

Chen, Y.-S. (1996). *Ausländische Studierende in der BRD: Anpassung fernostasiatischer Studierender an das Leben in Deutschland.* Münster, NY: Waxmann.

Clyne, M. G. (1987). Discourse structures and discourse expectations: Implications for Anglo-German academic communication in English. In L. E. Smith (ed.), *Discourse across cultures: Stategies in World Englishes,* pp. 73–84. New York: Prentice-Hall.

Ehlich, K. (1999). *Alltägliche Wissenschaftssprache.* Info DaF. 26(1): 3–23.

Eβer, R. (1997). "Etwas ist mir geheim geblieben am deutschen Referat." *Kulturelle Geprägtheit wissenschaftlicher Textproduktion und ihre Konsequenzen für den universitären Unterricht von Deutsch als Fremdsprache.* München: iudicium Verlag.

Grieswelle, D. (1978). *Studenten aus Entwicklungsländern: Eine Pilot-Studie,* Vol. 1. München: Minerva Publikation. Beiträge des Instituts für Soziologie.

Hayes, J. R., & Flower, L. (1980). Identifying the organization of writing processes. In L. W. Gregg & E. R. Steinberg (eds.), *Cognitive Processes in Writing,* pp. 4–30. Hillsdale, NJ: Erlbaum.

Krings, H. P. (1989). Schreiben in der Fremdsprache - Prozeßanalysen zum "vierten skill." In G. Antos & H. P. Krings (eds.), *Textproduktion: Ein interdisziplinärer Forschungsüberblick,* pp. 377–436. Tübingen: Niemeyer.

Kruse, O. (1993). *Keine Angst vor dem leeren Blatt: Ohne Schreibblockaden durchs Studium,* 3rd edition. Frankfurt a. M.: Campus.

Projektgruppe Ausländerstudium (Bockhorni, R., Ferdowsi, M. A., Schädle, W.,
    Steinitz, R., unter der wissenschaftlicher Leitung von Opitz, P. J.). (1987).
    Ausländerstudium in der Bundesrepublik Deutschland. 2. revised edition. Baden-
    Baden: Nomos Verlagsgesellschaft.
Rosen, R. (1997). *Leben in zwei Welten: Migrantinnen und Studium.* Frankfurt a.M.:
    IKO-Verlag für Interkulturelle Kommunikation.
Ruhmann, G. (1995). Schreibprobleme - Schreibberatung. In J. Baurmann & R.
    Weingarten (eds.), *Schreiben: Prozesse, Prozeduren und Produkte,* pp. 85–106.
    Opladen: Westdeutscher Verlag.
Ruhmann, G. (1996). Exkurs: Schreibblockaden und wie man sie überwindet. In K. D.
    Bünting, A. Bitterlich, & U. Pospiech (eds.), *Schreiben im Studium*, pp. 108–119.
    Berlin: Cornelsen Verlag.
Skillen, J.-A. (1985). Psychosoziale Probleme ausländischer Studenten: Interventions-
    möglichkeiten innerhalb einer zentralen Studienberatungsstelle. *Zeitschrift für
    Theorie und Praxis der Studien- und Studentenberatung,* 1(2): 27–36.

12

Language Learning Centers

Bridging the Gap Between High School and College

Gerd Bräuer

INTRODUCTION

Since the appearance of audiolingual methodology (Omaggio Hadley, 1993), language laboratories are well known in FL and L2 education in this country. Despite of their undoubted contribution to the development of language teaching and learning, the term "lab" nowadays also triggers memories about a place where students disappear behind technology, separated from each other, delving head first into the electronic environment and fighting a lone battle with linguistic requests from mysterious authorities. In this article I want to introduce the Language Learning Center (LLC), which at first glance, with respect to its name, might appear similar but actually embodies a great difference from the conventional laboratory model.

Let me first explain what an LLC is and what purpose I see in its existence. I then introduce its physical appearance and further define specific goals for the learning behind the different activities. Based on those more practical aspects, I then briefly outline the theoretical framework of the LLC model and conclude with an example of how to use such a place for language learning that can help bridge the gap often found between high school and college.

THE LLC: WHAT FOR?

Two questions seem vital in current foreign language education: (1) How to motivate high school students in a growing anglophone world to learn a foreign language and to continue learning it in college, and (2) how to instill a quest for learning beyond formal fulfillment of requirements and for lifelong language use and continuing improvement, even outside institutionalized education?

As the larger context, I see two general problems in foreign language education. First is the separation of languages in school curricula. Acquiring a new language can cause many novice learners, who might possibly spend years at this level, to suddenly feel as if they don't know anything. It seems as if they have to learn not only how to speak, read, write, and listen but also how to think. In their eyes, they don't even know how to learn, although they have conceptional knowledge about all those aspects in their first language. Unfortunately, not enough conscious use is made of this prior knowledge in traditional foreign language learning settings (see Collins in this volume).

The second general problem in current foreign language education is the lack of visibility of learning, and I mean *visibility* here also in a literal sense. The pressing need for knowledge about foreign languages and cultures in today's world is not experienced urgently enough, nor what language learning actually means and how its complexity can be dealt with (process visibility), nor the results of the learners' effort (product visibility).

Let me propose here that the High School Language Learning Center model provides possible answers to the questions cited earlier and suggests solutions to the problems just indicated.

The main purpose of the LLC lies in bridging the gap between high school and college, pulling strings tight between the different phases of a learner's biography and thereby creating long-term motivation for learning beyond the demands of individual institutions. Putting this into action calls for interactive connections among aspects that have traditionally been seen as separate:

- Team-teaching: coordination of content and methods
- Collaborative learning: projects between students
- High school tutoring: the college foreign language major's internship

- Training of teaching assistants: through high school and college faculty
- Theory goes practical: the teacher-researcher exchange
- Expanding the growing internationalization at the college toward high school: high school joins international events at the college
- Community outreach: international book fairs and writing contests organized jointly by high school and college

From this list of aspects, the LLC model is seen to be about *connecting* people or, more precisely, about *networking* among language practitioners—teachers and students, at both the high school and the college level.

As a result, the LLC seems to be an ideal place for numerous ways to *make language education visible* through purposeful practice. Creating individualized meaning for the effort spent often produces both a strong motivation for learning in general and, more specifically, a strong desire for acquiring a new language. This positive effect is boosted by *the existence of different languages* in such a facility. In a multilingual and multicultural environment, the opportunities for language education in its fullest complexity are plentiful, and they include strategic learning toward becoming an independent and lifelong language practitioner. Here, knowledge is not presented by teachers as a stumbling block for students on their way to a desired grade, it rather emerges from collaborative problem-solving done for the sake of continuing with the next task: learning to be a better language tandem partner, a college student tutor in high school, for example, or a more efficient member of a research project group.

WHAT DOES AN LLC LOOK LIKE?

Generally speaking, an LLC is a place where people share an effort to promote language learning, foreign languages as well as English. The underlying goal is to create and use a learning environment that stimulates language acquisition in a natural yet purposeful way. I can picture John Dewey's slogan "learning by doing" displayed over the entrance of such a facility.

Let's have a look at the physical appearance of the center as an important addition to other existing learning environments:

Furniture

- small and large tables for individual and group work (social aspect)
- a couch, a few armchairs grouped around a coffee table (inviting, casual character)
- shelves with books, magazines, and newspapers in English and foreign languages (comparative aspect)

- a few portable flip charts (spontaneity)
- exhibit boards featuring students' work (exemplary aspect, goal-oriented)

Manual Equipment

- manual printing sets of different kinds (kinesthetic aspect)
- a few typewriters (acoustic aspect)
- art supply (visual aspect)
- a large collection of artifacts from different cultures (tactile aspect)

Electronic Equipment

- overhead and slide projectors (presenting)
- TV and video camera (documenting)
- computers with Internet access and language learning software (connecting)
- printer and scanner (making visible)

As the list of fixtures suggests, the LLC invites discovery through the senses and the intellect and encourages lively exchange. Here, *experiencing* language and *experimenting* with language, *constructing* and *reconstructing* knowledge, are in the forefront compared to other learning environments where presenting and processing knowledge are predominant. Speaking with Gerald Graff (1992), in the LCC I see *conflicts* taught—and the process of finding possible solutions. As a result, insights are closely linked to the learner's personal experience. He or she has engraved meaning into the knowledge produced, something that has been determined by educators to be longer lasting than firm know-how handed down just to be swallowed.

WHICH GOALS ARE PURSUED WITH AN LLC?

Even though the aforementioned function of the center already indicates a certain type of learning, I want to further outline its specific goals for language education. The following overview of aspects the LLC is aiming for should be read with the previous list of furniture and equipment in mind as an invitation to envisioning ways to put those goals into practice:

The general goal is *whole language learning* (Halliday, 1978; Newman, 1985; Heald-Taylor, 1991), including the promotion of:

- naturally connecting reading, writing, speaking, and listening
- experiencing and producing language in a variety of different forms and formats (from reading a newspaper to videotaping)
- improving understanding of the *other* (cross-cultural experience)

- experiencing languages across the curriculum (problem-based projects)
- self-responsibility for learning (determination of what and how I want to learn)
- collaborative skills
- the study of languages beyond the classroom
- the preparation for lifelong (language) learning

WHAT IS TO DO THERE?

Based on the goals and the material provided, I envision students working on the following projects and activities. One disclaimer, though, needs to be spelled out clearly: Not everything will be possible at once and in any school. What can be accomplished has to be determined carefully, according to the prerequisites of each individual site:

- Internet projects (pen pals)
- International school newspaper
- Research and art projects
- Creative writing workshops
- Exhibits
- International coffee hours
- Printing (posters, books), book binding
- Literary readings
- Drama workshops
- International book fairs for the community
- Writing contests with other schools

THEORETICAL FRAMEWORK

Let me briefly identify the conceptual roots and the groundwork of the Language Learning Center model. They lie, as indicated by my earlier reference to John Dewey, in aspects of experiential pedagogy (Dewey, 1938). Others lead back to European reform pedagogy, where the so-called *Lernwerkstätten* (learning workshops) as places for project-based discovery learning were inspired and to which initiatives such as the New Math and Science movement in the United States have strong ties. Here, specifically in regard to the reflective aspect (diaries, learning logs, portfolios) of a learning approach that swings between theory and practice, Jean Piaget's model of cognitive development (1970), with learning through assimilation of (concrete) experiences into existing (abstract) concepts as its centerpiece, certainly comes into play.

Other conceptual roots can be recognized by looking at the center's peer-work (see also Weissberg in this volume) and tutoring (see also Büker in this volume), collaborative group effort (Brooke, Mirtz, & Evans, 1994) and facilitating (Branscombe, Goswami, & Schwartz, 1992) as coming from writing pedagogy, and the promotion of the process and product liaison as leading to the theoretical framework of composition studies (Perl, 1994). The variety of learning stimuli certainly resembles aspects of Howard Gardner's multiple intelligences approach (1993) and Stephen Pinker's theory of language instinct (1994), motivating different types of learners in the development of individual learning styles as a continuing interplay between the intellectual and the emotional resources of the student (Goleman, 1995).

The matrix of all this is David A. Kolb's learning circle (Kolb, 1984, p. 42) making dynamic connections among active experimentation, concrete experience, reflective observation, and abstract conceptualization. If I had to characterize the activities going on in an LLC with a single word, I would choose *discovery* and further define the term with Stephen Fishman as something that is "not a logical, orderly process, nor primarily a cognitive one, but is, in important ways, emotional: a unifying passion bringing together previously disparate experiences to yield personal reconstruction" (Fishman, 1998, p. 8).

PRACTICAL ASPECTS

Although I cannot yet refer to an LLC in place as a permanent institution, I want to provide a practical example for the concept of holistic learning, based on my previous collaboration with high schools. With this example I want to point out *in action* the potential of the center's theory-practice learning approach for language acquisition.

I teach a semester-long course in which my third-year college students produce a play in German for public performance. The play selection is done in collaboration with the German teachers of the local high schools. While we prepare the production, high school students read and discuss the play in class. A list follows of small-group projects high school students have done in collaboration with the college play production. I slightly revised the tasks in the light of the LLC model.

1. Build a model of the stage setting that will be used for the production of the theater play at the college. The model will be on display in the LLC until the play performance.
2. Interview the college student actors about their roles and, based on that and your knowledge of the script, write descriptions of the characters of the play. Suggest to the college class, with the help of drawings or collages (etc.), costumes and props for the characters.
3. Meet with college students for rehearsal sessions to support their efforts, and check on their script knowledge, pronunciation, and acting. Give

oral feedback during rehearsal, and write a summarizing comment for the college student afterward.

4. Based on your work on stage setting, character development, and costumes/props, set up an exhibit about the play and its production in order to prepare other high school students to join the performance at the college.

5. Write individual reviews about the performance and, based on those, organize a post-performance discussion with the cast in the LLC.

These projects have proven to boost the students' motivation to get involved personally, mainly because of deeply meaningful language use and its high visibility, but also due to the additional spark of collaborating with a very different group of learners, representing either (the high school as) a place where people came from and still can identify/sympathize with or (the college as) a place where many (high school) students aspire to be in the near future. In this regard, projects involving an LLC can help keep the goals of both levels of education in perspective and maintain continuing feedback—from peer, tutor, and teacher—about quality performance.

The advantage of work done under the roof of an LLC is also noticeable on the instructor's side, in both high school and college. A situation that is somewhat similar to team-teaching, the essential coordination of content and methods creates a number of moments where both parties (student and teacher) benefit from each other's expertise, individual reflection, and feedback.

Last, but not least, projects in collaboration between high school and college also reinforce community outreach—the performance of the play mentioned earlier always attracts high school and college-related audiences—making visible that bridging the gap between the two levels of education needs the effort and support of many.

REFERENCES

Branscombe, A. N., Goswami, D., & Schwartz, J. (eds.). (1992). *Students teaching, teachers learning.* Portsmouth, NH: Boynton/Cook.

Brooke, R., Mirtz, R., & Evans, R. (1994). *Small groups in writing workshops: Invitations to a writer's life.* Urbana, IL: National Council of Teachers of English (NCTE).

Dewey, J. (1963/1938). *Art as experience.* New York: G. P. Putnam's Sons.

Fishman, S. (1998). *John Dewey and the challenge of classroom practice.* New York: Teachers College Press.

Gardner, H. (1993). *Frames of mind.* New York: Basic Books.

Goleman, D. (1995). *Emotional intelligence.* New York: Bantam Books.

Graff, G. (1992). *Beyond the cultural wars: How teaching the conflicts can revitalize American education.* New York: Norton.

Halliday, M. (1978). *Language as social semiotic: The social interpretation of language and meaning.* Baltimore: University Park Press.

Heald-Taylor, G. (1991). *Whole language strategies for ESL students.* Carlsbad, CA: Dominie Press.

Kolb, D. A. (1984). *Experiential learning: Experience as the source of learning and development.* Englewood Cliffs, NJ: Prentice-Hall.

Newman, J. M. (ed.). (1985). *Whole language: Theory in use.* Portsmouth, NH: Heinemann.

Omaggio Hadley, A. C. (1993). *Teaching language in context*, 2nd edition. Boston: Heinle.

Perl, Sondra (ed.). (1994). *Landmark essays on writing process.* Davis, CA: Hermagoras Press.

Piaget, J. (1970). *Science of education and the psychology of the child*, translated by Derek Coltman. New York: Orion Press.

Pinker, S. (1994). *The language instinct.* New York: HarperCollins.

IV

Preparing the Future of Language Education

13

Foreign Language Teacher Education Through Immersion

Workable Practices in Action

Tony Erben

INTRODUCTION

The greatest change that has affected LOTE[1] education in Australia in the last decade has been the priority given to foreign language learning (Lo Bianco, 1987), the importance given to attaining second language proficiency (Leal, 1991), and most of all, the push by state governments to bring foreign language learning into the forefront of mainstream education (Braddy, 1991). Many schools and school systems have independently seized hold of the new ideas and demands brought about by recent changes in LOTE education and have adapted these to their local environments (Di Biase & Dyson, 1988). LOTE teachers are increasingly obliged to teach in non–teacher-centered LOTE programs and acquire specialist skills to operate successfully in these new teaching environments (Erben, 1998). Teaching through immersion is one such environment that is increasingly gaining acceptance in Australian school systems.

Unfortunately, pre-service LOTE teacher education institutions have tended to lag behind their primary and secondary counterparts in establishing innovative LOTE pre-service programs to equip future LOTE teachers with the necessary skills, knowledge, and proficiency to operate in the various LOTE programs now extant and to adapt to the changing demands in the profession (Leal, 1991; see also Schleppegrell in this volume).

This chapter outlines how a teacher education degree program delivered through Japanese immersion to English native-speaking students at Central Queensland University (CQU) in Australia has capitalized on the pedagogical attributes/qualities inherent within an immersion approach to facilitate the professional development of student teachers. Specific potentials for the foreign language curriculum are subsequently discussed.

Theoretical Underpinnings of Immersion Education

Theoretical considerations underpinning immersion education draw on a wide range of disciplines including (though not in order of importance) anthropology, education, psychology, sociology, and linguistics, which in turn incorporates the fields of neurolinguistics, psycholinguistics, sociolinguistics, and second language acquisition. Paulston (1992, p. 146) remarks that by drawing on such a diverse array of disciplines, research into bilingual education (and thus immersion education) leaves itself open to the conceptual and theoretical problems of research in those disciplines. While there is no denying that the accepted theoretical tenets of immersion education have been subject to criticism (for a summary see Baker, 1993), these tenets continue to offer immersion teachers, school administrators, and parents a plausible and justifiable explanation for the overall success of immersion education.

In the next section, the Central Queensland University (CQU) concept of immersion is defined from a much broader theoretical perspective. The aim is to justify the construction of a conceptual framework providing a more appropriate means to understand the effectiveness and attributes of immersion education and how these are operationalized through a series of workplace education practicums.

TOWARD A REDEFINITION OF IMMERSION

In order to better appreciate the effectiveness of immersion under various educational conditions, it is necessary to understand the nature of immersion. The interpretation of immersion provided in the literature has been given a largely linguistic and/or sociolinguistic bias. These perspectives are considered inadequate. In order to reconceptualize the meaning of immersion and to identify the attributes of immersion programs, one needs to appeal to the idea of complexity, context, and the conditions of immersion delivery, as reflected in Baker (1993), who states: "A recipe for success is unlikely to result from one ingredient. A great variety of factors act and interact to determine whether bilingual education is successful or not. . . . It makes more sense to consider the wider variety of conditions" (Baker, 1993, p. 172), and, "There is difficulty in pinpointing the crucial interacting factors that create an effective immersion experience" (Baker, 1993, p. 176).

Bartlett and Erben (1995) unraveled some of this complexity in a study centering on a university teacher education program through immersion (Baker, 1993), in which up to 80 percent of the curriculum is delivered through the medium of a second language (Japanese). As Harley and associates (1990, p. 58) point out, "It is important to emphasize that the pedagogic orientation of classrooms is not determined by any one feature, but by a cluster of interrelated features." These initial investigations indicated that through the direct and indirect incorporation of explicitly "Japanese" elements into lessons, that is, "life practices which exist in a variety of spaces and ways of behaving," students were being *immersed* in a system of beliefs, meanings, actions, and multiple identifications that inextricably allowed them to extend their perception of culture beyond a notion of their own ethnicity. They were exposed to more powerful and complex ideas of ideology, social formation, and representation. By being immersed in an environment of specifically "Japanese" knowledge, the immersion student teachers engaged with their learning through an array of cultural experiences.

THE MULTIDIMENSIONAL ATTRIBUTES OF IMMERSION AND THE PROBLEMATIC OF TERMINOLOGY

If immersion is to be accepted for the multidimensional phenomenon that it is, can one then divorce language from its cultural, contextual, and/or knowledge-assigned dependency? If one can't, then when using such terms as "partial-" or "full-immersion" in connection with language alone (as happens in the literature), the role played by the other attributes/qualities of immersion are unduly marginalized. Similarly, if the use of the term "partial" implies a definition based on language delivery time, then does that mean that when curriculum delivery through the second language stops, immersion stops occurring? The Bartlett and Erben study showed that immersion takes place in an immersion program even when the language of delivery is not the second language. Consequently, Bartlett and Erben advocate a concept of immersion based on the widest possible interpretation.

In another case in point, is there a need to elaborate the meaning of the "bi-" in such terms as "bilingual," "bicultural," and/or "biliterate" education? What does the process of "bi-" as used in bilingual education in fact mean? Some notion of duality is implied, though it may be queried whether this duality signifies a separation of two distinct sets of knowledge, cultures, and languages in the sense that each occurs as an accumulation of discrete skills, like something that one would add to one's repertoire or collection? Obviously, one cannot talk in terms of absolutes or mastery, when the process of becoming "bilingual," "bicultural," and/or "biliterate" can only be described along a continuum in terms of emergence. Baker (1993, p. 8) suggests that there are pitfalls in making arbitrary cutoff points about who is bilingual, bicultural, or biliterate, especially when measured against criteria consisting of competence and performance, attitude, and experience. "a bilingual's language competences are evolving, dynamic, interacting and intricate. They are not simple dichotomies, easily compartmentalized and static" (from Harley et al., 1990; cited in Baker, 1993, p. 12). While there might be a measure of interdependency among levels of bilingualism, biculturalism, and biliteracy, proficiency gained in one area, such as bilingualism, does not necessarily entail an equal, commensurate, or simultaneous level of proficiency gain in the areas of biculturalism or biliteracy, and vice versa.

In order to overcome somewhat narrow interpretations of immersion as a method of instruction, I offer the following as a way to make sense of immersion, particularly within a professional degree program at the university level: It is underpinned by four knowledge bases, which are (1) discipline content knowledge, (2) pedagogical knowledge, (3) professional knowledge, and (4) personal development knowledge.[2] Specifying what the participating student is actually immersed in, one may identify four areas characterized as *language, culture, context,* and *content knowledge.*

By understanding the interplay of these four attributes as a process within different classroom environments, different learning experiences, different group dynamics, and different practica and subject contexts, one can ultimately document the outcomes and student achievement levels in the two immersion programs through what might be called an immersion filter (Figure 13.1).

The Language Attribute

The first defining attribute of immersion, the language attribute, is viewed not just as a device to facilitate communication but also as a mechanism of

The Immersion Filter

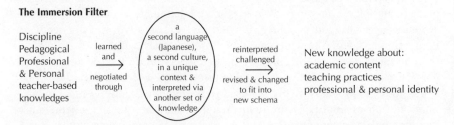

Figure 13.1 Representation of an immersion filter in a teacher education program

and for socialization. In this process, culture and language become intimately intertwined, so much so that culture (our beliefs, skills, experiences, and group identifications) acts as a filter through which language is exchanged. This filter is more complex when the interlocutors either are or are in the process of becoming bilinguals.

The Culture Attribute

The relationship of language to culture is a complex one, where "the imperatives and meanings of culture cannot be understood at the symbolic level of language" alone (Kalantzis, Cope, & Slade, 1989). Kalantzis and associates point out that culture functions at three levels. In the first instance, culture is the "sum of the various descriptions through which people make sense of and reflect their collective experiences." Second, it is necessary to incorporate within the idea about culture, "notions of mass, class, ideology, myth and social formation"; and at the third level, culture reflects a "whole way of life, a slab of social reality, always carried around by the same set of people." Cultural immersion in the CQU teacher education immersion degree programs is identified as immersion in a Japanese ethic, a Japanese set of experiences, a Japanese way of perceiving, but also in a cultural agenda of change, challenge, and advocacy against education for reproduction. That is, unlike more traditionally educated LOTE teachers, LACITEP graduates tend to see themselves agents of change in the pedagogy of LOTE.

Context as Attribute

Language is intimately associated with culture; indeed, to be able to function competently in any language, one must have acquired a certain level of sociocultural knowledge about the communicative conventions of the target group whose language one is learning. However, the interdependency of language and culture is shaped by the contexts within which communicative conventions are exercised. These contexts are not only physical but social-psychological; they are real as well as imagined. In education, the dynamics of any given context can and does shape the outcomes of learning (Seddon, 1993). Intertwined with the culture and the language of learning, immersion in various contexts imposes a set of "frames" that in any education program can govern and constrain curriculum implementation.

In a teacher education program, student teachers reflect upon the curriculum in an attempt to negotiate new knowledge and take ownership of what they consider relevant and pertinent to the context of their learning. Ultimately, their decisions will be transferred to and shape their own teaching careers. Particularly relevant to the context of learning, the context within which one is immersed, is the notion of "state" conceived as frame/context/state of being.

Notions of context are thus important in investigating the development of the student teacher's identity through an immersion teacher education program, especially since the shaping of a student teacher's identity will influence curriculum representations when that person eventually becomes involved in the process of curriculum delivery.

The Content Knowledge Attribute

Once a syllabus designed for a mainstream monolingual class has been reworked for delivery in a foreign language, the content is intrinsically changed. The degree of change may be plotted along a continuum. At one end of the spectrum, any content delivered through immersion may in general terms emulate, but not totally mirror, a mainstream curriculum. At the other end of the spectrum, it may solely reflect in design, delivery, content, philosophy, culture, and context the Geist (spirit) of the target language and country. This idea is represented graphically in Figure 13.2. The content of any curriculum may fluctuate between these two extremes on an ongoing basis. It can never be thought of as static. Immersion in and through a set of knowledge bases is intimately linked to language immersion, cultural immersion, and the context of immersion. The movement along the "knowledge immersion continuum" or, in other words, the specificity of the immersion curriculum is thus driven by the interdependence between the four attributes of immersion (language, culture, context, and knowledge). An immersion curriculum can never be considered the same as a mainstream curriculum.

In the context of the CQU teacher education immersion degree programs, there is another dimension to the issue of content knowledge. While one must consider immersion education as a process of immersion through a second language, another set of cultures, a context, and an array of knowledges, one must also come to terms with the knowledges that comprise a teacher's competence. In order to achieve a level of competence that will enable a teacher to carry out the task of teaching satisfactorily, a teacher needs to engage and develop proficiency in the four areas of discipline knowledge, pedagogical knowledge, professional knowledge, and personal knowledge (see Bartlett & Erben, 1995). It is these areas that have been used to underpin the curriculum of the actual CQU teacher education immersion degree programs.

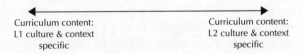

Curriculum content: Curriculum content:
L1 culture & context   L2 culture & context
specific   specific

Figure 13.2 A continuum indicating the limits of L_1/L_2 infusion into a curriculum

USING A DEGREE DELIVERED THROUGH IMMERSION TO GRADUATE PROFICIENT LOTE TEACHERS

The Bachelor of Education (LOTE) and the Bachelor of Professional Education (Japanese) programs began as pedagogical experiments to develop and implement an effective means to graduate teachers with sufficient professional knowledge in primary/secondary education and communicative competence in Japanese language and culture to meet the goals of the Queensland LOTE Initiative (Braddy, 1991) and growing employer demands (COAG, 1994). The vehicle through which such efficiency was to be achieved was based on a conception of language immersion. It was anticipated, on the one hand, that the delivery of a program of studies through immersion in a second language (L2) would greatly increase student L2 contact time, thereby significantly increasing students' opportunities to acquire the L2. On the other hand, the maxim "two for the price of one" became a reality, in that the two immersion degree programs would allow students to complete a traditional teacher education curriculum yet graduate with multiple majors.

The B. Ed. (LOTE) and the B. Prof. Ed. (Japanese) became in effect the first immersion initial teacher education degree programs in the world to employ language immersion (Japanese) as a means to graduate multiskilled primary and secondary teachers specialized and proficient in the areas of Japanese language, primary/secondary education, Asian literacy, immersion pedagogy, and one other discipline area of the student's choice. Seven years after the implementation of the first LACITEP[3] program, immersion at the university level, specifically within a teacher education context, may be seen as an uncomplicated label for what is actually a multidimensional and complex phenomenon (Cazden & Snow, 1990), of which language is only one part.

THE LANGUAGES AND CULTURES INITIAL TEACHER EDUCATION PROGRAM (LACITEP)

LACITEP aims to equip LOTE teachers to be able to meet the growing demands in the profession by graduating teachers trained in generalist elementary and secondary schooling with a specialization in LOTE (Japanese) pedagogy. By creating such a pool of multiskilled LOTE teachers who have a solid grounding in immersion teaching practices, both the Bachelor of Education (LOTE) and the Bachelor of Professional Education (Japanese) programs have aimed to set a standard for the direction that university LOTE teacher education should take in order to equip LOTE teachers for the twenty-first century.

The LACITEP curriculum follows an immersion tradition tracing its roots back to the St. Lambert experiment of 1965. However, immersion at the university level is basically still in its infancy. Differences include the following:

1. Adults (at least past the age of seventeen) and not children are involved in the immersion process.
2. The nature of university work makes it impracticable for immersion to start at the university level if students have had no prior second language experience.
3. Beginning university immersion students need to be acclimatized (or retrained) if their prior second language learning routines are well established but inappropriate for learning through immersion.
4. Unlike elementary school immersion, students at university participating in an immersion program have numerous immersion teachers.
5. In an initial teacher education program, immersion students have the additional opportunity of learning the L2 by reflecting on the L2 through the process of practice teaching.

There are five course components in the LACITEP programs (Figure 13.3), consisting of:

1. Foundation Studies
2. Discipline Studies
3. Teacher Development Studies
4. Curriculum Studies
5. Practicum Experiences

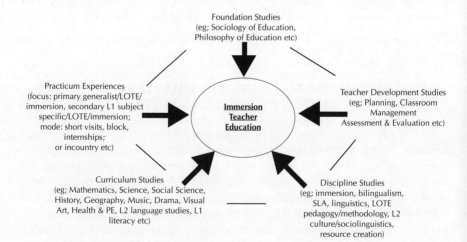

Figure 13.3 The four-year Bachelor of Education (LOTE)

LACITEP COURSE STRUCTURE

The aim of LACITEP is to deliver a minimum of 50 percent of curriculum subjects through the medium of Japanese. In effect, a subject is either (a) totally delivered through language immersion, (b) delivered in such a way that the lecture is given in English and the tutorials or seminars are given in the L2, or (c) totally delivered through the medium of the L2. The mode of delivery depends on the nature of the subject.

Figure 13.4 indicates those subjects involved in language immersion. Subjects that are darkly shaded are delivered through 100% language immersion. Subjects that are lightly shaded are offered through a combination of the L1 and the L2. In practice, this consists of a 3-hour plus 1-hour or a 2-hour plus 2-hour L2/L1 split, usually in favor of the L2, where the lecture is in English and the tutorials are in Japanese. Those subjects shaded in white are delivered through the medium of English.

PRACTICUM EXPERIENCES

In order to keep in line with the types of changes advocated by recent reports dealing with foreign languages and employment issues (Leal, 1991; Finn, 1991; Mayer, 1992), the CQU teacher education immersion degree programs aim to expand the learning opportunities for students at every possible juncture. The concept of immersion as it is enacted within these

Sem				
1	Professional Practice 1 (one day visits, 2 week block + SMS)	Development and Disability	Health & PE Curric Pedagogy	Effective Communication in a LOTE
2	English Curric & Pedagogy I	Teaching, Learning & Planning	Study of Society and Env Curric & Ped	Teaching through a LOTE
3	Professional Practice 2 (SMS + In-country)	Math Curric & Pedagogy I	Second Language Teaching Methodologies	Negotiating Meaning through a LOTE
4	English Curric & Pedagogy II	Gender as a Social Justice Issue	Second Language Acquisition	Using a LOTE in Cultural Settings
5	Language, Education & Professional Understanding	Science Curric Pedagogy	Bilingualism & Immersion Education	Raising Communicative Competence in a LOTE
6	Professional Practice 3	Math Curric & Pedagogy II	Studies in Language & Culture	Using LOTE in Workplace Settings
7	Economy, Education & Management	Arts Curric Pedagogy	Communication, Culture & Difference	LOTE Curriculum & Pedagogy
8	Professional Practice 4 (4-5 week block, in-country, and/or internship)	Identity, Curriculum & Learning Environments	Student Needs & the Supportive School Environment	Research in Linguistics and Cultural Acquisition

Figure 13.4 Bachelor of Education (LOTE) program of study

programs is enhanced and challenged through the numerous and varied practicum experiences within the degrees. Of all the components in the degrees, it is the practicum that allows the students to engage fully with the knowledge they have acquired in the content classes through immersion (see also Bräuer in this volume on practicum/internship).

Designing an immersion initial teacher education program that matches and keeps the interest of all students, fosters their overall growth and development, and provides ample opportunities for meaningful input and output is a necessary ingredient for success. The education of a reflective teacher is also of vital importance, particularly in the light of concerns about what occurs currently in practice teaching, namely, the socialization of the student into the status quo by the use of what is essentially an apprenticeship model (Price, 1989). It is hoped that the series of practicums built into the program will facilitate the students' interactions in the second language and offer each student a wide array of practice teaching environments.

Recent studies into the practicum component of pre-service immersion teacher education indicate that it is preferable for student teachers to attempt immersion teaching after having experienced success in regular monolingual and foreign language classes (Majhanovich & Grey, 1992). The CQU teacher education immersion degree programs have such sequenced built-in practicums. These offer students ample opportunity for observation and time to build confidence in mainstream monolingual and foreign language teaching, before having to deal with actual immersion teaching itself. By having such a variety of experiences and methods made available to them, future teachers can adopt the teaching techniques that most suit the circumstances and best cater to the individual needs of the school language learner.

In both the Bachelor of Education (LOTE) and the Bachelor of Professional Education (Japanese), students are required to complete a number of block practicum experiences in schools over the course of the degree program. The teacher development focus of each practicum differs from semester to semester. In order to gain expertise in all areas of specializations (primary, secondary, Japanese, immersion, Asian Studies, plus one other discipline area), students are advised to conform to the school types, as outlined in the recommended practicum schedule shown in Figure 13.5.

Elementary LOTE attachments across the state occur where appropriate supervision is available. The LOTE Japanese clusters that already operate are used to provide both support and supervision. These attachments include Distance Education, Independent Schools, Catholic Schools, and State Schools.

There are several kinds of practical experiences other than the block practicums. During the second semester in Year 1 and subsequently in the first semester in Year 2, students are required to visit schools one day per week. Ten such visits take place in the first semester, and ten occur in the second semester. Students are required to carry out tasks that relate back to first-year

1ST YEAR:	Sem. I and II	DISCIPLINE AREA	
Saturday Morning School		(LOTE)	10 half days
One day School		(Elementary/Secondary)	10 days
Professional Practicum 1		(Elementary/Secondary)	10 days
2ND YEAR:	Sem. III and IV	DISCIPLINE AREA	
Saturday Morning School		(LOTE)	10 half days
In-country		(LOTE)	20 days
Paraprofessional Work		(LOTE)	10 days or more
3RD YEAR:	Sem. V and VI	DISCIPLINE AREA	
Professional Practicum 3		(Elementary/Secondary)	25 days
4TH YEAR:	Sem. VII and VIII	DISCIPLINE AREA	
Professional Practicum 4		(LOTE + Discipline area)	25 days or
In-country/Internship		(LOTE + Discipline area)	25 days
	TOTAL =		approx. 135 days

Figure 13.5 Practicum schedule

curriculum subjects. The one-day visits are intended to acclimatize students to school procedures and provide students with their initial experiences in teaching (Kindt, 1995).

As part of the practicum experience, the idea of a Saturday Morning School (SMS) has been devised for Year 1 and Year 2 immersion student teachers. This school operates at Central Queensland University's Rockhampton Campus on a Saturday morning and is open to the wider Capricornia community. The composition of these classes consists of beginner learners of any age group as well as family groups.

The subjects Professional Practice 1 and Second Language Teaching Methodologies are integrated into and articulate with the experiences of the SMS practicum and provide the theoretical focus of what Eltis (1992) describes as a practicum-driven curriculum. In preparing lessons for the SMS, the immersion student teacher is expected to intake new ideas, develop lesson plans, deliver lessons, and videotape lessons, which are subsequently deconstructed after the event in Second Language Teaching Methodologies tutorials. SMS also provides the immersion student teachers the opportunity of team-teaching with registered LOTE teachers.

In order to train teachers who are capable of teaching in a number of different environments as well as achieving fluency in work-related competencies, the SMS is structured in such a way that the student teachers themselves have an opportunity to run the school. A school executive (Principal, Deputy Principal, Curriculum Advisors, and Resource Aide) establishes SMS policies and guidelines to which all immersion student teachers conform. The SMS is implemented for two 10-week blocks. After each five-week module, a new executive is elected. In other words, for every five-week unit of teaching, one immersion student teacher takes on the role of the SMS principal, another takes on the role of the deputy principal (as well as being the de facto school accountant), three immersion student teachers become curriculum advisors, and one becomes a resource person, while the remaining students take on the role of classroom teacher. These roles are rotated at the end of each five-week period of work.

Under the supervision of the academic coordinator, the SMS is administered by first- and second-year immersion student teachers. In this way, the student teachers are able to learn school administrative, managerial, and accounting procedures, which under normal circumstances are not possible in an in-school practicum (Erben, 1993).

During Year 2 there is the possibility of students carrying out another form of practical experience, namely, paraprofessional work for the Catholic Education Office, Rockhampton Diocese. The work is carried out on a voluntary basis. It is thought that such experience will be invaluable to the overall development of the immersion trained student teachers.

The most important form of practical experience is the *in-country component,* which provides experience with the types of language used by Japanese children in elementary schools in Japan. It also provides real experience in teaching LOTE across the curriculum. The in-country component is an important linking device in the immersion programs. The experiences that take place during the student's visit to Japan provide the basis for the focus of the next semester's core Japanese classes.

Leal (1991) insists that in order to maintain adequate standards of language competence and pedagogical training, future tertiary language programs and teacher training programs should contain provisions for in-country experiences and recommends that by 1998 a period of residence in the target language country become a compulsory requirement. In the second year and/or the fourth year of the LACITEP immersion programs, all students may spend 2–3 months (extendable to 5 months) in Japan. Due to equity issues, the in-country component as proposed is extended to students on a voluntary basis.

During this time, LACITEP student teachers are placed in a Japanese elementary school as a Teacher Assistant. In addition, all students undergo intensive Japanese language study. All students are billeted to Japanese families.

This in-country component is viewed as the initial stage in a lifelong process of ongoing visits to the country of the target language. It is hoped that students will establish contacts and links to people and institutions in Japan that will promote future periods of residence and/or teaching in Japan.

The students are encouraged to go to Japan, rather than have the clear choice of going or not going. For those who undertake the in-country component in Japan, Professional Practicum 2 is noted down on the practicum report as having been completed in Japan, in a Japanese primary school.

In addition to the practicum experiences, the immersion degree programs incorporate an "Advanced Professional Practice." A key objective of the Advanced Professional Practice is to provide school-based teaching experience and knowledge for student teachers. The Advanced Professional Practice is a separate component from Fieldwork. Students may apply to undertake a tour of teaching duty in Japan.

LACITEP PRACTICUM EXPERIENCES ANALYZED

In 1999, an extensive case study investigation was undertaken of LACITEP students involved in the Saturday Morning Japanese School. Data retrieved from an array of data collection tools indicate that LACITEP students and staff, school personnel, and community members who come into contact with the program acknowledge the benefits of the diverse array of practicum experiences in developing pedagogically well-informed teachers.

LACITEP students were able to explore this issue through ongoing taped group interaction sessions, through informal interviews, and through critical reflective portfolios in which they reflected on their experiences as teachers in the Saturday Morning School and school-based practicums and through which they were able to consider their developing understanding of the work of teachers.

Student comments included, "I'm grateful for the immediate immersion into the classroom situation because it makes this entire course a true teacher training course—not an 'academic' course with a bit of prac here and there," and, "Being able to work in a class like a teacher opened my eyes to the time involved in lesson organization." Also, "Prac teaching helps to increase my confidence; teaching a variety of different ages and people, watching other people teach, etc., helped me think about my own personal philosophy of education."

The challenge of sound pedagogy is clearly a major concern of students. Most students in the LACITEP programs express a certainty that more practice will facilitate the improvement and understanding of the processes of teaching: "LACITEP pracs allow me to realize the importance of not only the ways to improve my teaching and meaningful interaction, but also the importance of extra knowledge of the subject."

Not all data indicated complete student satisfaction with the immersion experience. Some students voiced concerns that the contextual attribute of immersion does in fact interfere in facilitating the development of appropriate pedagogical strategies for Australian schools. Furthermore, some students in the initial stages of the program found it difficult to identify the value of their own experience as a LACITEP student and draw on this as a generalist teacher, the difficulty being one of perspective and familiarity with making connections. Subsequent interview protocols revealed that by the second year of the program, students were generally much more confident and positive about their potential to envelop the competency required for a career in the teaching profession. The continued extensive practical contexts of the program were highlighted as the main facilitating medium by which this would be achieved.

Saturday Morning School is the LACITEP students' first real teaching experience within a structured educational program. As described earlier, the school is administered by the LACITEP students themselves. Its objective is to provide LACITEP students an opportunity to develop an independent teaching style while gauging the complexities of managing a curriculum and administering it to a school population of over one hundred people (people from the community of Rockhampton who come to CQU to learn Japanese in the Saturday Morning School).

Throughout the seven years in which the LACITEP degree programs have operated, one feature from which student teachers have increasingly benefited is the ability to transfer what and how they learn, the professional discourses they acquire, and the teacher-based literacy abilities to other contexts. It is to this notion of transferability that I now turn.

TRANSFERABILITY THROUGH IMMERSION

In order to understand better the process of transfer from the immersion program to a range of other educational contexts, selected students were interviewed over a period of twelve months. The interviews were a form of dialogue consisting of informal talks with students and staff, which were subsequently recorded and annotated. Students also provided unstructured journals, in which immersion students were asked to reflect upon their own studies and practical teaching experience. The purpose of this dialogue was to seek a shared understanding of how and where transfer of knowledge and skills took place. A collaborative approach to meaning-making served the interests of the methodological framework of investigation. This section serves to highlight, explore, and discover collaboratively the understandings that students and staff have arrived at through their participation in LACITEP.

LACITEP seeks to promote an immersion context that is linguistically defined through the delivery of up to 75 percent of course content through the medium of Japanese and is contextually defined in complex social and pedagogical relationships. There is an expectation that this difference (teacher education through immersion) promotes the development of different skills and knowledge. Furthermore, it is recognized that the skills that are developed are not devoid of "values" or attitudes. This section deals with how these skills and knowledge and the values that frame them are transferred productively from one academic context to another academic context, from one teaching setting to other teaching settings, and from one learning environment (immersion) into the practical environment for which student teachers aim to prepare themselves. The focus is on the professional and personal knowledge bases of the program.

The first issue that emerges is *shared responsibility for learning*. Students record a strong sense of group cohesion early in the program as they seek to support one another in their new environment. There are immediate mutual needs for support and assistance where differing levels of L2 proficiency or cultural awareness, teaching experience, artistic talent, organizational skills, and content knowledge are pooled and shared for personal and group benefit. The LACITEP students' needs to reflect and consider their learning process in relation to strategies, skills, and knowledge required to "survive" are immediate, because the context of their learning is different from previous contexts (that is, high school). This need for support and to address the development of shared responsibility is approached through a range of discussion forums (formal and informal) and the development of journal writing as a reflective strategy for professional development. These methods demonstrate that the students' capacity to shoulder responsibility for their learning remains a key area of development in the first semester and one that provides the foundation for continuing personal and professional development in the program.

LACITEP instigates a greater range of ways to organize curriculum content and its delivery according to subject matter, language instruction, and other related resource concerns. Students experience diverse approaches to teaching, organizing, and disseminating information and stimulating learning processes, which are subsequently reflected in the application of similarly diverse "practices" by the students themselves in their teaching roles. From interviews with lecturers and tutors working in both the English medium and the Japanese medium, it is observed that LACITEP students demonstrate a greater range of ways to develop and use teaching/learning resources in the classroom.

One lecturer related how "immersion students bring a knowledge/awareness of language as communication, vitality of communication through language which is immediately useful to drama curriculum." He went on to say, "The benefits of immersion for drama are clear. Students are inherently interaction oriented [which] enhances/facilitates interaction in drama. The immersion experience/language learning experience facilitated their use and transfer of drama pedagogy/curriculum content." The implications for non-language aspects for drama were similarly expressed by the drama lecturer:

"Immersion enriches the drama curriculum, extends and challenges the current mainstream to look beyond current topics and utilize drama in this culturally enriching and informative way."

The lecturer for the subject *Developing Communicative Competence in a LOTE* saw the applicable benefits of immersion: "Immersion students as developing language learners and as immersion teachers are aware of the need to break down the message to build the concept from experience and hypothesis testing. This is their own learning experience through immersion." She went on to say that this skill of breaking down the message to rebuild the concept from experience promotes "immersion students to demonstrate imaginative, innovative ways of developing and using teaching/learning resource materials."

The clear distinction in comprehension levels of L2 delivered content in the class appears to have instigated a heightened awareness among LACITEP students to plan for mixed-ability groups and other content subjects also. LACITEP students recognize that the core ingredient in their teaching effectiveness is comprehensible communication. As students interested and stimulated by language learning, they are able to transfer this principle to their teaching practice in other areas.

Language awareness and perception of communication as a core principle of the teaching-learning continuum constitutes the amalgam strengthening the link between content and delivery knowledge.

DEVELOPMENT OF INDIVIDUAL NEEDS, INTERESTS, AND CAPACITIES

Clearly, two main issues emerge in relation to the development of a LACITEP student teacher's knowledge base. The first relates to the opportunities students in the LACITEP program perceive they have in order to develop their needs, interests, and capacities in the manner in which they are used to learning. Students enrolled in LACITEP enter the program with a wide range of vocational agendas. The majority of students envisage their future work as teaching; some identify with generalist elementary teaching outcomes, while others are particularly interested in LOTE. A minority of students whose vocational interests lie in areas of business and tourism see education as a means to an end. These students enroll in LACITEP with a view that its training in Japanese communication can place them advantageously to seek work in their identified profession outside education.

Nevertheless, the context-rich and practicum-diverse nature of LACITEP does provide opportunities for students to explore and enhance knowledge, skills, and understandings about their specific areas of interest, particularly in the second and third years of the program, in such subjects as "Research in Linguistic and Cultural Acquisition" and "Studies in Language and Culture" as well as in the in-country practice teaching component and Saturday Morning School. The following comments were written by LACITEP student teachers in their journals in relation to their individual needs as student teachers and how they have professionally developed through their participation in Saturday Morning School. The students express how their SMS experiences are transferred to their individual professional and personal needs in the following ways.

Professional

"I've learned that education is a combination of teaching skills and student participation."

"I believe I must establish my own philosophy and goals of education and what I think is important to teaching."

"SMS draws on everything I have learned—at SMS we can experiment with lessons, but when at School we have to do what the teacher presumably tells us."

"How to teach on the spot confidently. Ways of making lessons more enjoyable."

"Techniques in learning how to teach, without being self-conscious."

"Many different teaching strategies encourage learning on different levels."

"It gave us a certain competency in organizing a venture on our own."

"From classroom observations we picked upon good/bad teaching strategies."

"Insight into learning styles, insight into classroom situation."

"We got an idea about the time involved in lesson preparation."

"The need for managing resources."

"Gaining competence in speaking in front of a group."

"Being able to monitor student progress."

"How to make lessons fun."

"I think it has demonstrated how teachers and other staff members have to successfully participate together to get the job accomplished—gives me a sense of being a part of a functioning organization."

"I've gotten practice in writing interesting and appropriate lesson plans for a range of age groups."

Personal

"The Course should give me the potential to be a great primary teacher."

"The utmost important thing is to have communication and be able to communicate within all aspects of the school hierarchy."

"Knowledge not difficult to acquire but difficult to implement."

"Becoming more definite."

"Teachers do a lot of work—I have learned more about myself—learned where my strong and weak points are."

"It (SMS) brought everyone together because we had to come together."

"How to work with others, listen to their points of view. How to say no to people without feeling guilty."

"I've found through my experiences in the SMS, I have come to appreciate the positions of teachers. I realized how much planning and organizing go into the preparation of a lesson—which I think I could improve on !"

The second issue in relation to the development of individual needs relates closely to the first, but being focused on the individual needs of self, it relates to the individual needs of others. From the very early stages of the program, LACITEP students indicate a keen sense of the difficulty of catering for diverse abilities, skills, talents, and interests in their teaching. This is a feature of LACITEP students' ability to relate back to their own experience as a diverse class group challenging the creativity of their lecturers. Again, it is the experience of their own learning as students in the immersion stream and the process of reflection and critical consideration of this learning experience that is proving to assist LACITEP student teachers to "work through" and develop their own understandings about what they do in their own teaching.

The extracts from the journal and interview data demonstrate the transfer of students' experience as students in the LACITEP program to their work as teachers—not as mimics, but as experimenters, innovative teacher-researchers, exploring the notion of pedagogy/androgogy by participating in teaching "through doing comes learning" and determining the links for themselves between content and how they teach it.

Apparent also are the ever-present attributes of immersion as enhancers of the process of transfer. It is the precise combination of the contexts, culture, knowledge, and language of LACITEP that permeates the program and enriches the transfer of learning across curriculum areas and across roles.

IMPLICATIONS OF USING IMMERSION TO TRAIN TEACHERS

How Does Immersion Used Within a Teacher Education Program Facilitate or Constrain Language Development?

Immersion should not be considered an educational panacea that automatically induces high levels of language proficiency in students who participate in immersion programs. Numerous other factors do mitigate whether students are successful in their language learning or not. What immersion does do is to provide the teacher and the learner with a stimulus, a medium, and an environment that can greatly support the learner in the language acquisition process. If conditions are right, student teachers can gain immediate benefits from being in an immersion teacher education program. Language proficiency may thus improve in this order: comprehension > speaking > reading > writing. Immersion facilitates learning because it allows students to learn the second language when they are ready to learn it. Immersion does this by providing students with a range of comprehensible input in a variety of situations, it provides students with language scaffolds and encourages students to be proactive in their own learning. It also allows students opportunities for output, which is crucial if second language acquisition is to be facilitated. Furthermore, different curriculum areas promote differing thematic interactions, which facilitate proficiencies not only in the four macroskills to varying degrees but also proficiencies in Basic Interpersonal Communication Strategies (BICS) and Cognitive-Academic Language Proficiency (CALP).

What Types of Language Competencies Are Developed by Student Teachers?

Immersion students are able to develop very sound grammatical competencies. They learn how to converse on a wide range of topics and develop teacher-talk skills in Japanese. Sociolinguistic competencies develop as well, though not so spectacularly. Students may develop sound passive skills in a variety of sociolinguistic registers, though they may be actively conversant in only plain, polite, and formal registers. Because LACITEP student teachers are immersed in a cultural, contextual, and knowledge base specific to Japan and Japanese, student teachers acquire a very fine-tuned cultural sensitivity. They also develop good paralinguistic skills. Discoursal competency improves with higher-level-proficient students. It seems that lack of grammatical competence in the early stages of language learning does impede the cohesion and cohesiveness of texts delivered in Japanese.

First-year LACITEP students need to be reconditioned for language learning in an immersion context, because most school leavers have a particular view of themselves as language learners and of language that may not "sit well" with successful learning through immersion. Immersion promotes LOTE student teachers to think of themselves as communication teachers (i.e., teachers of a linguistic, sociocultural system of meaning, interpreting, and perceiving), not just language teachers. Immersion can never re-create a microcosm of the target country in the classroom completely or perfectly. However, it does lend itself to mirror the target country in an Australian context more fully than a classroom where the language is taught as object. In order to acquire competencies in the areas just cited, both the teacher and the learner need to contribute to the creation of a learning situation that will facilitate this.

What Is the Nature of Language Use in LACITEP?

Immersion provides various scaffolds or platforms that the student teacher can use to interact in the L2. The use of the L2 is high in all content immersion classes, though affective factors such as stress, tiredness, and motivation may lower the amount of L2 use in classes. Less-proficient students seem to be hesitant to speak in class, even though these students need most to converse to aid their language development. Some content classes lend themselves more to class activities, whereas others are organized more on a group or pair activity basis. Group work promotes the use of the L2 in classes, though it also gives students an opportunity to sneak in some English.

LACITEP student teachers feel that the process of practice teaching is one factor that definitely encourages student teachers to use their L2 and to reflect on their L2 development. Students also uniformly seem to agree that the implementation of language immersion should be graded and guided. It should be graded in the sense that a minimum/maximum of 50 percent of classes should initially be offered in immersion only in the first semester of the first year of study, slowly increasing as students get used to university life and the pedagogy of immersion language delivery. It should be guided in the sense that support structures need to be in place, to give students systematic help to develop their language proficiency. Last, students need to familiarize themselves with immersion to be able to benefit from it. This involves a process of retraining and getting the students to use more communicative strategies to promote greater language use.

Classroom interaction in the L2 needs to be stimulated by the teacher, though interactions need not necessarily be based solely on teacher-student discourse; indeed, student-student negotiation is just as important if not more beneficial for student language development. The immersion experience does not stop when the class is over; language interactions in the L2 outside the classroom need to be promoted.

How Do the Process or Participants of Language Immersion Mediate Decisions About Curriculum Design, Content, or Delivery?

Immersion used within a teacher education degree program is definitely more work for students because they have to negotiate a curriculum through the medium of two languages, and it is more work for the teachers because they have to design materials for use in the immersion classroom and simultaneously provide for meaningful comprehensible L2 input and stimulate L2 interaction. Immersion does change the content of the curriculum because it is mediated through a second language. From the balancing of these three factors—student proficiency, teacher competency, and content—any number of curriculum patterns and delivery modes can and do occur. LACITEP is unique to CQU; in any other tertiary setting, its components and level of effectiveness may not be the same.

In order to stimulate interactions in the L2 and about the content in a way that facilitates learning of content and language, seminar and tutorial-style delivery modes are more preferable than lectures. On average more teacher-student contact time is necessary when delivery occurs through immersion than when the same subject content is delivered through the medium of the L1. Finally, as a multidimensional phenomenon, it is necessary for immersion teachers to rework the curriculum so that it can be delivered through the L2 in a way that is comprehensible and meaningful.

The following is a summary of the main points that have arisen out of the knowledge outcomes data. They are reviewed in terms of the four original issues utilized in the research framework.

How Successful is the Transferability through Immersion Phenomenon?

Student teachers actively transfer perceptions, ideas, and strategies acquired through one language system and apply/use them when learning through the medium of another language system. They become adept at transferring analytic skills developed in one area to help them understand concepts of another subject area better. These same learning strategies are readily employed to facilitate student teachers' own teaching.

What Benefits are Gained from All the Practical Teaching Experiences?

Effective and efficient learning benefits LACITEP student teachers in their roles as teachers. Feedback from LACITEP students' teaching endeavors would indicate that their teaching is highly successful. Students are able to draw on their combined skills and utilize them in a classroom as individual teachers or as a group of teachers. It is imperative that in order to graduate multiskilled teachers an array of practical experiences be provided. These should be sequenced and allow the student to develop pedagogical skills in line with their own level of professional development. Practicum experiences should also encourage student teachers to utilize the types of discipline knowledge that will aid them in teaching endeavors. Such knowledge includes the following:

1. proficiency in the four macroskills (minimum level ASLPR 3) and four linguistic competencies
2. sound training in applied linguistics and second language acquisition
3. structured school experiences incorporating pre-service, internship, and induction years

4. appropriate cultural knowledge
5. training in teaching cultural content and skills
6. training as a second language teacher
7. substantial in-country experience

Each practicum experience provides student teachers with differing skills and competencies. At all costs, traditional apprenticeship models of teacher training must be avoided. To further facilitate L2 proficiency, high levels of immersion delivery and an in-country component are advisable. Immersion teacher educators need to model a variety of teaching practices that will encourage the immersion student teacher to foster his or her own eclectic approach to teaching.

What Level of Academic Achievement Can Be Reached Using an Immersion Approach to Teacher Education?

Students' level of academic achievement does not seem to be compromised by the fact that students negotiate the curriculum through the medium of a second language. All external performance indicators undertaken to date show that relative to students involved in the same area of study, immersion students achieve equally as well in all subject units.

CONCLUSION

The LACITEP program provides an exemplary answer to the call for change. First, the LACITEP program graduates multiskilled and versatile teachers giving school authorities the option of employing generalist primary school teachers or specialist LOTE/Immersion teachers or both. Second, LACITEP addresses the issues raised in both federal and state reports on LOTE proficiency and teacher training. Last, and above all, LACITEP seeks to graduate informed, highly proficient, and well-trained LOTE/Immersion teachers who can cope with the demands that education in the twenty-first century will bring and carry on the momentum of change for a brighter, more educated multilingual Australia.

NOTES

1. Languages Other Than English, or LOTE, is the term used in Australia to designate foreign language education.

2. *Discipline content knowledge* refers to substantive knowledge of disciplines other than education. This includes, for example, music, physical education, and mathematics. *Pedagogical knowledge* includes categories of general pedagogical knowledge, pedagogical content knowledge, curriculum knowledge, and management. *Professional knowledge* emphasizes contexts and also incorporates knowledge of educational contexts and knowledge

of learners. *Personal development knowledge* is more akin to that espoused and articulated by Eraut (1994), whereby participants who undertake learning on particular knowledge areas personalize that learning as their own. Personal knowledge informs professional judgment and becomes embedded in performance.

The significance of context generally in education (Seddon, 1993) must not be underestimated. Its relevance to a personal knowledge base and to the CQU immersion degree curricula needs to be underscored. On this point, Eraut (1994, p. 22) argues along the following lines:

> ... the influence of context on knowledge use, arguing first that the nature of the context affects what knowledge gets used and how. Three types of context are distinguished: the academic context; the organizational *context of policy discussion* and talk about practice; and the *context of practice* itself. New concepts and ideas brought into these contexts have to be transformed in order to become usable in contextually appropriate ways; and this transformation can also be viewed as a form of learning which develops the *personal knowledge base* (my italics) of the professional concerned. Therefore it is inappropriate to think of knowledge as first being learned then later being used. Learning takes place during use, and the transformation of knowledge into a situationally appropriate form means that it is no longer the same knowledge as it was prior to it first being used. It also follows that learning to use an idea in one context does not guarantee being able to use the same idea in another context: transferring from one context to another requires further learning and the idea itself will be further transformed in the process.

3. At CQU, we refer to the two immersion degree programs as the LACITEP programs. For ease of reading I will refer to both as LACITEP from here on in. The first of the LACITEP immersion degree programs was established in 1993. It was a four-year Bachelor of Education (LOTE), which graduated Japanese and elementary school specialists capable not only of teaching the whole primary school curriculum as well as teaching Japanese but also of teaching the whole curriculum through the medium of Japanese. In 1999, a second immersion degree, the Bachelor of Professional Education (Japanese), was established. While still being delivered through the medium of Japanese, this degree graduates students with specializations in secondary school education plus one other discipline area (e.g., business, tourism, computers, science, etc.).

REFERENCES

AACLAME. (1990). *Bilingual education in Australian Schools. Bilingualism: Who? What? Why?* Australian Advisory Council on Languages and Multicultural Education. Canberra, AGPS.

Allen, P., Fröhlich, M., & Spada, N. (1984). The communicative orientation of language teaching: An observation scheme. In J. Handscome, R. A. Orem, & B. P. Taylor (eds.), *On TESOL '83*. Washington:TESOL.

Baker, C. (1993). *Foundations of bilingual education and bilingualism.* Clevedon, U.K.: Multilingual Matters.

Bartlett, L., & Erben, T. (1995). *An investigation into the effectiveness of an exemplar model of LOTE teacher-training through partial immersion.* A report for the Innovative Languages Other Than English Project, Federal Department of Employment, Education and Training of Australia.

Braddy, P. (1991). *Languages other than English: A Statement by the Minister.* Department of Education, Queensland. Government Printing Service (QGPS).

Carr, W., & Kemmis, S. (1986). *Becoming critical: Education, knowledge and action research.* Geelong: Deakin University Press.

Cazden, C. B., & Snow, C. E. (eds.) (1990). *English plus: Issues in bilingual education.* Newbury Park: Sage Publications.

Council of Australian Governments (COAG). (1994). *Asian languages and Australia's economic future.* A report prepared for the Council of Australian Governments on a proposed Asian languages/studies strategy for Australian schools. Queensland Government Press (QGP).

Department of Employment Education and Training (1991). *Australia's language: The Australian language and literacy policy.* Canberra: Australian Government Printing Service (AGPS).

Di Biase, B., & Dyson, B. (1988). *Language rights and the school.* Sydney: ICEC FILEF Italo-Australian Publications.

Eltis, K. (1992). Reshaping pre-service teacher education: Establishing a practicum-driven curriculum. *Journal of Teaching Practice, 2*(2): 53–72.

Eraut, M. (1994). *Developing professional knowledge and competence.* The Falmer Press. London. Washington, DC.

Erben, A. (1993). Teacher training through immersion. *Australian Association of Language Immersion Teachers,* 1(August) (inaugural issue).

Erben, A. (1993). The importance of the practicum in teacher development. What happens in an immersion teacher training program? *Australian Association of Language Immersion Teachers,* 1(August).

Erben, A., Cox, R., & Phillips, S. (1993). Training generalist primary school teachers through partial immersion in Japanese. Final project outline. Faculty of Education, University of Central Queensland.

Erben, T. (1998) The virtual immersion classroom and audiographic technology: A different linguistic bath? Paper presented at the WorldCALL Conference. University of Melbourne, 13–17 July.

Finn Report. (1991). *Young people's participation in post-compulsory education and training.* Report of the Australian Education Council Review Committee. Canberra: AGPS.

Goodenough, W. H. (1971). *Culture, language, and society.* Reading, MA: Addison-Wesley.

Harley, B., Allen, P., Cummins, J., & Swain, M. (1990). *The development of second language proficiency.* Cambridge: Cambridge University Press.

Harmstorf, I., & Cigler, M. (1985). *The Germans in Australia.* Melbourne: AE Press.

Kalantzis, M., Cope, B., & Slade, D. (1989). *Minority languages and dominant culture: Issues of education, assessment and social equity.* London: Falmer Press.

Kindt, I. (1995). *Bachelor of Education/Bachelor of Teaching (Primary) School Experience Handbook.* Faculty of Education, Central Queensland University.

Leal, B. (1991). *Widening our horizons.* Report of the Review of the Teaching of Modern Languages in Higher Education. Canberra: Australian Government Printing Service.

Lo Bianco, J. (1987). *National policy on languages.* Canberra: Australian Government Printing Service.

Lyster, R. (1990). The role of analytic language teaching in French immersion programs. *Canadian Modern Language Review,* 47(1): 159–176.

Majhanovich, S., & Grey, J. (1992). The practicum: An essential component in French immersion teacher education. *The Canadian Modern Language Review,* 48(4): 682–695.

Mayer Committee. (1992). *Employment-related key competencies for postcompulsory education and training.* A Discussion Paper. Australian Education Council and Ministers for Vocational Education, Employment and Training. Melbourne: AGPS.

Nicholas, H., Moore, H., Clyne, M., & Pauwels, A. (1993). *Languages at the cross-roads*. Report of the National Enquiry into the Employment and Supply of Teachers of Languages Other Than English. Melbourne: National Languages and Literacy Institute of Australia (NLLIA).

Paulston, Christina Bratt, ed. (1992). *Sociolinguistic perspectives on bilinugal education*. Clevedon; Philadelphia: Multilingual Matters.

Price, D. (1989). The Practicum: A recent review of the literature. *South Pacific Journal of Teacher Education,d 17(2)*.

Rebuffot, J. (1993). *Le point sur . . . L'immersion au Canada*. Quebec: CEC Press.

Said, E. (1993). *Culture and imperialism*. London: Chatto and Wiondus.

Said, E. (1978). *Orientalism*. London: Penguin.

Seddon, T. (1993). *Context and beyond: Reframing the theory and practice of education*. The Falmer Press, London, Washington, DC.

Singh, M. G. (1995). Edward Said's critique of orientalism and Australia's "Asia Literacy" curriculum. *Journal of Curriculum Studies,* 27 (559–620).

Stern, H. H. (1978). French immersion in Canada: Achievements and directions. *Canadian Modern Language Review*, 34(5).

14

Technology in Language Teacher Training

The New Challenges of Multimedia-Based Content, Technology-Enhanced Language Learning, and Computer-Mediated Communication

Lawrence F. Glatz

THE STATE OF CURRENT RESEARCH

Owing to the extremely rapid, widespread deployment of computer technology in such a relatively short time, few publications to date have discussed the changes in teacher training programs necessary because of this remarkable transformation. The references presented in this chapter do show that current research on technology in language pedagogy is enlivened by the creativity of individual practitioners, who then reflect upon their use of multimedia-based content (MBC), technology-enhanced language learning (TELL), and computer-mediated communication (CMC) (see also Gonglewski and

Lee in this volume). This chapter builds on the two most recent and valuable contributions by Kassen and Higgins (1997) and Scott (1998), whose ideas are discussed in the section on teacher training involving technology.

The Perspective of a Practitioner

Drawing on the most recent scholarship available, as well as experience acquired from instruction with MBC in undergraduate German language and culture courses and extensive exploration of these issues in the author's undergraduate seminar on Multimedia and Second Language Acquisition, this chapter presents viewpoints formulated as a practitioner, which must await the judgment of long-term research efforts and the experience of other practitioners. The suggestions and ideas offered here are the synthesis of practice and reflection, which itself is a key component of training teachers to effectively use technology. Reflection on practices improves them (Kassen & Higgins, 1997).

The Role of the Teacher

The following assertion in an important article by Kramsch and Andersen puts the challenge of MBC in perspective:

> What multimedia thrusts upon us as never before is the necessity to keep text and context in constant tension with one another. The computer with its unlimited capacity, rather than challenging our analytic and interpretive responsibilities, seduces us into believing that the truth is just around the corner of the next "text" that will fill the ultimate gap in our understanding. But this universe of spoken, visual, written, and printed texts is not self-explanatory. As a medium, it can only substitute itself for the living context and foster the illusion that context is nothing but an assembly of texts that get illuminated in unmediated fashion by juxtaposing them with other texts. Contrary to folk wisdom, understanding has not been made more immediate through the advent of multimedia technology. Rather, it has become more mediated than ever, with a mediation that ever more diffuses and conceals its authority. The role of education, and foreign language education in particular, is precisely to make this mediation process visible. (Kramsch & Andersen, 1999, p. 39)

The very important process of mediation means that the role of the teacher in instruction is not endangered by the rapid deployment of MBC, but rather that the need for the teacher to effectively mediate learning materials is even greater with MBC.

Today's Language Learners

Language learners of today—both in the environment of traditional instruction and by independent efforts—are increasingly computer literate. Two labels accurately fit this audience: They are visually literate and entertainment oriented. This generation is capable of working well with MBC and in a TELL environment but also demands much of the materials, in terms of graphic user interface (GUI), help functions and navigational ease, and of the instructor mediating them (Gölz, 1999). Although computer-assisted language learning (CALL) materials have existed since the 1960s (Levy, 1997), the tremendous leap to multimedia and Internet-based resources is having a greater impact. An expanding amount of interactive materials on the World Wide Web (WWW), MBC on CD-ROM or DVD, and exciting CMC options such as archived discussion boards, chatrooms, and email are all transforming the ability to learn a foreign or second language effectively (Bush, 1997). Because today's language learners are so technologically sophisticated, they respond to materials and methods that give sensory stimulation and genuine feedback.

INTERACTIVE, LEARNER-CENTERED INSTRUCTION

Growing from a basis in CALL, recent MBC and TELL materials, resources in the WWW, and CMC technology will continue to transform the role of teacher and empower interactive, learner-centered language learning. While the practical advantages of MBC and TELL lie both in the presentation of culturally rich materials and in interactive feedback, the next generation of teachers needs to find adequate means of acquiring technological knowledge and skills, within specific language training programs leading to teacher certification or graduate language programs, in order to work most effectively with students.

This discussion approaches the problem eclectically by suggesting specific innovations in material for pedagogical courses and general recommendations for instructors training students, the basis of which stresses exploration, implementation, and reflection. It assumes that the current task-based instructional paradigm, which seeks meaningful contexts for speech acts, is a viable theoretical basis for language learning (Savignon, 1983; Hadley, 1993). One ever-present question is the appropriate starting point for this discussion: Are the new technological options really necessary for students to learn in the most pedagogically effective manner?

How Effective Are MBC and TELL?

In one well-documented case, students using a multimedia computer-assisted language learning system (MCALL) at the Universiti Malaysia Sarawak, with absolutely no instructor help, earned significantly higher TOEFL scores, at a reduced cost to the institution,[1] than students who were in conventional, instructor-led classes (Soo & Ngeow, 1998). Questions concerning their competency in oral proficiency, the nature of the motivational factors involved, and the perhaps dubious quality of the instructors aside, the question of what students do achieve in a teacher-mediated format of MBC is of vital interest. Although the results of teacher-mediated MBC are still dramatically challenged by some scholars (Roche, 1999), the effectiveness and enjoyment of MBC involving an instructor in the language learning process are claimed by both students and teachers in many surveys and studies (Bush, 1997). The best argument for implementing MBC and TELL lies in their unique strengths.

The Strengths of MBC and TELL

The strengths of MBC are that sound, still image, video, and hypertext are superior to a course based on a textbook, because the learner has the visual and aural input of real speech in a context (Pennington, 1996; Levy, 1997). The use of interactive exercises in a TELL setting, which give better, immediate feedback based on the learner's answers, is also superior to the completion of material that must be evaluated later. Self-paced learning with MBC and TELL, within the successful task-based instructional paradigm[2] involving interaction with an instructor and other students, has become an effective course format.

Examples of beginner-level MBC materials include video clips of dialogs and interviews, which a learner can use repeatedly, and often have many "help"[3] features that explain the language the learner sees, hears, and reads. This pattern of repetition, combined with meaningful "help" on demand, is extremely effective in improving listening ability (Joiner, 1997). Examples of effective cultural resources include hypertexts illustrating the unique traditions and values in a given culture, as well as biographical and historical materials. The material that governments, organizations, and businesses place in the WWW can also be adapted for language learning (Green, 1997; Glatz, 1998; Walz, 1998).

Multimedia materials are especially helpful with intermediate-level learners, because progress at the level beyond beginner seems slow and student frustration is often high. Hypertext for intermediate-level learners is a dramatic advancement, because it allows learners to hear passages, to see the related images, and to use the extensive help features. The result of hypertext usage is rapid acquisition of vocabulary (Chun & Plass, 1996) and an improved ability to read (Martinez-Lage, 1997). Reading is an important vocabulary builder (Roche, 1999) and greatly accelerates the ability to comprehend speech, a factor in communicative competence. The entertaining aspect of multimedia is also motivating for learners. Both independent individual learning and shared learning in groups are options with hypertexts.

MBC learning experiences are culturally rich, visually oriented, and less frustrating than the traditional textbook-based instruction. The positive results of MBC materials include an increased ease of oral comprehension and reading ability, an emphasis on speaking in context, as modeled for example in video clips, and grammatical information integrated into the useful passages presented as hypertext. The use of MBC also lends itself to cooperative learning. Concentrated work on specific vocabulary, with which students have difficulty, is possible. The greatest benefit is in the use of better, immediate feedback in TELL, which helps to maintain continued interest in learning. Learners who use MBC and TELL materials are truly a new generation.

TEACHER TRAINING INVOLVING TECHNOLOGY

The issue of training instructors to effectively work with important technological options will be divided into four parts in this discussion: (1) the challenges of MBC and TELL, (2) the challenges of CMC, (3) the role of distance education and online instruction, and (4) recommendations for improving teacher training curricula.

The Challenges of MBC and TELL

The new MBC and TELL instructional options challenge students and instructors with many exciting, difficult, and unresolved issues involved in converting traditional pedagogical methodology to effective practices mediated by computer technology. These issues relate to two areas of language instruction: (1) presenting course content to the learner and (2) enhancing each individual's learning processes with feedback. The topic of evaluating each individual's academic achievement by means of assessment technology, which could include testing by means of traditional-type questions (true/false, multiple choice, etc.) in a computer format, which also logs answers and calculates scores, is an important issue, but beyond the scope of this discussion.[4]

New teachers must become aware of the MBC and TELL materials available for their given language of instruction and fluent in their practical use. Instead of assuming the practice of passive implementation of commercially packaged content and interactive exercises, often without a direct link to classroom practices, teachers now being trained need to be introduced to and gain solid experience with the following six pedagogical considerations: (1) the theory and practice of evaluating MBC and TELL materials, (2) the theory and practice of mediating the social context of multimedia, (3) the interface of culture and language, (4) the role of individual learning styles, (5) the role of cooperative learning, and (6) the basics of creating MBC and TELL materials, especially interactive exercises, available to students on local networks, distributed on the WWW, or on transportable media storage systems, such as CD-ROM or DVD.[5]

Evaluating MBC and TELL Materials. The challenges of implementing MBC and TELL materials must be preceded by active involvement in exploring and evaluating MBC and TELL materials, in regard to both technical and pedagogical concerns (Kassen & Higgins, 1997; Scott, 1998). Questions as to whether the given materials can account for diverse learning styles, or offer an array of "help" options, or have a range of level-appropriate scenes or exercises must be given equal weight with questions as to whether the graphic user interface (GUI) is logical and inviting or whether the video clips can be effectively interrupted and repeated (Plass, 1998). In the process of learning to evaluate MBC and TELL materials, students training to be instructors attain the necessary level of technical comfort with computer operation. Knowing when a program or a computer is not functioning correctly can be very important, especially if the number of computers or the time for student use is limited.

A teacher training model suggested by Kassen and Higgins (1997), which they label the Language Learning Technology (LLT) module, stresses that learning to teach with MBC and TELL materials involves five distinct phases: preparation, familiarization, exploration, integration, and synthesis. Underlying each phase is the important opportunity for reflection on theory and practice, yielding both knowledge and skill. The end result is technological options integrated into the learning experience for students, from which the instructor can better evaluate other MBC and TELL materials for possible selection.

Scott (1998) emphasizes that graduate teaching assistants (TAs) would do well to relate the technological capability of MBC or TELL materials to underlying pedagogical theories. Scott correctly views three basic learning modes—the sequential, the relational, and the creative—for each of which different materials are designed. It is also recommended that teachers in training develop research skills for studying how students react to MBC and TELL and their performance with various learning environments. Such inquiry is still quite unevolved, but will influence the development of future MBC and TELL materials (Chapelle, 1998). Scott's analysis complements the ideas of Kassen and Higgins, also finding that the need for reflection in adopting technology to be crucial.

The following four points are meant to focus on pedagogical concerns that future teachers confront in both evaluating and implementing MBC and TELL materials, followed by the more difficult area of creating such materials. Each area not only involves a keen concern with the *how* of technological options. It should be emphasized that teachers must also reflect on the *what* and *why* of the materials in a learning environment (Tedick & Walker, 1995).

Mediating the Social Context of MBC. That students being trained to teach a foreign or second language should understand the problematic creation and implementation of multimedia is extremely important (Kramsch & Andersen, 1999). Because MBC is itself a mediated social context for language learning, altered and interpreted by the attempt to depict language usage, the crucial role of the teacher to explain and amplify the full cultural background of the material is not diminished, but increased. Although MBC is a much improved starting point for productive classroom interaction, over textbooks, it offers much more detailed material to the student and can therefore be overwhelming.

The student enters into an exploratory mode of learning that must be mediated by the instructor for full understanding. Practical examples of successfully mediating the social context of MBC include (1) interpreting the appearance and actions of people, (2) interpreting the patterns of interaction between people, (3) interpreting locations and living spaces, and (4) interpreting important objects. Mediation of these four aspects contributes to the acquisition of information in order to compare and contrast both the cultural and socioeconomic background of the MBC with that of the individual learners. What may be depicted as common or ordinary, special or unusual, must be explored for its contextual background *and* its language usage.

Understanding the language used by the people in the given MBC, though the primary goal of the learner, is but one part of the material. The language is made living, but subject to even greater scrutiny. The competent teacher learns how to use the entire offering for positive learning by exploring with students all the nonverbal material that MBC provides. In focusing then on language usage, which is best understood in terms of this larger contextual background (Frommer, 1998), the teacher has mediated this material and related it to the specific language used.

The Interface of Culture and Language. Word order, verb tenses, and vocabulary usage in meaningful speech acts do not reflect the grammatical order that textbooks seek to impose on a language. The teacher must often mediate the language presented in MBC for effective student understanding. An important part of this role involves the active exploration of the interface of culture and language in the many situations presented in MBC. The use of formal and informal address, for example, is lifted from being a grammatical emphasis to a cultural reality with the students truly being able to recognize the social context behind the language they see and hear.

Because the interface of culture and language is less visible to those who have insight into a particular linguistic region, either as native speakers or acquired through periods of residency, no activity is more useful to the future teacher than the refreshing experience of working as a beginning language learner with MBC. This process is revealing and enables one upon reflection to be more aware of those aspects of culture that place language in a unique contextual background that must be mediated for full understanding (Kramsch & Andersen, 1999).

The Role of Individual Learning Styles. The nature of an individual student's reaction to any learning environment reflects unique and often complex motivation and personality, and the fit between classroom dynamics and the individual student's learning style can influence language acquisition (Meunier, 1998). While learning style preferences vary and reflect personality differences, MBC and TELL materials are actually a means to bridge the learning style preferences of various learners in a class. An instructor using MBC and TELL materials can balance activities that involve linear and concrete thought processes with those that are more interpretative and open ended.

Although the use of TELL materials is at times more problematic, as the nature of the given interactive exercise and feedback may not fit well with an individual's learning style, the key to effective use of MBC and TELL materials is to assume that any given computer activity is only one of many learning tools in working toward a specific goal. Some learners will indeed find TELL in general more effective for them than others, just as some learners will respond more positively to a certain type of TELL activity than another (Levy, 1997). Practical examples of successfully accommodating individual learning styles include (1) stressing target vocabulary items by means of activities involving all four skills, (2) supplementing difficult grammatical points with additional oral practice, and (3) introducing tasks that involve negotiating meaning, bridge information gaps, and have many possible means of completion or allow creative answers. The challenge of MBC and TELL materials for the instructor is not so different from that of traditional methodology: to be able to monitor student progress toward language acquisition and to provide additional material or activities when necessary.

The Role of Cooperative Learning. The practical implementation of MBC and TELL provides rich opportunities for cooperative learning, whereby students work as partners or in small groups on tasks involving not only listening and reading, but also speaking and writing (Beauvois, 1998). The product of such work can then be taken up in classroom activities. Approaching MBC as a learning environment for students in isolation, alone at a workstation, fails to play to its strength as an engaging and entertaining medium that allows productive partner and group activities that help all participants. Partners and groups, separated geographically, could in fact meet solely in the context of the same cyberspace learning environment (Hoven, 1999).

Beyond the real-world limitation of perhaps not having enough workstations for each learner, which could then be made into an advantage, the use of cooperative learning strategies reinforces the mediated nature of MBC, owing to the interpretative nature of video clips and images. Practical examples of successful cooperative learning strategies include the following: (1) adopting techniques from the use of video in the classroom, such as previewing activities and description activities of images or video clips without sound, (2) basing role-play activities in small groups on the given situations introduced in MBC, and (3) adapting dialogs and interviews presented in MBC for team writing assignments. Many assignments for individual completion can be the basis of cooperative learning activities. The dynamic contexts of MBC naturally provide excellent material for subsequent class discussions.

Creating MBC and TELL Materials. Few instructors or creators of multimedia have the personal experience of extensive language learning in such interactive visual environments as are now available. Many teachers have also never been trained to evaluate and implement MBC and TELL materials. There is still, in general, a lack of institutional support for such training. The perception that authoring software is very difficult also remains a stumbling block. Multimedia is often not integrated into the curriculum and outcomes, but fulfills a supplemental role. Although rapid changes in hardware and software do occur, the stability of the WWW is a bright spot for development efforts. Digitizing existing materials (pictures, slides, music, texts, etc.) for use as language learning resources on the WWW, especially on cultural topics, has been a realistic goal for many instructors and programs, although substantial efforts do require the use of an advanced relational database (Pusack & Otto, 1997). The effort at creating cultural resources online and directing learners to authentic materials on the WWW is already highly developed (Green, 1997; Glatz, 1998; Walz, 1998). The creation of more comprehensive multimedia materials, with advanced interactive exercises giving useful feedback, is an ongoing challenge.

The need for future teachers to learn to be fluent in the creation of MBC and TELL materials can be best addressed in a course format that combines students with a technical background with language students.[6] The instructional format could also be an interdisciplinary team-teaching one, with faculty from a language discipline and from the appropriate technical department, such as instructional design, technical communications, or computer science. A good introduction to the process of design grows from evaluating MBC and TELL materials and should continue by offering practical experience in placing materials on the WWW. Such a course would have an emphasis on completing group projects for language learning. Because several WYSIWYG editors[7] for the Hypertext Markup Language (HTML) as well as many exercise templates available in PERL, Java, or Javascript software languages exist in the case of the WWW and because the multimedia authoring software choices also include numerous templates and media editors, the core of such a course could take many directions. The ingredients for success, however, would be an emphasis on incorporating various learning styles into the group projects and designing projects of an appropriate scope.

The Challenges of CMC

The options of CMC also challenge students and instructors with many exciting, difficult, and unresolved issues involved in converting traditional pedagogical methodology to effective practices mediated by computer technology. These issues relate to two areas of language instruction: (1) facilitating and monitoring interaction with students and (2) facilitating and monitoring interaction between students.

The first implementation of CMC by instructors can be daunting. The instructor is confronted with the issue of preparing students both technically and in terms of the expectations of their active participation. It must be remembered that the effectiveness of technological adaptation is determined in each instance by the level of comfort the participants bring or attain in regard to the requirements posed by such new methodology. No training for instructors in this endeavor is better than the active learning experience of using CMC in teacher training courses as forums for ideas, for experimentation, and for reflection.

The function of CMC can be considered in two ways. The first function is the facilitating of language production in level-appropriate forums, and the second function is the monitoring of language use in order to focus on form and offer corrective feedback in a positive manner. The primary choices in CMC methodology are the options of having either synchronous or asynchronous communication and the degree of instructor facilitation and monitoring. The advantage of synchronous communication is that the student input is rewarded with feedback quickly in the form of the responses by other students and/or language models, which can be stimulating and maintain the energy of a discussion. This communication is true cooperative learning. The disadvantage is the grammatical inaccuracy that occurs and must be tolerated.

The advantage of asynchronous communication is in the time and effort students can expend in increasing grammatical accuracy. The choice of instructor and language model involvement as a means of facilitating discussion in either type of forum has an impact on the communication. A key question is how to offer feedback without dampening the communicative drive, which allows for less grammatical accuracy. One means is to have individual student input in a CMC forum later reviewed by an instructor for the purpose of returning this input to that individual with error corrections and/or explanations. Another is to have the general problems of several students observed by the instructor discussed in comments and explanations received by all students. Research indicates that the use of CMC can be a means to reduce stress in communication as well as to facilitate self-expression (Beauvois, 1998). The use of CMC is also an excellent source of reading material, in which the students are involved actively (Bernhardt & Kamil, 1998).

The specific CMC technology involved can allow students to form and engage in smaller group discussions within a forum, with individual students joining and leaving as desired, much like the natural interaction of people at a social gathering. The use of email is another example of asynchronous CMC. The main difference between forms of CMC and classroom conversation is in the ability of the participants to make self-corrections to utterances during production and review that production later (Beauvois, 1998; Kelm, 1998). A full research agenda, however, must be undertaken to understand the nature of the learning occurring in this type of interaction (Ortega, 1997).

A comparison of experiences of students and instructors involved in the innovative use of CMC technology indicates several common themes. Various CMC tools available for local networks and on the WWW facilitate proactive learning and enhance the nature of cooperative learning. The convenience of asynchronous communication, allowing for flexibility in balancing work, school, and family schedules, is also a significant benefit. Although technological skill, as employed for example in engaging in group work electronically, is not the focus of academic achievement, the skills and experiences involved will serve students well in the changing world of employment and lifelong learning.

CMC requires more active learning on the part of the student and enhances cooperative learning among students. In general, because the products of student work are placed in the more permanent forum of electronic bulletin boards or the WWW, which are subject to later review by both students and instructors, the students exhibit a greater interest in meaningful expression in discussions and assignments. Students in CMC have, in fact, been determined to be more productive in the target language (Beauvois, 1997). The future of CMC will be explored, discussed, and debated in the classrooms, the synchronous chatrooms, the asynchronous electronic bulletin boards, and the email of those instructors and students who participate in expanding the active vocabulary of what constitutes this new language of academic interaction.

DISTANCE LEARNING AND ONLINE INSTRUCTION

Evolving out of distance learning courses, based largely on materials on videocassette and teleconferencing, but now incorporating computer technologies, the possibility of language learning in an online-only instructional format may be realized in the coming years. Only if instructors and students can fully utilize CMC options, including advanced audio capabilities, will this format be so effective as to challenge the face-to-face interaction between instructors and students and between students themselves (Gölz, 1999). The latter is of special consideration. The use of email by a class, for example, that does meet face-to-face will necessarily be different from the communication via email of students who only have only this contact. The mediating role of instructors is, however, still an assumption of distance learning and online instructional options.

The unique ability of online exercises to give real, if not individual, feedback is also of note. Whereas the weakest link in distance learning courses is that individual correction of student work is often very delayed, with a long time between student involvement in the task and the student receiving feedback on the completed task (Gölz, 1999), the use of templates to place language exercises in the WWW offers a superior learning experience in distance learning courses. The interactivity of such exercises means that the learning system is functioning as a tutor in the process of completing level-appropriate work. This capability can also be used in courses with regular meetings, so that the teacher in the classroom is engaged primarily in more constructive interaction. The online-only instructional format remains at this time problematic.

IMPROVING TEACHER TRAINING CURRICULA

While many programs have relied on a one-semester course covering the basics of foreign language pedagogy, with the element of computer technology being an additional but small component in recent years, a thorough review of this curriculum is warranted. A transformation worthy of the enormous changes in instructional practice due to MBC, TELL, and CMC requires a new format. The traditional methods course, covering all material in one semester, would be best altered to integrate the study of the role of computer technology into all aspects of the traditional skills of listening, reading, writing, and speaking (Bush, 1997). A second course exploring the critical nature of the mediated social context of multimedia, perhaps even specific to one language of instruction, would then also be required, one in which students started creating MBC and TELL materials.

The state of current language learning materials also shows several important needs, which future teachers will participate in resolving. The need for developers who are teachers, trained in the theory of the mediated social context of multimedia, is foremost. The need for more MBC directed at target audiences based on age, level of instruction, and incorporating diverse learning styles, is crucial. The need exists for detailed analysis of learning patterns in order to improve materials (Chapelle, 1997). The need for partnerships between high schools and institutions of higher education is evident, so that the progressive path of language learning takes an effective hold at an earlier age. Because the need for language learning is strong in the highly mobile, communication-oriented world of the Information Age and because important advances in multimedia resources and technology suitable for language learning are greatly helping to meet the challenging requirements of language learners, the teachers of the future must master the technological palette available.

The future will bring more, better, and integrated commercial multimedia product lines, which will often be of a hybrid nature, integrating the latest media storage, such as DVD, with interactive websites. Easier authoring software will help instructors create useful units for the unique needs of individual and/or group language learners. More and better resources on the WWW will be accessible at greater speeds due to increased bandwidth, a key component for quality distance and independent language learning. A solid understanding of the productive implementation of MBC, TELL, and CMC technologies must be integrated into teacher training in the depicted manner, in order for the mediated nature of such instructional options to be used to the best possible advantage.

SUMMARY

While the need for students being trained to teach a foreign or second language to understand the problematic creation and implementation of MBC and TELL is extremely important, technology will not endanger the role of teacher. Empowering interactive, learner-centered language learning brings even greater challenges, but also greater rewards. New teachers, fluent in the materials available for their given language of instruction and in their practical use, will not simply passively implement commercially packaged content and interactive exercises.

Well-trained teachers, who understand the theory and practice of mediating the social context of multimedia, the role of individual learning styles, the interface of culture and language, the role of cooperative learning, and the basics of creating their own content and interactive exercises, will be able to meet the challenges of technologically sophisticated learners. While the practical advantages of MBC, TELL, and CMC lie both in the presentation of culturally rich materials and in interactive feedback, the next generation of teachers must critically adapt these technological options to the needs of their specific language programs. The specific innovations in pedagogical courses and general recommendations for faculty guiding students embarking on the path to second language teaching in this new millennium made here are meant to enliven the discussion on the role of the teacher and of technology in foreign and second language instruction.

NOTES

1. The remarkable increase in the efficiency of technology, as illustrated by the ever-decreasing cost of digital technology in relation to the performance supplied (Bush,

1997, p. 322), is a factor more directly of interest to the administrators who will be supporting language teaching. The reduced cost of technology, as a reason to implement it, does present a positive line of argument with which language instructors can influence such administrators.

2. The task-based instructional movement since the 1980s, with communicative competence as the primary goal of language learning, complements MBC and TELL philosophically because it regards active language usage as the primary goal of interaction between teacher and students (Savignon, 1983; Hadley, 1993). Textbook exercises have little part in such dynamic instruction, but a basis in MBC does.

3. Help features can be specific lexical items, such as providing an accurate translation for the given context; grammatical explanations, such as noting the use of the subjunctive form of a verb; or contextual notes, such as explaining that the use of a given slang term is perhaps appropriate only with friends or family.

4. The practice of using MBC but relying on pencil-and-paper testing is not invalid, because of the greater expression possibilities of this format, which should indeed be tested. The use of Oral Proficiency Interviews (OPI) is a time-intensive procedure, but the single best means to test real communicative competence. A computer-assisted version of this method does not yet exist.

5. The selection and deployment of specific media storage systems is an important factor, as the generation of the laserdisc and laserdisc player is rapidly being replaced, leaving many programs that adopted them quickly at a high cost with outdated, unsupported technology. The stability of the WWW, in which a simple Hypertext Markup Language (HTML) page remains accessible, but for which new extensions are added without affecting simpler HTML pages, is of note.

6. This format has been successful at several institutions, including the author's college.

7. WYSIWYG editors allow the material on the computer screen of the creator to be exactly what the student will view: What You See Is What You Get.

REFERENCES

Beauvois, M. (1997). Computer-mediated communication (CMC): Technology for improving speaking and writing. In M. Bush (ed.), *Technology-enhanced language learning*. Lincolnwood, IL: National Textbook.

Beauvois, M. (1998). E-Talk: Computer-assisted classroom discussion. In J. Swaffar, S. Romano, P. Markley, & K. Arens (eds.), *Language learning online: Theory and practice in the ESL and L2 computer classroom*. Austin: Labyrinth. Retrieved August 17, 1999, from the World Wide Web: http://labyrinth.daedalus.com/LLO.

Bernhardt, E., & Kamil, M. (1998). Enhancing foreign culture learning through electronic discussion. In J. Muyskens (ed.), *New ways of learning and teaching: Focus on technology and foreign language education*. Boston: Heinle & Heinle.

Bush, M. (1997). Implementing technology in language learning. In M. Bush (ed.), *Technology-enhanced language learning*. Lincolnwood, IL: National Textbook.

Chapelle, C. (1997). CALL in the year 2000: Still in search of research paradigms? *Language Learning & Technology,* 1(1): 19–43. Retrieved August 17, 1999, from the World Wide Web: http://polyglot.cal.msu.edu/llt/vol1num1/chapelle/default.html.

Chapelle, C. (1998). Multimedia CALL: Lessons to be learned from research on Instructed SLA. *Language Learning & Technology,* 2(1): 22–34. Retrieved August 17, 1999, from the World Wide Web: http://polyglot.cal.msu.edu/llt/vol2num1/article1/index.html.

Chun, D., & Plass, J. (1996). Effects of multimedia annotations on vocabulary acquisition. *Modern Language Journal,* 80(2): 183–198.

Frommer, J. (1998). Cognition, context, and computers: Factors in effective foreign language learning. In J. Muyskens (ed.), *New ways of learning and teaching: Focus on technology and foreign language education.* Boston: Heinle & Heinle.

Glatz, L. (1998). Business German and the WWW. *PEALS: Journal of the Colorado Congress of Foreign Language Teachers,* 35(2): 10–21.

Gölz, P. (1999). Bridging the gap: Distance education courses on the Web. *IALL Journal of Language Learning Technologies,* 31(1/2): 17–23.

Green, A. (1997). A beginner's guide to the Internet in the foreign language classroom with a focus on the World Wide Web. *Foreign Language Annals,* 30(2): 253–264.

Hadley, A. (1993). *Teaching language in context: Proficiency-oriented instruction,* 2nd edition. Boston: Heinle & Heinle.

Hoven, D. (1999). A model for listening and viewing comprehension in multimedia environments. *Language Learning & Technology,* 3(1): 88–103. Retrieved August 17, 1999, from the World Wide Web: http://polyglot.cal.msu.edu/llt/vol3num1/hoven/index.html.

Joiner, E. (1997). Teaching listening: How technology can help. In M. Bush (ed.), *Technology-enhanced language learning.* Lincolnwood, IL: National Textbook.

Kassen, M., & Higgins, C. (1997). Meeting the technology challenge: Introducing teachers to language-learning technology. In M. Bush (ed.), *Technology-enhanced language learning.* Lincolnwood, IL: National Textbook.

Kelm, O. (1998). The use of electronic mail in foreign language classes. In J. Swaffar, S. Romano, P. Markley, & K. Arens (eds.), *Language learning online: Theory and practice in the ESL and L2 computer classroom.* Austin: Labyrinth. Retrieved August 17, 1999, from the World Wide Web: http://labyrinth.daedalus.com/LLO.

Kramsch, C., & Andersen, W. (1999). Teaching text and context through multimedia. *Language Learning & Technology,* 2(2): 31–42. Retrieved August 17, 1999, from the World Wide Web: http://polyglot.cal.msu.edu/llt/vol2num2/article1/index.html.

Levy, M. (1997). *Computer-assisted language learning: Context and conceptualization.* New York: Oxford University Press.

Martinez-Lage, A. (1997). Hypermedia technology for reading. In M. Bush (ed.), *Technology-enhanced language learning.* Lincolnwood, IL: National Textbook.

Meunier, L. (1998). Personality and motivational factors in computer-mediated foreign language communication (CMLFC). In J. Muyskens (ed.), *New ways of learning and teaching: Focus on technology and foreign language education.* Boston: Heinle & Heinle.

Ortega, L. (1997). Processes and outcomes in networked classroom interaction: Defining the research agenda for L2 computer-assisted classroom discussion. *Language Learning & Technology,* 1(1): 82–93. Retrieved August 17, 1999, from the World Wide Web: http://polyglot.cal.msu.edu/llt/vol1num1/ortega/default.html.

Pennington, M. (1996). The power of the computer in language education. In M. Pennington (ed.), *The Power of CALL.* Houston: Athelstan.

Plass, J. (1998). Design and evaluation of the user interface of foreign language multimedia software: A cognitive approach. *Language Learning & Technology,* 2(1): 35–45. Retrieved August 17, 1999, from the World Wide Web: http://polyglot.cal.msu.edu/llt/vol2num1/article2/index.html.

Pusack, J., & Otto, S. (1997). Taking control of multimedia. In M. Bush (ed.), *Technology-enhanced language learning.* Lincolnwood, IL: National Textbook.

Roche, J. (1999). Multimedia in language instruction: Challenges and solutions. *IALL Journal of Language Learning Technologies,* 31(1/2): 45–52.

Savignon, S. (1983). *Communicative competence: Theory and classroom practice.* Reading, MA: Addison-Wesley.

Scott, V. (1998). Exploring the link between teaching and technology: An approach to TA development. In J. Muyskens (ed.), *New ways of learning and teaching: Focus on technology and foreign language education.* Boston: Heinle & Heinle.

Soo, K., & Ngeow, Y. (1998). Effective English as a Second Language (ESL) instruction with interactive multimedia: The MCALL Project. *Journal of Educational Multimedia and Hypermedia,* 7(1): 71–90.

Tedick, D., & Walker, J. (1995). From theory to practice: How do we prepare teachers for second language classrooms? *Foreign Language Annals,* 28(4): 499–517.

Walz, J. (1998). Meeting standards for foreign language learning with World Wide Web activities. *Foreign Language Annals,* 31(1): 103–114.

15

Challenges in Language Teacher Training

Mary J. Schleppegrell

As a fresh graduate with a master's degree, Sarah got a job teaching composition to immigrant students in a U.S. university composition program. Her students come from mixed first language backgrounds, but all are graduates of American high schools who need to further improve their English for university work. Their interests span a range of academic disciplines. Sarah's primary responsibility is to help them improve their writing and grammar so that they can pass the university's composition exam.

Paul's job is in a community college in California, where he teaches a variety of skills courses (listening/speaking, reading, writing, grammar) to students at a wide range of proficiency levels and from a variety of language backgrounds. Some are in job training programs, and some are planning to go on to university. He follows the program's curriculum, but often has to adapt materials to the specific groups of students taking his classes.

Mary works in an Intensive English program affiliated with a local university. She teaches a variety of courses, including English for specific purposes (ESP). As her students typically come to the United States in groups from the same country, they share a first language. The program and students expect Mary to be a cultural informant about life in the United States as well as to teach her students English.

Jeanie's job is at an adult school run by the local school district. She works with immigrant students who have recently arrived in the United States and are beginners in English. Many of them are not literate in their native languages. They want to learn "survival skills," including the language they need to find jobs, locate housing, and negotiate with their children's schools. Jeanie teaches in churches or other settings without classroom equipment, and where attendance is irregular. She often finds that the assigned textbooks are inappropriate or too difficult for her students.

Doris got a job at a university in China after graduation. She teaches seven two-hour classes, all with different preparations, including oral skills, extensive reading, and writing. The textbooks she has been assigned to use are in Chinese and English. Teaching extensive reading is difficult with the limited materials that are available, and students have to be encouraged to write more than very short texts. Many of her students have good knowledge of English grammar, but want to develop English communication skills.

Hsueh-chu returned to her native Taiwan after graduation, where she is teaching English in a university program. She would like to employ the communicative methods that she learned about during her training program, but the institutional expectations and her junior status make it difficult for her to introduce new approaches.

Jeff joined the Peace Corps, where his assignment sent him to Morocco to teach English to classes of up to 120 students at a time. The examination-driven curriculum frustrates him in his attempts to introduce new material or use different methods from the translation and grammar review that his students are used to.

Erin also went overseas. Her job is with two private language schools in Portugal, where her classes are held at businesses before work, at lunchtime, and in the evenings. Some of her ESP students are highly motivated, while others are not. As the program has no set curriculum, Erin has complete responsibility for planning lessons. Requiring homework is impossible, and attendance is often poor because the students have other responsibilities that come before English. Students are goal-oriented and complain when the lessons do not seem relevant to what they believe they need.

In our applied linguistics master's degree program, we are confronted with the challenge of providing a curriculum that can prepare graduates for this wide variety of possible job opportunities. This chapter discusses these challenges (see also Erben in this volume) and some ways that our program is trying to address them in preparing future teachers for such a range of possible teaching contexts.[1]

CHALLENGES OF DIVERSE CONTEXTS

Table 15.1 outlines the special features of the types of language teaching programs that employ our graduates. It shows how the students' characteris-

Table 15.1 Features of Language Teaching Settings

Type of School	Student Characteristics	Curriculum Focus	Instructional Challenges
University in United States	Immigrants, International students	Academic focus	Teaching for high-level academic achievement
	Usually advanced level	Reading and writing skills	
Community Colleges in United States	Immigrants, International students	Academic and employment focus	Teaching a variety of levels to students with varied goals
	Level varies	Variety of skills	
Intensive English programs in United States	International students	Academic focus	Teaching a variety of skills and levels
	Level varies	Variety of skills	
		Cultural topics	Providing cultural information
Adult schools in United States	Immigrants	Survival skills focus	Teaching beginning level students without literacy skills
	Beginning, intermediate levels	Listening/speaking skills	
	Some not literate in L1	Cultural topics	Teaching under difficult circumstances (assigned materials not always appropriate, facilities may be temporary, attendance may be irregular)
University outside United States	Students from homogeneous first language backgrounds	Academic focus	Teaching where academic norms and procedures are unfamiliar; may be British English norms
	Level varies; often different levels of speaking and listening than of reading and writing	Variety of skills	Teaching students who have no interaction with native speakers
	Students often have good knowledge of grammar rules		Materials may be limited, grammar-based, or outdated
Language school outside United States	Students from homogeneous first language backgrounds	Employment focused; often ESP	Teaching students who have no interaction with native speakers
	Level varies	Variety of skills	Materials may be unavailable or not appropriate; often British English norms
	Interests and motivation for learning English vary		Teaching mixed levels; attendance may be irregular

tics, the curriculum focus, and the instructional challenges of the teaching assignments differ from one type of institution to another. It also shows that the settings in which new teachers will work range from academic to very informal, some in second language and some in foreign language contexts. The students with whom teachers we are training will work range from illiterate immigrants to highly proficient international students seeking Ph.D.'s from U.S. institutions, to university students or businesspeople in their home countries. The kinds of curricula we need to prepare teachers to work with range from academic programs with a set series of materials and tasks to very open-ended programs with no set curriculum. In addition, norms may be British rather than American. The instructional challenges in these settings also vary widely, with small classes and large, with current or outdated materials, and with a variety of expectations regarding culture and its role in English teaching. Preparing teachers to be effective in this range of possible assignments is a challenge to our program, as each of the different settings suggests a different set of goals and objectives for teacher preparation.

An added challenge is that the teacher trainees themselves come from a diversity of backgrounds and experiences. A significant number are nonnative speakers of English, reflecting the fact that more English teachers worldwide are nonnative speakers than native speakers.[2] Native speakers and nonnative speakers typically have different needs, as they have different implicit and explicit knowledge of English, different cultural backgrounds, and different expectations for themselves as future teachers. Of course, beyond the broad generalizations we can make about native speakers and nonnative speakers, each individual student brings a different set of prior teaching experiences and familiarity with other cultures.[3]

This means that a teacher-training program has to address a wide range of issues in preparing a diverse group of students to teach in such varied potential contexts. This chapter addresses some of those issues, including (1) the appropriate research base to draw on to prepare teachers; (2) curriculum issues such as the levels to prepare teachers for, the materials to prepare them to use, and the methods and approaches to introduce and to give teachers for practice; and (3) the complex role of culture in language teaching. Following a discussion of these issues, this chapter presents some strategies that our program uses to respond to these challenges.

The Research Base

The process of language acquisition is different for learners in different environments. Language learning populations in different contexts present teachers with a wide range of profiles in terms of their skills, goals, and motivations; research done in one context may not be generalizable to other, different contexts. This means that the theoretical understanding of the process of second language acquisition (SLA) that we present to prospective teachers needs to be rich enough to account for the wide range of contexts in which these teachers will work. Each SLA study investigates learning processes in particular kinds of learners, so that the conclusions and recommendations of any particular research study may not be general to other SLA contexts. Scarcella (1996), for example, points out that much of the research on which Krashen's (1982) influential hypotheses about SLA are based was done on foreign students in the United States. These hypotheses, then, may not be useful in explaining the learning processes of long-term immigrant students who have well-developed spoken English skills, but lack writing skills—the students whom Sarah, mentioned earlier, teaches.

Nayar (1997) makes a similar point, arguing that the research base for second language teaching is not always relevant to foreign language teaching contexts.[4] Nayar compares language learning environments in different contexts and concludes that "[t]he socio-cultural and affective domains of language learning as well as the political and economic factors that control language policy, language use, language availability, and teaching conditions" are so different "as to make many of the socio-linguistic principles, theoretical assumptions, and pedagogical practices of one . . . ineffective [or] inoperable in the other" (1997, p. 24). Engaged in foreign language teaching, teachers like Doris, Hsueh-chu, Jeff, and Erin will need different strategies and different understanding of learning processes than their peers who teach in second language settings.

Research based on the narrow context of ESL in the United States thus may be limited in its validity for generalization to other contexts. Sridhar and Sridhar (1992) and Kachru (1994) provide critiques of SLA theory that focus on how standard presentations of the processes of SLA typically ignore data from learners in bilingual and multilingual contexts. Although these researchers focus specifically on contexts of indigenized world varieties of English, such as in India, many of the issues they raise are important to consider in preparing teachers for other contexts as well. For example, do we assume that the goal in language teaching is for students to acquire native-like competence in the target language? If so, how is "native-like competence" to be understood? Does it include native-like performance of speech acts and genres? If so, what is the "native-like" target? Speech acts and genres are cultural, emerging from social interaction and conventions that have been established in particular speech communities. Native speaker norms may be irrelevant when the students' primary interlocutors will be other nonnative speakers of English. A focus on acquisition in native contexts assumes that learners are immersed in the target language, that their mother tongue has little social role, and that its use interferes with communication (Sridhar, 1994). But this is not the case for many learners who will use English in their own cultural and social contexts, where English may alternate with or supplement the use of other languages. In such cases, the L1 does not just serve the interference or facilitation roles that are typically ascribed to it. Instead, features of learner language that might appear to be "errors" in the context of English monolingual settings may be universally shared and appropriate in the English as a foreign language context, where they mark membership in a particular community of speakers (Sridhar & Sridhar, 1992).[5]

Some of the accepted major constructs of SLA theory, such as interlanguage, also need to be reconsidered. Sridhar suggests that the term *interlanguage* leads us to view most learners as unsuccessful, since they never achieve "native-like" proficiency. Instead, he argues, many learners are successful bilinguals who learn the language skills they need for the full range of communicative contexts in which they find themselves, none of which may involve native speakers of English. Sridhar argues for "a more functionally oriented and culturally authentic theory, one that is true to the ecology of multilingualism and views the multilingual's linguistic repertoire as a unified, complex, coherent, interconnected, interdependent, organic ecosystem" (1994, p. 803).

A further critique of SLA theory questions the view that the ideal motivation for success in language learning is "integrative." Recent research has shown that, in many contexts, students succeed in learning English with only instrumental motivation (Oxford & Shearin, 1994). Dörnyei (1990) focuses on foreign language learning, rather than second language learning and suggests that instrumental motives significantly contribute to motivation in foreign language learning, and that the nature of motivation also varies as a function of the level of proficiency to be attained.

Many of the findings of second language acquisition research need to be considered in light of the populations on which the research was done and reinterpreted in terms of the particular students with whom a teacher is working. Prospective teachers need to be critical readers of research who can identify what is valuable and what is irrelevant to the contexts in which they will be teaching.

Curriculum Issues

Our understanding of the contexts for which we are preparing teachers affects a host of curriculum issues, including the skills we prepare them to teach and the methods and approaches they learn to implement. This section discusses these concerns for training programs that wish to prepare teachers for a wide range of contexts.

Govardhan, Nayar, and Sheorey (1999) report on a survey of job responsibilities listed in published advertisements for EFL teachers. The prospective teachers' duties included "teaching, advising, counseling, tutoring, developing curricula, working in a language lab, directing writing programs, training teachers, directing research, preparing materials, and even providing general academic leadership" (p. 117). Courses they may be called on to teach included "listening, speaking, reading, writing, composition, English or U.S.

literature, syntax, general linguistics, English grammar, morphology, semantics, and pragmatics " (p. 117). Govardhan and associates note that teachers are also "expected to develop curricula, prepare placement and achievement tests, supervise other foreign teachers, and translate materials" (pp. 117–118). They suggest that many new teachers in EFL settings will confront "large classes, lack of teaching aids, undertrained local teachers with low English proficiency, unfamiliar educational bureaucracies, antiquated examination systems, and lack of congruence between the educational ideologies and practices of the visitors and hosts" (p. 116). This means that our teacher trainees need to be prepared to take into consideration "the educational culture of the target country, the status and role of English in the curriculum and the society, the language(s) of the students and their attitude toward English, and the availability (rather, the lack thereof) of instructional resources" (p. 116). How do we prepare teachers to cope with this range of tasks and issues?

Teacher training programs typically take a "four skills" approach, preparing students to teach listening, reading, speaking, and writing. But it is difficult for a program both to provide the same degree of focus on all four skills and to prepare teachers to work with students at all levels in each skill area. In addition, students also need to learn to teach vocabulary and grammar and to deal with cultural topics. In each of these areas, the target context for teaching greatly affects what students will need. For example, academic learners in second language contexts may have well-developed oral skills, but need extensive grammar instruction for writing. Academic learners from foreign language learning backgrounds, on the other hand, may know grammar well, but need to develop fluency in the target language. Beginners may need a particular focus on listening comprehension. Foreign language learners may prefer to develop good reading skills.

Teachers also need to be prepared to teach at all levels, but it is very difficult for training programs to provide experiences that expose future teachers to a range of beginning to advanced students. The need to develop teaching skills for a program's practicum context typically focuses teacher trainees on working with a particular group of learners on particular skills, and it is difficult also to prepare them to teach students at other proficiency levels or to focus on skill areas not relevant to their practicum teaching. The teaching practicum also occurs in either a second language or a foreign language environment (in our case, a second language setting), so it is difficult to foreground the requirements of the other teaching context.

The role of grammar teaching is a case in point. Teachers in foreign language teaching contexts need to be credible grammar teachers, since often their students are learning the language with a focus on grammar rules. On the other hand, in second language teaching contexts, the role of grammar teaching is often deemphasized, and teachers need to be able to provide opportunities for interaction and development of fluency through authentic communication activities.

Teachers also need to understand the different roles that input may have in language learning in different settings. In foreign language learning contexts, input for language learning may be available only in the classroom. This calls for different approaches and different focuses for activities from what is possible when input is available to the learner through practice opportunities outside the class.

Complicating these matters further are the different needs of native and nonnative speakers. Liu (1998) suggests that nonnative speakers have different needs in pedagogical grammar courses, since they typically already have good formal knowledge of English and need practice in its use, while native speakers often have little formal knowledge and need to learn the terms and generalizations that will enable them to present grammar to learners. The variety of the language in which to prepare students to teach also varies according to the setting. Benson (1989) points out some differences between British and American English, for example. Many of these differences are not familiar to native speakers of American English. Benson suggests that teacher-training programs need to enable teachers to adapt to settings where the language norms are British.

Teachers also need skills in curriculum development and lesson design for situations in which they have few materials. They need to be able to examine the materials they are assigned to teach and determine their relevance and usefulness for the group they will work with. Auerbach and Burgess (1985), for example, demonstrate the kind of sensitivity to materials that teachers who work with adult immigrant second language learners need in order to avoid stereotyping them as fit only for entry-level job opportunities. In some contexts teachers may be asked to teach with few or outdated materials. The teacher who has been prepared in a training program that is well stocked with the latest materials may not know how to cope. On the other hand, those who will teach in materials-rich environments need to be knowledgeable about what is available and have experience using a variety of materials and approaches, including computer-based instruction. They need to be able to work with a variety of media and state-of-the-art technology and equipment if they are to be competitive for jobs in well-funded schools.

The methodologies we introduce to prospective teachers are also not universally applicable. Most language teaching programs now focus on communicative approaches and prepare teachers to stimulate classroom interaction through experiential activities, group work, and other tasks that promote language use. While important in many contexts, such approaches are not universally appreciated or employed. Burnaby and Sun (1989), for example, report on the views of twenty-four Chinese (PRC) teachers, who cite numerous constraints on implementing Western methods in their classrooms. Li (1998) reports similar findings in his survey of and interviews with Korean teachers, who point out differences between second language teaching and foreign language teaching that make it difficult for them to adopt communicative methods. Liu (1998) argues that SLA methodologies need to address the issues that face nonnative speakers teaching in their own countries, where large classes and different expectations in foreign language teaching environments call for different methods from those expected in second language settings. Ignoring traditional methods, according to Liu, shows a disregard for "differences in socio-economic conditions, educational ideologies and systems, and other factors that help define teaching conventions" (1998, p. 4).

Training programs need to prepare teachers to work with students in diverse environments, where teachers need different kinds of skills and knowledge about language learning and teaching. Simple issues like keeping the class working in English, especially in small group situations, don't even come up where we have classes of students with mixed first languages. But for teachers working in foreign language teaching environments or in intensive programs or other contexts where their classrooms have speakers from one language background, these are key issues.

All these curriculum issues, then, including which skills to focus on, which level of proficiency to provide practice with, how to treat grammar and other topics comprehensively, and which methodologies and approaches to introduce, are important considerations for teacher training programs. Choices in each of these areas provide future teachers with different experiences and knowledge and prepare them for different kinds of teaching assignments.

The Role of Culture

Finally, the role of culture in language teaching is a major issue for teacher training programs. A focus on the role of culture includes consideration of which cultural issues should be presented in the classroom and what kinds of generalizations about culture need to be taught and practiced. In addition, the culture of the institution in which prospective teachers will work is also part of the cultural context and may require teachers to develop new understandings about the role of the teacher and how teachers might address a range of pedagogical issues in different teaching contexts. This section discusses these points and the challenges they present for teacher training programs.

Different contexts call for different perspectives on the role of culture in language teaching. Although we typically think of language and culture as being inextricably intertwined, in the context of English teaching it is important to consider what the "culture" of English is. English is a world language, and the norms and expectations for speakers in different cultural contexts are not the same as those expected in English-speaking contexts. In our case, we need to prepare teachers to help students understand cultural issues relevant to life in North American contexts, but they also need to understand that teaching about that culture may not be relevant for students who are learning English for other purposes than to integrate into life in North America or other English-speaking countries.

Nayar (1997) suggests that sociopragmatic issues involved in, for example, complimenting behavior, which may be important for students in second language contexts, are nonissues in other contexts, where complimenting behavior has different norms and expectations, even when English is used. Nayar suggests that where English is taught in a second language environment, with opportunities to use the language outside of class, and where the goal is to integrate into the native English-speaking community, English is often taught "as an emancipatory step toward the privilege of admittance into and full participation in the target society, for socioeconomic respectability and upward mobility" (p. 17). But of course this is not the context in which English is learned around the world. We need to make our teachers aware of these different ways of thinking about teaching sociocultural and pragmatic functions of language.

An additional cultural issue is the institutional culture in which the future teachers will work. We need to prepare our students to present themselves credibly in academic institutions both in their own cultures and in different cultures. This involves basic questions about the role of the teacher. Is the teacher a facilitator of learning or a repository of knowledge? How should a teacher present himself or herself, and how will students in other cultural contexts view this presentation of self? What makes a teacher credible in the U.S. context is not the same as what makes a teacher credible outside the United States. Related concerns include dealing with plagiarism, cheating, and other issues that are often seen quite differently in different contexts. Prospective teachers need to understand that there is more than one way to think about all of these issues.

Summary

We have seen that it can be problematic for future teachers if they are exposed only to research that has been done with certain kinds of learners and are taught methodologies that prepare them only for particular situations such as the second-language learning context. We need to prepare teachers for classes of mixed and homogeneous first language students, for students at different levels of proficiency, for situations that are both materials-rich and materials-poor, and for teaching in different cultural contexts. They need to be able to teach all language skills in a variety of settings. By being conscious of the different needs and contexts that the teachers we are preparing will face, we can help our students develop a more flexible approach to their profession that will enable them to continue learning and adapting to different contexts of teaching.

STRATEGIES FOR ADDRESSING THESE ISSUES

Of course, there is no one way to address these issues, and no program is likely to be able to prepare every student for every possible teaching context. But in our program we rely on three major strategies to help our future teachers begin to understand the complexities of the field they are entering. First, rather than present one way of thinking about language acquisition and one methodology for teaching, we draw on a range of research and encourage students to develop basic principles to inform their teaching. We encourage students to think about the basis of research findings and examine the relevance of particular findings for language acquisition in different contexts. Second, we provide an integrated theory and practicum course sequence that gives students a range of teaching experiences and allows them to explore issues and concerns that they know will be relevant to the contexts in which they envision themselves teaching. We do not promote a particular method-ological approach, but instead encourage teachers to explore a variety of approaches and ways of teaching and consider how different approaches might meet different learner needs. Finally, we work with student teachers to help them set their own goals for their teaching and monitor their own progress toward those goals, empowering them to be reflective teachers who can adapt to different teaching contexts. Throughout our training program, we highlight issues of culture and examine how cultural assumptions may need to be adapted or modified for different teaching situations and how teaching about culture will take different forms in different contexts.

Drawing on a Range of Research

Our students read a range of research on second language acquisition and consider the different characteristics of the learners in the research popula-tions. It is particularly easy for us to point out the differences between the newly arrived international student population on our campus and the immi-grant students who are graduates of U.S. secondary schools but who still need assistance with their language development to be effective in university-level work. Our students observe these different populations and have practicum experiences where they interact with them and come to understand the different profiles and needs of these students in terms of the language skills they most need to develop, their need for and interest in cultural information about the United States, and their goals and purposes for improving their English.

Teacher trainees benefit from an approach that gives them a broad perspective on what promotes language acquisition in different settings. We expose our students to a wide range of language teaching research and then encourage them to develop a set of principles that they can apply in choosing the approach they will take in any particular setting. In reading published research, students focus on the contexts in which different studies have been done and advice has been developed and consider how the research and advice may or may not apply to different populations. For example, reliance on comprehensible input as a stimulus for further language acquisition seems valuable and necessary with an international student population in a second language setting. But as the prospective teachers interact with immigrant students who are fluent in spoken English but exhibit serious deficiencies in their writing, they come to see that comprehensible input may no longer be the key issue and that contextualized focus on form can help students write the academic registers that are required for success in educational contexts. Rather than promote a "method" of language teaching, we encourage students to develop good understanding of what promotes language learning and then to draw on that understanding to develop the appropriate approaches for the contexts in which they find themselves.

An important aspect is encouraging our students to focus their own research on teaching-related topics of interest to them. We present them with a wide range of journals and other research resources that address language acquisition and language teaching issues and encourage them to select research topics relevant for contexts in which they envision themselves teaching. In this way, students can prepare themselves for the settings in which they see themselves teaching. Sharing this research then informs everyone in the program. Our students have carried out thesis research on such topics as promoting global education in Japan, developing ESP courses for Taiwanese, and preparing listening comprehension workshops for newly arrived international students in the United States. They have conducted research on various language skills and topics such as contrastive rhetoric or discourse analysis. These research projects enable all the prospective teachers in our program to broaden their knowledge and experience and consider issues from a variety of perspectives.

Integrating Theory and Practice

Theoretical understanding is important, but it is through the actual practice of teaching that students begin to develop their own personas as teachers and come to understand the uses and limits of theoretical knowledge. Our program offers three quarters of supervised practicum teaching, with the practice teaching linked to our theory and methods sequence of courses that are taken concurrently with the practicum. The theory and methods courses raise issues that can be explored in the practice teaching assignments and highlight approaches that will enable our students to work in varied contexts. Our approach to pedagogical grammar, for example, works to help teachers develop skills both in explicit grammar teaching and in focusing on accuracy in a fluency-based approach.

Over the course of an academic year, students experience different contexts of teaching and focus on different skills. During their first quarter, students teach newly arrived international graduate students, focusing on listening and speaking skills at the same time that they read and learn about basic principles and approaches to language teaching. As novice teachers themselves, they are provided with lesson plans and materials and guided in what they teach. They also engage in observation tasks with a very different group of ESL learners, the immigrant undergraduate students. This gives them a context for comparison of different learner populations from the very beginning of our program.

During the second quarter, our methods course focuses on curriculum, materials, and syllabus design. The student teachers take more responsibility for their practicum teaching, choosing a skill area such as reading or listening and developing their own mini-courses. They draw on a variety of resources, exploring their particular skill area in depth and familiarizing themselves with the range of resources available. Those interested in technology, for example, can investigate computer-assisted language learning, while those planning to teach in settings with few resources can explore ways of using simple resources to design lessons and activities (see, for example, Schleppegrell & Bowman, 1995). Teachers share what they have learned with their peers in the methods course, giving all of them the benefit of the in-depth work that each has done in a particular area.

The teachers we prepare need to be able to assess what is needed in a particular context and have the resources to be able to take the skills focus or content focus that fits the setting in which they are teaching and adapt it to the level of the learners they are working with. To make this possible, the prospective teachers learn how to conduct a needs assessment that gives them information about students' purposes for learning and current proficiency levels (Schleppegrell, 1991). Equipped with skills for assessing students' needs, they can make curriculum and methodology decisions that are appropriate for the particular circumstances in which they may find themselves. Following this needs assessment, the teachers develop their own syllabi and experiment with a variety of approaches to lesson design.

As part of their practicum experience, students also employ a problem-posing approach to help them learn more about their students and develop appropriate activities. We use problem-posing as a technique for exploratory research to inform teachers about learning processes and cultural issues and to help them make curriculum decisions. Problem-posing, an approach developed by Paolo Freire in the context of adult literacy programs (Freire, 1991), employs a dialogic approach that enables a learning community to share diverse viewpoints about a particular issue. This reveals the richness of the varied cultural perspectives in most classrooms, helping teachers to enrich their knowledge about their students and to examine their curriculum decisions in light of that knowledge. Student teachers in our practicum program conduct a problem-posing activity and reflect on it (see Schleppegrell, 1997a,

1997b, for details). This gives them a greater awareness and consciousness about their students' reactions to their teaching and makes the student teachers more self-sufficient. Cultural issues inevitably surface through this process and stimulate valuable discussion among the teacher trainees.

During the third quarter, student teachers have the option of doing an off-campus practicum, where they can teach at a local community college, adult school, or intensive English program. This experience provides them with an opportunity to work with yet another group of learners and levels. When students are doing practicum teaching with advanced students, as they typically do when they work in a university setting, it is difficult to bring in issues relevant to low-level students. Working in other settings introduces them to a wider range of learner levels and concerns. Although even varied practicum experiences still provide only a limited view of the whole field of language teaching possibilities, the variety of learners with whom the student teachers work and the increasing responsibility that they take on in developing their syllabus and lessons gives them an introduction to the wealth of contexts and learner types that they may work with in the future.

Setting Goals for Teacher Development

The most important way we adapt our program to the different contexts and settings in which our students will be teaching is by encouraging them to set individual goals for the development of their teaching skills. At the beginning of each quarter, we engage in activities that enable each student teacher to set his or her own goals in the areas of lesson organization and content, time management, classroom interactional patterns, and assessing their students' performance. They develop a list of their goals for development of their teaching skills during that quarter and then write a reflection on each of the lessons they teach, in which they analyze their progress on those goals. This gives opportunities for nonnative speakers to focus on different issues than the native speakers and for all students to develop the skills they think will be most important for them.

Throughout the practicum experience, student teachers are observed by experienced teachers and by their peers. Before the peer observations, they identify issues that they would like their classmates to give them feedback on. This experience gives them confidence in their own abilities to give and get feedback once they are finished with the training program. In addition, student teachers videotape their teaching on a regular basis and reflect on their performance.

Setting goals for themselves and then monitoring their own progress on those goals helps student teachers gain confidence. They are typically well aware that they need to work in a variety of areas to improve their teaching and are often overwhelmed by how many issues need to be attended to at the same time in the classroom. Looking at their development in the different areas they have identified and setting goals for improvement in each area gives them ways to see how incremental changes in their approach can lead to steady growth in their skills and confidence.

CONCLUSION

There is no one way to teach language and no one way to train language teachers for the myriad of contexts in which they may find themselves after graduating from a program. But feedback from our former students encourages us to believe that by promoting critical reading of and reflection on research findings, providing a variety of teaching experiences in a training program integrated with courses in theory and methods, and encouraging them to reflect in structured ways on their teaching and set goals for improvement, we enable them to be more effective teachers who will continue learning even as they assume their professional responsibilities. In the diverse world of language teaching possibilities, this seems to be the best way to prepare teachers for any teaching context.

NOTES

1. The K-12 teaching context is not addressed in this chapter. Although our program does have students who have K-12 credentials and who will return to teaching in this context as ESL specialists, K-12 teaching requires additional credential work and so is not a focus of our teacher training program.

2. Liu (1998) reports that about 37 percent of TESOL students in the United States are international students and suggests that their needs are typically not well served by teacher training programs.

3. The labels native speaker and nonnative speaker obscure a host of complexities when applied to those who have learned English and other languages in a variety of different contexts, as pointed out by Davies (1991), Kachru (1994), Kachru & Nelson (1996), and Liu (1999), among others. Medgyes (1992) identifies some of the advantages that nonnative speakers have in language teaching. For example, they serve as models of successful language learners, know effective learning strategies, and can anticipate language difficulties, where they share the learners' mother tongue.

4. The terms second language and foreign language are themselves problematic when applied to English, as pointed out by Nayar (1997). He reviews how these terms developed and then outlines differences in contexts for learning English that go beyond this dichotomy. He suggests a three-way distinction: English as a Second Language, English as an Associate Language, for countries like India where English is an institutional language, but where identification and assimilation into a native-speaking community is not assumed, and English as a Foreign Language.

5. Cook (1999) addresses some of these concerns, suggesting that the focus should be on the L2 user rather than on native speaker norms and that this can be accomplished by incorporating goals based on L2 users in the outside world, bringing L2 user situations and roles into the classroom, using the students' L1 in teaching activities, and drawing on descriptions of L2 users or L2 learners rather than descriptions of native speakers as sources of information.

REFERENCES

Auerbach, E. R., & Burgess, D. (1985). The hidden curriculum of survival ESL. *TESOL Quarterly*, 19(3): 475–495.

Benson, M. (1989). Differences between American English and British English: A challenge to TESOL. *TESOL Quarterly*, 23(2): 351–355.

Burnaby, B., & Sun, Y. (1989). Chinese teachers' views of western language teaching: Context informs paradigms. *TESOL Quarterly*, 23(2): 219–238.

Cook, V. (1999). Going beyond the native speaker in language teaching. *TESOL Quarterly*, 33(2): 185–209.

Davies, A. (1991). *The native speaker in applied linguistics*. Edinburgh: Edinburgh University Press.

Dörnyei, Z. (1990). Conceptualizing motivation in foreign-language learning. *Language Learning*, 40: 45–78.

Freire, P. (1991). The adult literacy process as cultural action for freedom. In M. Minami & B. P. Kennedy (eds.), *Language issues in literacy and bilingual/multicultural education,* pp. 248–265. Cambridge, MA: Harvard Educational Review.

Govardhan, A. K., Nayar, B., & Sheorey, R. (1999). Do U.S. MATESOL programs prepare students to teach abroad? *TESOL Quarterly*, 33(1): 114–125.

Kachru, B. B., & Nelson, C. L. (1996). World Englishes. In S. L. McKay & N. Hornberger (eds.), *Sociolinguistics and language teaching,* pp. 71–102. Cambridge: Cambridge University Press.

Kachru, Y. (1994). Sources of bias in SLA research: Monolingual bias in SLA research. *TESOL Quarterly*, 28(4): 795–799.

Krashen, S. (1982). *Principles and practice in second language acquisition*. Oxford: Pergamon Press.

Li, D. (1998). "It's always more difficult than you plan and imagine": Teachers' perceived difficulties in introducing the communicative approach in South Korea. *TESOL Quarterly*, 32(4): 677–704.

Liu, D. (1998). Ethnocentrism in TESOL: Teacher education and the neglected needs of international TESOL students. *ELT Journal*, 52(1): 3–10.

Liu, J. (1999). Nonnative-English-speaking professionals in TESOL. *TESOL Quarterly*, 33(1): 85–102.

Medgyes, P. (1992). Native or non-native: Who's worth more? *ELT Journal*, 46(4): 340–349.

Nayar, P. B. (1997). ESL/EFL dichotomy today: Language politics or pragmatics? *TESOL Quarterly*, 31(1): 9–37.

Oxford, R., & Shearin, J. (1994). Language learning motivation: Expanding the theoretical framework. *Modern Language Journal*, 78: 12–28.

Scarcella, R. (1996). Secondary education in California and second language research: Instructing ESL students in the 1990s. *CATESOL Journal*, 9(1): 129–152.

Schleppegrell, M. (1991). English for specific purposes: A program design model. *English Teaching Forum* (October): 18–22.

Schleppegrell, M. (1997a). Teacher research through dialogic inquiry. *Canadian Modern Language Review*, 54(1), 68–83.

Schleppegrell, M. J. (1997b). Problem-posing in teacher education. *TESOL Journal*, 6(3): 8–12.

Schleppegrell, M. J., & Bowman, B. (1995). Problem-posing: A tool for EFL curriculum renewal. *ELT Journal*, 49(4): 297–307.

Sridhar, K. K., & Sridhar, S. N. (1992). Bridging the paradigm gap: Second-language acquisition theory and indigenized varieties of English. In B. B. Kachru (ed.), *The other tongue: English across cultures*, pp. 91–107. Urbana: University of Illinois.

Sridhar, S. N. (1994). A reality check for SLA theories. *TESOL Quarterly*, 28(4): 800–805.

Author Index

Subject Index

About the Contributors

Gerd Bräuer is an Assistant Professor of German Studies at Emory University. He taught German as a foreign language in Prague (Czech Republic) and in Eugene and Portland, Oregon. At the University of Oregon he held a postdoctoral fellowship sponsored by the Deutsche Forschungsgemeinschaft (DFG). His research interests are writing pedagogy and second/foreign language pedagogy. Most recent publications include *Schreibend lernen* [Writing to Learn], 1998, *Writing Across Languages,* 2000, and *Reflexive Praxis* [Reflective Practice], 2000.

Stella Büker has an M.A. in German as a foreign language and has also studied linguistics and history at the University of Bielefeld (Germany). She has been teaching internationally and is currently involved in the Writing Consultation Program for foreign students at U.B. Her research interests include pedagogy of academic writing, foreign language acquisition, and communication analysis.

Timothy G. Collins is assistant professor of English as a second language at National-Louis University, Chicago, and has taught ESL, EFL, and Spanish in Spain, Morocco, and the United States. He holds a Ph.D. degree from

University of Texas at Austin. His research interests include theater arts in elementary ESL, ESL in adult education, work force ESL, and school-to-work initiatives in ESL.

Tony Erben is currently Senior Lecturer in the Faculty of Education at Central Queensland University (CQU). His interests include bilingual, immersion, and foreign language education as well as applied linguistics. He has published in the area of immersion education and is heavily involved in foreign language teacher training in Queensland.

Lawrence F. Glatz is an Assistant Professor of German at the Metropolitan State College of Denver. After receiving an Honors B.A. in German from the University of Pennsylvania in 1984, he pursued graduate study in German Literature at the Pennsylvania State University. He was awarded an M.A. in 1988 and a Ph.D. in 1995. In addition to teaching courses on German language and culture, German literature and civilization, and German for business, his interests include the pedagogical use of multimedia and computer technology in language instruction. His professional affiliations include active involvement in the American Association of Teachers of German (AATG), the American Council on the Teaching of Foreign Languages (ACTFL), the International Association for Language Learning Technology (IALLT), the Colorado Congress of Foreign Language Teachers (CCFLT), and the Modern Language Association (MLA).

Margaret Gonglewski (Ph.D., Georgetown University) is Assistant Professor of German and Language Program Director in the department of German & Slavic Languages and Literatures at the George Washington University in Washington, D.C. She has published articles on issues in language program direction, the professional development of graduate students, and the use of technology in language learning and teaching. She is author of the testing program and website for the introductory German textbook *Treffpunkt Deutsch*.

Christine Galbreath Jernigan is a lecturer in the Curriculum and Instruction department of the University of Texas at Austin. After receiving her B.A in English and French literature at Wake Forest University, she completed her Ph.D. in Foreign Language Education at U.T. Austin. As a doctoral student she taught Portuguese language courses in the Spanish and Portuguese department. She recently completed a motivational and cultural training workshop for teachers of English in Minas Gerais, Brazil, and is currently teaching "Sociocultural Influences on Learning" and "Social Studies Methods" to undergraduate education majors. Her research focuses on teaching culture in the foreign language classroom and on language learning motivation.

Adam Knee holds a doctorate in cinema studies and a certificate in TESL and has taught English language and academic writing classes in the United States and abroad. He is an assistant professor in the department of English at Tamkang University Taiwan.

Lina Lee is assistant professor of Spanish at the University of New Hampshire, where she coordinates the Basic Language Program, trains teaching assistants, teaches foreign language teaching methods, and supervises foreign language interns. She has published articles in the areas of portfolio assessment and Internet technology for teaching foreign language and culture in *Hispania, Foreign Language Annals, CALICO*, and *Northeast Reports and Newsletters*. She is the author of websites for the Spanish textbooks *Mosaicos* and *Puentes*.

Kathleen N. March is professor of Spanish at the University of Maine. She has written numerous articles on Latin American, Spanish, and Galician literature. Her interests in linguistics are in applied linguistics, bilingualism, and sociolinguistics. She teaches courses in Spanish, multiculturalism, and women's studies. She coordinates the beginning Spanish program and the Critical Languages Program of self-instructional courses in less commonly taught languages.

Frank A. Morris is currently a Ph.D. student in Hispanic linguistics at the University of Minnesota. His research interests include first and second language acquisition, second language pedagogy, bilingualism, dialectology and Spanish in the United States. Frank received an M.A. in Hispanic literature from the University of Minnesota and a B.A. in history and English at the University of Iowa.

Beverly Moser holds a doctorate in German from Georgetown University, with a research focus in second language writing. In her work directing the basic language program in German at the University of Tennessee, Knoxville, she began developing strategies for enhancing enrollment in German, which form the basis of her discussion in this volume. She was awarded the college's Faculty Advising Award in 1996 in recognition of her advising program. She is the author of an intermediate-level German textbook, *Schemata*, that bridges the gap between basic language instruction and the upper division, and she publishes in the area of second language acquisition. In 1997, she joined the faculty of Appalachian State University in Boone, North Carolina, where she teaches all levels of German and occasional courses in Applied Linguistics.

Mary J. Schleppegrell is Associate Professor of Linguistics and Director of English as a Second Language and the M.A. program in applied linguistics at the University of California, Davis. Her research interests include teacher training and language teaching pedagogy, as well as discourse analysis of the features of academic registers.

Jean Marie Schultz received her doctorate in Comparative Literature from the University of California at Berkeley, where she has been coordinator of the intermediate French program since 1986. Her most active field of research focuses on foreign language writing. She has spoken at numerous conferences and given workshops in writing and critical thinking. She has published in the *Modern Language Journal, French Review*, and the Cambridge University Press series in Applied Linguistics.

Robert Weissberg is Associate College Professor at New Mexico State University, where he directs the International Intensive English Program. His areas of interest are adult second language acquisition and second language writing.